000897

Routledge studies in business organizations and networks

Thinking Organization

Edited by Stephen Linstead and
Alison Linstead

LONDON AND NEW YORK

First published 2005
by Routledge
2 Park Square, Milton Park, Abingdon, Oxon OX14 4RN

Simultaneously published in the USA and Canada
by Routledge
270 Madison Ave, New York, NY 10016

Routledge is an imprint of the Taylor & Francis Group

Typeset in Garamond by Wearset Ltd, Boldon, Tyne and Wear
Printed and bound in Great Britain by MPG Books Ltd, Bodmin

British Library Cataloguing in Publication Data
A catalogue record for this book is available from the British Library

Library of Congress Cataloging in Publication Data
A catalog record for this book has been requested

ISBN 0-415-33364-4

Contents

Figures

Contributors

Martin Brigham is a Lecturer in the Department of Organization, Work and Technology (formerly the Department of Behaviour in Organizations) at Lancaster University Management School, Lancaster University. He is also an associate member of the Centre for the Study of Technology and Organization at Lancaster University. His current research interests concern the relationship between technology and social and organization theory and ethnographies of information systems.

Steven Connor has taught since 1979 at Birkbeck College, where he is now Professor of Modern Literature and Theory. He is currently Academic Director of the London Consortium Master's and Doctoral Programme in Humanities and Cultural Studies. He is also the College Orator. He currently supervises postgraduate research students working on Beckett, Paul de Man, theories of parody and pastiche, the philosophy of literary intention, the history of sound, the cultural history of gravity, twentieth-century sound art and contemporary music culture. He is a regular radio broadcaster. His interests include ventriloquism, on which he published *Dumbstruck: A Cultural History of Ventriloquism* (Oxford University Press, 2000), and he is continuing to develop an online archive of texts and images discussed in the book and relating to its subject. He has also recently published *The Book of Skin* (Reaktion Books, 2004). His current research is on the air.

Martin R. Fellenz lectures in Business Studies at Trinity College Dublin. He has an MBA from Bridgeport and a PhD from the University of North Carolina. His research interests include organizational behaviour and organization theory, organizational justice, flexibility, organizational learning, change and knowledge management.

Robert Grafton Small holds a CNAA doctorate on social aspects of consumption. Prematurely retired after posts in Marketing at Strathclyde and Organizational Symbolism at St Andrews, he has lately been associated with the University of Leicester's Management Centre, maintaining an active interest in original research and publishing regularly across disciplines.

Loizos Heracleous is a Fellow in Strategy and Organization at Templeton College, Oxford University. He gained his PhD at the Judge Institute of Management Studies, University of Cambridge. Loizos is the author of *Strategy and Organization: Realizing Strategic Management* (Cambridge University Press, 2003) and co-author of *Business Strategy in Asia: A Casebook* (Thomson Learning, 2004). He is a Senior Editor of *Organization Studies* and serves on the editorial boards of the *Journal of Applied Behavioral Science*, the *Journal of Management Studies* and the *Asia Pacific Journal of Management*. His research is published or forthcoming in over thirty-five research papers in international journals, including the *Academy of Management Journal*, *Harvard Business Review*, the *Journal of Management Studies*, *Human Relations* and the *Journal of Applied Behavioral Science*. His research has received two Best Paper awards from the US Academy of Management, in 1999 and 2004.

Jean-Marie Jacques took his PhD in science and in management sciences (psychosocial). He is now Professor at the University of Namur (Facultés Universitaires Notre-Dame de la Paix, Belgium) and Director of the Research Center for Crisis and Conflict Management (ReCCCoM) in the same university. He is also visiting professor at the University of Freiburg (Germany) and at the École Normale Supérieure de Cachan (Paris). He is a Member of the Académie Royale des Sciences de Belgique (Royal Academy of Sciences of Belgium) and Executive Secretary of the IGBP-Belgian Committee. He specializes in risk and crisis studies, particularly in perception of risk, cognitive sciences and research methodology. He has performed extensive field research in India, Indonesia, Namibia, Egypt, Spain, France and Belgium, and acts as adviser for several different international organizations.

Marja-Liisa Kakkuri-Knuuttila is Lecturer in Philosophy at the Helsinki School of Economics and *Dozent in* at the University of Helsinki. She has recently finished a six-year period (1998–2004) as a Senior Research Fellow at the Academy of Finland working on the project Epistemology and Methodology of Management Research. Her research in ancient philosophy has focused on Aristotle's dialectic, rhetoric and methods of inquiry (saving the phenomena). One aim of the Epistemology and Methodology of Management Research project has been to introduce Aristotelian methods and conceptions to organization and management studies. The approach in several of her investigations has been the 'naturalistic' one, emphasizing how the research is actually carried out rather than how it should have been carried out.

Donncha Kavanagh is Senior Lecturer in Management at University College Cork, part of the National University of Ireland. He has degrees from University College Dublin, the University of Missouri and Lancaster University. He has published in the fields of engineering, management, organization studies and marketing. His research interests include the pre-modern, the history of management thought, eschatology and the sociology of knowledge and technology. He is currently researching the translation of management technologies into higher education.

Kieran Keohane lectures in Sociology at University College Cork, where he took his BSocSc and MA. He obtained his PhD from York University, Toronto. His theoretical research interests include sociological analysis in the interpretive tradition: hermeneutics, phenomenology, psychoanalysis, classical and contemporary social theory, confluences between critical theory and post-structuralism, the conditions of postmodernity, and philosophical affinities in literature and poetics. He is also interested in cities and forms of urban life, identity, difference and social antagonism, political sociology, memory, fantasy, collective representations and the symbolic order. His publications include *Symptoms of Canada* (University of Toronto Press, 1997), an exploration of Canadian identity and national character informed by Lacanian psychoanalysis and the political theory of Laclau and Mouffe.

Carmen Kuhling is Lecturer in Sociology and the former director of Women's Studies at the University of Limerick. A Canadian by birth, she moved to Ireland in 1994 after having the good fortune to marry an Irishman, and received her PhD in 1998 from York University, Toronto. She has published in the area of cultural studies, psychoanalysis and popular culture, and her book *The New Age Ethic and the Spirit of Postmodernity* (Hampton Press, 2004) examines the rise of the New Age movement as a symptom of various crises of modernity.

Hugo Letiche is Professor of 'Meaning in Organization' at the University for Humanistics, Utrecht, the Netherlands, where he is Head of Department and Director of the DBA/PhD programme. He did his BA in the committee on general studies in the humanities at the University of Chicago, his doctor's (Master's) at Leiden University in conflict psychology, and his PhD at the Vrije University, Amsterdam, in adult learning. Previous appointments include Erasmus University, and part-time positions at Lancaster and Keele Universities in the United Kingdom specializing in international business, ethics and corporate governance. His research interests span organizational theory, organizational learning and change, philosophy and organization, and complexity theory and its applications. Recent publications have dealt with the work of Baudrillard, Luhmann, Lyotard and Serres. He is Associate Editor for Organization Studies of the journal *Emergence and Organization*, and is on the editorial boards of *Organization*, the *Journal of Organizational Change Management* and *Culture and Organization*.

Alison Linstead is Senior Lecturer in Critical Management Studies at the University of York. She has previously worked at the Universities of

Durham, Essex and Leicester. She holds a BA in Business Studies, an MSc in Organization Development and a PhD in Management from Sheffield Hallam University. Her research interests include identity, where she has a joint-edited book *Organization and Identity* (Routledge, 2004, with Stephen Linstead) and a sole-authored book *Managing Identity* (Palgrave forthcoming); gender, where she recently edited a special issue of *Gender Work and Organization* titled 'Beyond Boundaries: Towards Fluidity in Theorizing and Practice' with Joanna Brewis; and change, where she has recently edited a special issue of the *Journal of Organizational Change Management* entitled 'Change in the Feminine: Women in Change'. She is also working on qualitative methods and feminine philosophy. She is an Associate Editor of *Gender, Work and Organization* and a member of the Steering Group of the British Academy of Management Special Interest Group on Identity.

Stephen Linstead is Professor of Critical Management Studies at the University of York, UK. He has previously worked at Durham Business School, where he was Professor of Organizational Analysis and Director of Research, and at the Universities of Essex, Sunderland and Wollongong (NSW), the Hong Kong University of Science and Technology, and Lancaster University Management School. He has particular research interests in language, anthropology and qualitative methods, gender and sexuality, aesthetics, postmodern thought and the work of Bergson and Bataille. Recent books include *Organization Theory and Postmodern Thought* (Sage, 2004), *Text/Work* (Routledge, 2002), *The Language of Organization* (edited, with Robert Westwood, Sage, 2001) and *The Aesthetics of Organization* (edited, with Heather Höpfl, Sage, 2000). He is currently working on laughter, Deleuze, play, postcolonial anthropology and a sole-authored book *Casual Organization Theory*.

William McKinley received his PhD in organizational sociology from Columbia University, and is currently Professor of Management at Southern Illinois University at Carbondale, Carbondale, Illinois. His research interests include organizational restructuring and downsizing, organizational change, organizational decline, epistemological issues in organization theory, and the sociology and philosophy of organization science. His publications have appeared in *Administrative Science Quarterly*, *Academy of Management Journal*, *Academy of Management Review*, *Academy of Management Executive*, *Journal of Management Inquiry*, *Organization*, *Organization Science*, *Accounting, Organizations and Society*, *Advances in Strategic Management*, *Management International Review*, *Journal of Engineering and Technology Management*, *Business Horizons* and other journals.

Joachim Maier has degrees in organizational science from Sweden and Switzerland, and is Lecturer in Design Culture at HGKZ (Applied University for Art and Design, Zurich, Switzerland). He is studying for his xiv Contributors

doctorate at the Universiteit voor Humanistieke, Utrecht, and formerly worked for the Lego Imagination Lab, Lausanne. He collaborates in Irganic GmbH (www.irganic.com), which provides consultancy on information design, graphics, code/gaming, community building, facilitation, solution-focused consulting, corporate therapy, large-group interventions and pop culture-based interventions. He co-developed and coordinates the virtual community www.nic-las.com, based on the application of Niklas Luhmann's ideas on social systems, communication and media theory and into the digital world. Other influences are Baudrillard, Deleuze, Giesecke, McLuhan and Žižek.

Iain Munro teaches information systems, operations and statistics in the Department of Management at St Andrews University. He previously worked at Warwick Business School and has BSc and PhD degrees from Hull University. He is completing a book called *Information Wars* and his publications have appeared in a number of international journals, including *Organization Studies* and *Organization*.

Frits Schipper studied physics and philosophy. He wrote his dissertation on an important problem in twentieth-century epistemology, namely, the relation of intuition and construction in the works of Carnap and Husserl. Nowadays he teaches philosophy of management and organization at the Free University of Amsterdam (Vrije Universiteit) and is coordinator of the new Master's programme in this field (which started in September 2004). He is very much interested in how philosophical reflection may contribute to management and organization, conceptually as well as in a more practical sense. He participates in two research groups at the Free University, namely, the philosophy group Knowledge, Normativity and Practice and a research group in the Department of Economics, and is involved in several networks of consultants. Among his themes of interest are rationality, creativity, knowledge management and (corporate) governance. His English-language publications have appeared in *Organization*, *Management Learning* and *Reason in Practice*.

Eero Vaara is Professor of Management and Organization at the Swedish School of Economics and Business Administration in Helsinki (Finland) and Visiting Professor Strategy at the École de Management de Lyon, France. Most of his research has focused on organizational change, industrial restructuring and globalization. He has in particular examined mergers and acquisitions from several kinds of theoretical and methodological perspectives. He has lately worked especially on narrative and discursive analysis in the context of dramatic organizational change. In addition, he has been interested in philosophical questions in organization and management research. His work has been published in leading international journals.

Anne Wallemacq is Professor at the University of Namur (Facultés Universitaires Notre-Dame de la Paix), Belgium, where she served as Head of the Department of Sciences of Management from 1998 to 2001. Her research interests are in the fields of organization, human resources management, sociological theory, cognitive cartography, crisis and conflict management, language, and perception. She is a member of the Commission 'Economische Wetenschappen in Bedrijfskunde' of the Funds voor Wetenschappelijk Onderzoek – Vlaanderen (Funds for Scientific Research) and a member of the International Advisory Network on Organizational Discourse. She has published in books and journals in both French and English.

Acknowledgements

An earlier version of Chapter 12 appeared as 'Organization as reply: Henri Bergson and casual organization theory', *Organization* 9 (1): 95–111. We are grateful to Sage Publications for permission to reproduce parts of it here.

1 Introduction

Are organizations good to think with? Thinking things through and thinking through things

Stephen Linstead and Alison Linstead

The heritage profession has become hip.

(Philosophy Online)

No doubt about it, philosophy is the new Rock and Roll.

(Banville 2001)

As we write this, it is some twenty-five years since Gibson Burrell and Gareth Morgan (1979) left the field in no doubt that philosophy is relevant and important to the analysis of organizations. Although theirs was a narrower focus than they would have taken had applied philosophy been their objective, by concentrating on the ontological and epistemological underpinnings of theory and method it not only presented itself in an interpretively convenient matrix, but became a towering citation index success. So there is really no excuse for what has been the relative neglect of philosophy, especially in its other branches, in organization studies until comparatively recently. In its turn, until recently philosophy has tended formally to treat anything to do with management with disdain, as part of the messy but necessary business of earning a living, and the study of organization has been damned by association (Laurie and Cherry 2001: 4).

But, of course, philosophy has always been there or thereabouts. Philosophy itself creates, brings people, things and concepts together, and *organizes* (Linstead and Mullarkey 2003; Linstead and Thanem forthcoming). For Socrates, philosophy was a form of "midwifery" that helps to bring new things into being, as opposed to a form of "pandering" that makes merely cosmetic changes to what is. Knowing the difference ought to be of critical importance to those involved in organization and management, whether entrepreneurs or with delegated responsibility for hiring potentially expensive consultancy with public money. Socrates' identification with a feminine activity of midwifery might also give us cause for reassessment in a world of organizations that remain dominated numerically, affectively and epistemologically by men, male psychologies and masculine rationalities (Wajcman 1998). While we could make a case for the connections between philosophy and formal organization going back to Plato's philosopher-kings, in the last century, in the period when the foundational texts of modern management were being crafted, Oliver Sheldon (1924) produced *The Philosophy of Management*, which, in contrast to the functional dominance of simple economic rationalism in the management writings, examined the purposes and responsibilities of modern industrial management. More recently, the emphasis on business ethics has seen a revival of interest in Aristotelian moral philosophy through the work of Alasdair MacIntyre (1981, 1989), and Richard Sennett's sociological philosophy has seen similar attention given to Aristotle's philosophy of character (Sennett 1999). Charles Handy (1989) has been borrowing snippets from philosophy for several years and styles himself a "social philosopher", which may perhaps be overstating the case but does indicate that he wishes to claim some more substantial foundation for his "guru" status than simple fashion. In 1990, another general treatment of philosophy in organizations appeared (Hassard and Pym 1990), and almost everyone from the pre-Socratics to the postmoderns has made an appearance of sorts in the management and organization literature since then. Whole books have been devoted to postmodernism and organizations (Boje *et al.* 1996; Hassard and Parker 1993; Linstead 2004) and one notable collection to Foucault alone (McKinlay and Starkey 1998). At the level of concepts, the term *deconstruction* is now part of the everyday language of managers, and the Aristotelian concept of *phronesis* has been recently reintroduced into management education (Clegg and Ross-Smith 2003) as well as social research that intends to make a practical difference (Flyvberg 2001). In the arena of strategy, while debate on the relative merits and contemporary relevance of Confucius (e.g. Rudnicki 1998), Sun Tzu (e.g. McNeilly 2000; Sunzi and Michaelson 2001) and Machiavelli's (e.g. Jay 1987/1996; McAlpine 1998) advice to leaders has rubbed shoulders in airport lounges with speculation on how Aristotle might have managed General Motors (Morris 1997), considerable impact has also been made by the rediscovery of the process philosophy of Bergson, Whitehead and Dewey, and this has combined with part of the work of Deleuze to generate interest in foresight and becoming in relation to immanent strategy (e.g. Chia 2004; Mackay and McKiernan 2004). Socratic Consulting as a method has an increasing group of subscribers, especially in the Netherlands, and it is even possible for executives with enough time and money to join an exclusive group spending a week sitting under a tree on the Greek island of Skyros at the feet of a consultant philosopher examining in mock-Socratic fashion their working lives.[1]

The chapters of this book have at their core contributions made to the meeting of the European Group for Organization Studies Standing Working Group on the Philosophy of Management at Lyon in July 2001. They shared a mutual objective: to explore philosophical issues of relevance to organization studies. Not with any particular objective of improving management or organizational efficiency, or of necessarily making organization studies more scientific, but recognizing that, to borrow from Socrates, the disciplinary field that leaves its own assumptions, suppositions and conditions of its self-consciousness as a discipline unexamined is impoverished to the imperilment of its claims to understanding. There was no particular commitment to analytical or continental approaches, functionalism or postmodernism, and there is evidence of all in the book. The only criterion was that positions be explicated with care and respect for other positions; we were not interested in soapboxes, panegyrics, simplistic or polemical critiques or in setpiece "debates" between positions, only that arguments be explicated with attention to detail and some reflexivity. There was no preference for rationalism or anti-rationalism, only relevance. We did, however, feel that organization studies had demonstrated a preference for rationalistic styles of inquiry that privileged "getting on top" of a subject (classic hypothetical-deductive methodologies in particular display this) over "getting among or amid" a subject (which ethnographic or inductive methodologies do), and we hoped to achieve a better balance (see Connor, this volume, Chapter 10). Additionally, thought styles that privilege getting on top of things also tend to demonstrate their obsession with controlling their subject matter by prediction, by "thinking things through". In his important work *The Savage Mind*, Claude Lévi-Strauss argued that primitive peoples' thought processes were not inferior to those of civilized modern peoples, just different and more concrete. Instead of thinking things through, they had a tendency to think through things. This improvization with ready-made objects in the world he called *bricolage* (Linstead and Grafton Small 1990). Recent usages of this term in organization studies (e.g. Kamoche *et al.* 2002) have translated it as improvization – a form of which it certainly is – and thereby overlook its material qualities as a form of concrete rather than abstract reason. People use *goods* to think with. For Lévi-Strauss, the civilized mind is distinguished not by the fact that it does not employ such reason, but by the fact that it characteristically seeks to deny that it does. In this volume we have been pleased to include two contributions (Connor and Grafton Small, Chapters 10 and 11) that not only demonstrate how such thinking is alive and well within the postmodern world, but embody it in their style of writing.

In addressing our question of whether organizations are good to think with, or alternatively whether an organization could be considered a good to think with, traditionally philosophy as a discipline has responded negatively, or at least by ignoring the question. The contributions to this book, we believe, offer evidence to suggest that the answer to both questions should be emphatically positive and that philosophy should develop organization and management as a field while in turn it should be drawn upon much more explicitly and reflectively by scholars in the field of management and organization studies. We present the evidence in three areas that we consider to be characteristic of the field: problems associated with representation of the "object" of organization [*representing* organization];

issues of knowledge construction, sociability and subjectivity [*knowing* organization]; and issues of emergence, complexity and change [the *becoming* of organization]. Each of the first two parts of the book begins with more positivistic approaches, while the third follows a different trajectory by drawing out some immanent and neglected aspects of previous approaches and analyses and turning them into agendas for the future – from the premodern to the virtual, the supernatural to the post-human. We will now introduce each of the chapters in turn.

For *Marja-Liisa Kakkuri-Knuuttila* and *Eero Vaara*, in Chapter 2, causation is one of the questions that still seems to divide social scientists and organization researchers. In brief, those in the naturalist camp tend to focus on causal explanations of different phenomena while those in the interpretive or constructive camp seem to reject the idea of causation altogether. In this chapter, the authors argue that this division, while understandable, is not necessary and rests partly on a problematic notion of causation developed during the so-called linguistic turn in social sciences. To uncover some of these problematic assumptions, they take a critical look at one of the most influential pieces of work paving the way for interpretive research in social sciences in general and culturally oriented organization studies in particular: *The Idea of a Social Science* by Peter Winch (1958). The main target of their criticism is the crude distinction – shared within the hermeneutical and phenomenological tradition – that natural sciences only deal with *external relations* while social studies deal with *internal relations*. According to this view, causation – which, following the Humean conception, has to deal with external relations – has no relevance in social studies focusing on internal relations.

In their analysis, they point to the inherent problems of a simplistic adherence to the Humean notion of causation. They suggest an alternative notion of causation which draws mainly from age-old Aristotelian ideas. Their alternative is based on the notion of *power* in the sense of *capacity*, which allows causation in singular instances. They argue that the ancient Stagirite's ontological distinctions yield an alternative that satisfies the Winchian and the interpretive scholar's demand for a contextualist and non-deterministic conception of causation. With this ontology, human skills and social causation in general can be grasped with the help of the same categories as the realm of nature, though requiring subtler distinctions. Their reflective exercise hence implies that in spite of important differences in goals and methodologies, traditional and interpretive research need not be seen as incompatible perspectives.

Anne Wallemacq and *Jean-Marie Jacques* in Chapter 3 address the question of how to represent language. The question, first of all pragmatic, is asked on the occasion of a project, carried out by the authors, of developing EVOQ©, a cognitive cartography program (Wallemacq and Jacques 2001). The particularity of this software program is that it tries less to grasp the articulation of concepts within a reasoning process than to isolate the semantic fields the speaker is situated in and copes with. The semantic field is the whole set of associations/opposites that orbit around the words. In the field of organization studies, the elicitation of these semantic fields is very illuminating since it makes apparent the perceptual system specific to an individual or a group. As a matter of fact, these semantic fields are carried on by language. It may be language as we mean classically, but it may also be the specific language spoken by an organization or a group. In this case, by "language" (which they call code, on ethnomethodologists' heels), not only do they mean new words, technical words or borrowed words that are specific to an organization, but also the specific use made of common words in this particular context, as well as their wake of associations.

Of phenomenological and post-structuralist inspiration, the software relies on a conception of language that does not match classical modes of representation in boxes and nodes or in branches and nodes. From a pragmatic angle, the question of knowing how to represent language has become eminently theoretical. It is a matter of finding a space for representation whose properties (echo) correspond to the conception of language borne by these currents of thought. In doing this, the authors have gone over "to the other side of the mirror", in an architecture of thought no longer functioning in terms of branches and nodes, or in terms of causes and effects.

For *Hugo Letiche* and *Joachim Maier* in Chapter 4, meanings, events and organizations "slide", or move about. Structurally pre-defined, seemingly rigid action (the "game") does not necessarily lead to stasis. How do we understand this combination of the *game's* closed structure and its ability to change itself? *Glissement* is a way to describe interaction between the logic of the game and the events of change and activity. *Glissement* can be understood as an aspect of identity (Robbe-Grillet), as a characteristic of gaming, as a subversive logic (Deleuze) and as an ebb and flow of signification/identity (Lacan). In this chapter, these definitions are first explored, then the film *The Matrix* is examined in terms of *glissement*. Because the film can be understood as a description of organization, as an animated computer game and as a study of the hyper-real culture of simulacra, it provides material for the conceptual exploration they seek. In the end, the authors oppose the matrix's gaming with their own play; these two senses of *glissement* are fairly irreconcilable.

Iain Munro in Chapter 5 addresses the question, what role does myth play in modern organization? If one takes the project of modernity seriously, then one would conclude that myths can be entertaining and possess a certain aesthetic value, but they have little role to play in a society properly governed by reason. But this, Munro argues, may be a little too simplistic an interpretation, as was perhaps most powerfully demonstrated in Nietzsche's analysis of morality. He observed that the Enlightenment philosophers attempted to replace dogmatic religious myths with a morality that had a rigorous foundation in reason, only to prove the very same beliefs they held in the first place (such as the prohibition against suicide and the strictures against following one's animal inclinations). For Nietzsche, in order to understand the world and wo/man, myth seems to be in some sense necessary. In the last century, Freud attempted to show that the human psyche is arranged according to a mythic structure, that of the Oedipus complex. He also took pains to point out that this was not a metaphysical argument, but was derived from scientific observation of many cases.

It is Munro's contention that crucial to the conditions of organization is the use of myth. Myth operates on many different levels. For example, myths may be positively encouraged within an organization to help create an organizational identity. This can be used to engineer an organizational culture by appeal to a history and lineage. But myths also operate in a more global fashion. For example, Adorno and Horkheimer highlight the mythic qualities of modernity and the rhetoric of the Enlightenment with respect to the myth of Odysseus. Also, Deleuze and Guattari have shown how the myth of Oedipus is not just a psychoanalytic device, but is central to the capitalist concept of desire and the capitalist institution of the nuclear family. Organization is a parasitic phenomenon that derives its energy from and turns itself against desiring machines. Desiring machines have no organization; they are simply flows of desire, the production of an unconscious in connection with other machines (both technical and social). These commentaries on the function of myth show that there is no such thing as organization *per se*, or rationality *per se*, and when we have come to believe otherwise, we have merely forgotten the mythic grounds of that organization or rationality. Munro does not therefore reject myth in favour of a rational theory of organization but offers a schizoanalytic theory of organization which parodies these myths.

Loizos Heracleous and *Martin Fellenz* in Chapter 6 raise and explore the appropriateness, applicability and appropriation of concepts transferred from other conceptual domains (e.g. ethnography, sociology, history and philosophy of science) to organizational analysis. They open up for debate and problematize a hitherto largely implicit and taken-for-granted situation in social science, and suggest exploratory directions and ideas for further debate. They discuss issues arising from conceptual appropriations and suggest at least three criteria for judging the appropriateness of the diffusion of "alien" concepts in organizational analysis: technical adequacy, paradigmatic adequacy and pragmatic adequacy. They explore two examples of such appropriations to illustrate these criteria: the concept of discourse as used in the philosophy of science, and the concept of culture from ethnography.

They argue that social science is characterized by a considerable rate of diffusion of concepts from one conceptual domain to another and by paradigmatic diversity. Influential scholars have argued against this diversity as a way of advancing the social sciences. Researchers have for the most part, however, been urged to utilize concepts from other conceptual domains in order to enrich their own, and both paradigmatic and methodological closure have been argued to be unproductive for advancement of the social sciences.

Discussions relating to the cross-utilization of concepts address such issues as differences in levels of analysis in the original and the new usages of the concept, as well as practical issues relating to social scientists' training, orientations and skills as factors encouraging certain approaches over others within and across disciplines. Published field and conceptual research, however, usually does not address either these or other fundamental issues arising from the appropriation of concepts from other conceptual domains.

The appropriation of concepts from source domains and their use in "target domains" raises important issues. For example, from a metaphorical perspective, given that most of the theorizing in social science is metaphorical in nature (Morgan 1980, 1983), and that our conceptual system is metaphorically structured (Lakoff 1990; Ortony 1979), the transfer of a key concept from the source to the target domain creates a metaphorical implication complex (the implications conceptually transferred by the source domain to the target domain) that currently remains unexamined. This implication complex, which is characterized by both actualized and potential connections and the creation of meanings deriving from such connections, operates subconsciously in both the authors' and the readers' minds to suggest frames for interpretation, in the case of the authors regarding their data and in the case of the readers regarding the text they are reading. If the implication complexes remain unexamined, confusion can result regarding what the author actually intends to say, and how the reader should interpret this. This begs the question of whether there are, could be or should be "criteria" of interpretive validation of such conceptual transfer.

Underlying this idea is the claim that there are better and worse appropriations, which is necessary if we share a concept of social science as a potentially cumulative endeavour with an actual subject matter outside itself, and the need for a common language and platform for debate. Heracleous and Fellenz propose that such criteria should be based not on some absolute measure of "goodness" of appropriations, but rather on indications that the social scientists concerned have explored and clarified their use of key concepts from other conceptual domains with regard to the three levels we have mentioned: technical adequacy, paradigmatic adequacy and pragmatic adequacy.

In Chapter 7, *William McKinley* argues that it has become commonplace to argue that knowledge is socially constructed, whether in science or in organization studies. However, with some exceptions, constructivists have not gone into much detail about how the construction process takes place. In organization studies, for example, little information has been provided by theorists working from a constructivist perspective about how organizational constructs attain an objectified status. This is an important issue, because from a constructivist viewpoint, construct objectification creates many of the phenomena that organizational researchers investigate. According to constructivists, phenomena such as "transactions", "isomorphism", "institutional fields", "power", "niches", "inertia", and so on are not intrinsic to unmediated organizational reality, but have their source in mental representations that extract a common element from a set of concrete observations. These constructs tend to transcend their status as mental representations, however, and attain an objectified status that portrays them as phenomena external to the mind. These are the "unobservables" that are espoused as appropriate objects of study by realists.

While organization theorists appear to have taken this objectification process for granted, the process is not necessarily as automatic or as trouble-free as one might assume. This raises the question of what independent variables influence the level of objectification attained by organization studies constructs. McKinley addresses that question by developing a theory of construct objectification in organization studies.

In the theory, the most important variable affecting the degree of construct objectification is the extent to which a construct has a standard definition that is shared among construct users. When a construct has a standard definition, the empirical domain of the construct takes on an intersubjective status that is outside any individual construct user's mind. Put another way, the empirical domain of the construct becomes aperspectival, and this aperspectivity fosters the objectification of the construct. By contrast, when users attach diverse definitions to the same construct, the empirical domain of the construct is more subjective; it differs from one user's mind to another user's mind. This subjectivity interferes with the articulation of the construct as a distinct object outside any individual mind, and – in constructivist terms – means that the phenomenon named by the construct is only partially externalized. Several organization studies constructs share the fragile status that results, which is attributable to the lack of cross-user convergence in definitions of the same construct.

McKinley identifies four exogenous variables that influence the degree of convergence across users in definitions of a given construct. The first of these variables is the nature of the media through which a construct diffuses, distinguishing specifically between "rich" media and "lean" media. Rich media help produce standardization in the definition of a given construct, and, through that standardization, objectification.

A second variable that affects definitional convergence is the degree to which the measures used to tap a construct are similar from study to study. Of course, similar definitions lead to similar measures, but the theory advanced here also assumes that the reverse is true. Constructs are often "carried" or "black-boxed" by their measures, so when measures converge, definitions are likely to as well, and the empirical domain of a construct achieves aperspectivity and becomes objectified. When operationalizations of the same construct differ across studies, definitions also tend to diverge, and the empirical domain of the construct becomes subjective and incompletely externalized.

A third variable influencing definitional convergence is the power structure of the discipline in which a construct is deployed. In disciplines where power is highly centralized, construct definitions developed or adopted by elites will have more force as standard templates. At the other extreme, when power is widely dispersed there will be more freedom for the individual scholar to conceptualize and define constructs as he or she chooses, thus generating more local idiosyncrasy in construct definition and correspondingly less objectification.

Finally, the type of interdependence characterizing a discipline's research activity is an important determinant of definitional standardization and resulting construct objectification. In disciplines where pooled interdependence (Thompson 1967) is the norm, scholars tend to operate autonomously, and the products of their research are aggregated to form the sum of available disciplinary knowledge. This is not conducive to standardization of construct definition across different users and to objectification of the phenomenon referred to by a construct. On the other hand, disciplines characterized by sequential or reciprocal interdependence have a pattern of research in which the output of one research project or theory paper feeds directly into another, and researchers are bound together by a well-developed scholarly division of labour. In this situation, there is a greater constraint towards definitional convergence among users of the same construct, and greater construct objectification

McKinley finally specifies testable propositions that are intended to be a focus for future empirical research, with the intention of improving our understanding of how organization studies is struggling to give birth to its phenomena.

Frits Schipper in Chapter 8 observes that knowledge management (KM) and related concepts such as the knowing organization are very popular nowadays. In this chapter, Schipper analyses different kinds of questions – concerning matters of act, meaning, orientation and (professional) identity – and relates them to KM. In KM, "how-questions" concerning matters of fact are very dominant, but the other questions get less attention. This is especially true of questions of meaning concerning knowledge, which bring up philosophical issues that are relevant.

Among the issues Schipper discusses are epistemic variety and knowledge quality. Epistemic variety concerns the many modes in which reality can be known (structural, hermeneutical, etc.). Knowledge quality is, *inter alia*, about aspects of truth and possible depths of knowledge. Schipper's conclusion is that, basically, KM is about finding one's way in the potential richness of knowledge. Simply asking "how" questions is of limited assistance in this; it is imperative that questions of orientation and questions of identity are addressed as well, which KM at present does not appear to be doing.

In Chapter 9, *Donncha Kavanagh, Carmen Kuhling* and *Kieran Keohane* advocate and demonstrate the value of science fiction as a potent way of "practicalizing philosophy". Science fiction narratives provide an ideal-typical setting through which theory can be represented, clarified and developed. They also help us link the abstraction of theory and the messiness of practice, while partly sidestepping the enigma whereby any study of the empirical world may merely reflect back the particular ontologies and epistemologies that constitute that world. In particular, these authors claim that the various *Star Trek* television series provide a powerful metaphor for understanding and teaching certain themes regarding modernity, including the possibility of universal progress through economic expansion (capitalism, colonialism), technological development (industrialism, positivism) and the possibilities for universal emancipation (democracy). They especially focus on the Borg Collective, a form of life that has become one of the most enduring and critical mirrors that *Star Trek* has held up to contemporary society, and which can be usefully understood as a metaphor for the dark side of instrumental rationality. The chapter draws on the various encounters between the starship *Enterprise* and the Borg to illustrate and engage with the diverse writings of Weber, the Frankfurt School, Habermas, Foucault and Haraway on modernity's continuing and ambivalent struggle with instrumental rationality.

Steven Connor in Chapter 10 introduces us to an approach that he calls "cultural phenomenology", a way of thinking through things rather than thinking things through, which gave us the subtitle for this introduction. The piece here is part of a series of radio broadcasts called "Rough Magic" (which can be listened to on RealPlayer from Steven's website at http://www.bbk. ac.uk/eh/skc/; scroll down to "Rough Magic"). Influences on this approach from philosophy abound, although the phenomenology owes more to Serres than to Merleau-Ponty, less to Heidegger than to Deleuze, the anthropology more to Augé than to Leiris. The project is cultural and communal, which is why it lends itself readily to thinking about organization. Connor's project would make a useful manifesto for the new qualitative organization theory as it aims to "enlarge, diversify and particularise" its object of study. As he explains, "instead of readings of abstract structures, functions and dynamics, it would be interested in substances, habits, organs, rituals, obsessions, pathologies, processes and patterns of feeling". This spanning of the anthropological and the psychoanalytic is at once "philosophical and poetic, explanatory and exploratory, analytic and evocative". Its achievements would derive from "the manner in which it got amid a given subject or problem, not . . . the degree to which it got on top of it".

Robert Grafton Small's work has always been amid and never on top of its object, and has given many interpreters difficulty because it so effectively embodies assemblage, collage and other stylistic devices that are often more compelling in theory than in execution. In another *tour de force* (Chapter 11), he weaves self and other into his own brand of cultural phenomenology, crossing literary, philosophical, political, artistic and economic boundaries seamlessly and at will, arguing that we are not what we consume but what we become by consuming. We are workplaces in and of ourselves, endlessly emergent, the object both of our own desires and of the objects we desire, suiting ourselves, however dimly, with what suits us. Our communities and our sense of belonging are similarly reproduced, through everyday exchanges of goods and the not so good, symbols and understandings. Drawing on his and others' personal experiences of enculturation, he discusses these forms of order and orders of forms against a backdrop of consumer ethnography and our mutual dependence on the retailed and the retold.

Stephen Linstead in Chapter 12 moves this emerging theme of embodiment casually back in the direction of philosophy as he argues for the continuing relevance and vitality of Bergson's work for contemporary organization studies. Bergson's corpus is reviewed, along with some suggestions as to his relevance for contemporary organization theory. It is argued that Bergson's work would view organization as part of its object, a process which is changed by that engagement, in non-dialectical conversation with it. Organizing, then, is a reply to the object, an act that creates its own possibility. Calculative and formalistic organization theory fails to take into account the importance of intuition as a form of knowing, responsive to the shifting nature of both its object and itself over time, which a *casual* organization theory, on Bergsonian lines, would do. Many of the concepts that organization theory takes as having objective status and whose qualities can therefore be measured in terms of strength, intensity, and so on – such as motivation, personality or culture – are seen in this way: thought *backwards* – as descriptions arising out of a process of *refocusing*.

Finally, the concept of change, which is addressed throughout Bergson's work, is discussed. However, there is no Bergsonian system or programme to be offered here (after all, an organization theory that views change as being an inescapable process must itself embody change in its own provisionality), merely an introduction to some of the rich veins of ideas in his work, and an invitation to engage with them. It is an invitation that, like all invitations, invites us to reply.

Martin Brigham concludes the volume, in Chapter 13, with a critical and creative exposition of time-based accounts of organizing, importantly prefigured by Bergson and Nietzsche. He claims that, despite their differing commitments, Bergson and Nietzsche share a number of important and overlapping concerns. First, both contend that the practical human condition is constitutively bound up with the spatialization of time into discrete entities and that this is useful "for prolonging the earthly dance". For Bergson, this privileges quantitative difference over qualitative difference; that is to say, it foregrounds individuation, abstraction and differences of degree over the indivisible, the heterogeneous and differences in kind. Second, Nietzsche describes the "prejudice of reason" as a condition based upon the metaphysical assumption that logical abstraction provides access to a realm of unity, permanence and being. For both Bergson and Nietzsche, representationalism needs to be rethought along the lines of Nietzsche's injunction that "[i]n so far as the senses show becoming, passing away, change, they do not lie".

Bergson's claim that space can only ever be homogeneous and Nietzsche's injunction of becoming raise crucial questions for organizing and organizations. Brigham contends that a critical exploration that ranges across Bergson's concern with quantitative and qualitative multiplicity, Nietszche's notion of reactive and active forces, and Deleuze and Guattari's claims of the molar and molecular provides for a reanimated sense of organizing that does not posit organizations as merely fictitious entities, as some varieties of perspectivism threaten to do. It is rather the concept of organizing as somehow ahistorical that is illusory, and it is from this argument that he develops the claim that the human is marked out by and is constituted through promises across space and time.

Brigham contends that this historically constituted promise-making ability is crucially related to technics: that is, that the technical is co-originary with and sets out the specificity of the human. This, then, critically implicates the becoming of the human condition with the calculation, regulation and simplification made possible by technical affordances; that is to say, the becoming of becoming of the human is always already a relation between affect, technical object and mind.

Such claims problematize Bergsonian accounts that set out space as homogeneous and Nietzschean-inspired claims to pure becoming, yet paradoxically provide, in a spirit true to both Bergson's and Nietzsche's endeavours, a *becoming that becomes*, which goes some way to providing the human with the practical resources for virtual futures that are both open, indeterminate and creative.

These, then, are our chapters, opening up a new field of the philosophy of organization – bridging the fields of management and organization studies while firmly eschewing all those varieties of philosophical guruism and philosophical kitsch that currently populate the field. Philosophy and organization studies have much to say to each other, and much to contribute to our understanding of the real world of organization and the problems of practice, which are not always as they might appear. In our concluding chapter, we consider the potential nature of this contribution and some ways forward.

Note

1 For a useful review of the state of activities across the board, see Laurie and Cherry (2001) in their introduction to the first issue of the journal *Reason in Practice*, now *Philosophy of Management*. The journal now co-organizes a well-supported annual conference at St John's College, Oxford.

A press release from *Philosophy Online*, 7 May 2001, http://www.alexhoward. demon.co.uk/Press%20Releases.htm (accessed 1 August 2004) reads:

Café Latte with a slice of Sartre? Could Aristotle run General Motors? Philosophy is going back on the street, into boardrooms, is available for consultation. Tom Morris is a premier league philosopher for companies in the Fortune 500. Lou Marinoff helped global power brokers philosophise at the World Economic Forum in Davos this year. Hundreds of 'Cafés Philos' proliferate in France and are growing rapidly elsewhere. This heritage profession has become hip.

Now you can buy time, from a philosopher online, to your very own PC. Alex Howard, a UK-based member of the American Philosophical Practitioner Association's Key Consulting Team, with five acclaimed books and thirty years experience to draw on, has become the first APPA certified philosopher to provide a commercial, professional, service online. He offers user-friendly access to philosophies, ancient and modern, at $125 per hour (or local currency equivalent) using secure payment via WorldPay.com. *'I help clients match the pressing questions they are asking to the ideas and philosophers best able to assist them.'*

Alex's own workplace is itself an integration of old and new: his hi-tech approach is based in an 1850 townhouse blending modern Dell with antique Delft. Alex is the very first certified philosopher to move into e-commerce. He won't be the last.

Philosophy is also going on holiday: you can join Alex face to face for a fortnight in September on the Greek island of Skyros (http://www.skyros. com). With like-minded enthusiasts you can explore questions and concerns that matter to you. *'People come for fun, relaxation, privacy, intimacy and a chance to take themselves and others seriously. Each complements the other. Skyros is ideal.'* Where better to philosophise than a Greek island?

We have no idea as to the effectiveness or helpfulness of this service – we haven't tried it or talked to those who have. But it isn't what we are trying to develop in this book.

References

Banville, J. (2000) "It's not that difficult, and it's good for you too", review of Alain de Botton's *The Consolations of Philosophy* (London: Pantheon Books, 2000) in *Irish Times*, 1 April 2000.

Boje, D., Gephart, R. and Thatchenkery, T. (1996) *Postmodern Management and Organization Theory*, Thousand Oaks, CA: Sage.

Burrell, G. and Morgan, G. (1979) *Sociological Paradigms and Organizational Analysis*, London: Heinemann.

Chia, R. (2004) "Strategy-as-practice: reflections on the research agenda", *European Management Review* 1 (1): 29–34.

Clegg, S. and Ross-Smith, A. (2003) "Revising the boundaries: management education and thinking in a postpositivist world", *Academy of Management Learning and Education Journal* 2 (1): 85–99.

Flyvberg, B. (2001) *Making Social Science Matter: Why It Failed and How It Can Succeed Again*, Cambridge: Cambridge University Press.

Handy, C. (1989) *The Age of Unreason*, London: Random House.

Hassard, J. and Parker, M. (1993) *Postmodernism and Organizations*, London: Sage.

Hassard, J. and Pym, D. (eds) (1990) *The Theory and Philosophy of Organization*, London: Routledge.

Jay, A. (1987) *Management and Machiavelli: Discovering the Principles of Management in the Timeless Disciplines of Statecraft*, New York: Random House (reissued in 1996, Englewood Cliffs, NJ: Prentice Hall).

Kamoche, K. M., Vieira da Cunha, M. and Vieira da Cunha, J. (eds) (2002) *Organizational Improvisation*, London: Routledge.

Lakoff, G. (1990) "The invariance hypothesis: is abstract reasoning based on image-schemas?", *Cognitive Linguistics* 1: 39–74.

Laurie, N. and Cherry. C. (2001) "Wanted: philosophy of management", *Reason in Practice* (now *Philosophy of Management*) 1 (1): 3–12.

Linstead, S. (ed.) (2004) *Organization Theory and Postmodern Thought*, London: Sage.

Linstead, S. and Grafton Small, R. (1990) "Organizational bricolage", in B. Turner (ed.) *Organizational Symbolism*, Berlin: Walter de Gruyter.

Linstead, S. A. and Mullarkey, J. (2003) "Time, creativity and culture: introducing Bergson", *Culture and Organization* 9 (1): 3–13.

Linstead, S. and Thanem, T. (forthcoming) "The trembling organization: order, change and the philosophy of the virtual", in M. Fuglsang and B. Meier (eds) *Gilles Deleuze and the Multiplicity of the Social*, Edinburgh: Edinburgh University Press.

McAlpine, A. (1998) *The New Machiavelli: The Art of Politics in Business*, London: John Wiley.

MacIntyre, A. (1981) *After Virtue: A Study in Moral Theory*, Notre Dame, IN: University of Notre Dame Press.

MacIntyre, A. (1989) *Whose Justice? Whose Rationality?*, Notre Dame, IN: University of Notre Dame Press.

Mackay, R. B. and McKiernan, P. (2004) "Exploring strategy context with foresight", *European Management Review* 1 (1): 69–77.

McKinlay, A. and Starkey, K. (1998) *Foucault, Management and Organization: From the Panopticon to Technologies of the Self*, London: Sage.

McNeilly, M. R. (2000) *Sun Tzu and the Art of Business: Six Strategic Principles for Managers*, Oxford: Oxford University Press.

Morgan, G. (1980) "Paradigms, metaphors and puzzle-solving in organization theory", *Administrative Science Quarterly* 25: 605–622.

Morgan, G. (1983) "More on metaphor: why we cannot control tropes in administrative science", *Administrative Science Quarterly* 28: 601–607.

Morris, T. V. (1997) *If Aristotle Ran General Motors: The New Soul of Business*, New York: Henry Holt.

Ortony, A. (1979) *Metaphor and Thought*, Cambridge: Cambridge University Press.

Rudnicki, S. (1998) *Confucius in the Boardroom: Ancient Wisdom, Modern Lessons for Business*, New York: Dover Books.

Sennett, R. (1999) *The Corrosion of Character: Personal Consequences of Work in the New Capitalism*, London: W. W. Norton.

Sheldon, O. (1924) *The Philosophy of Management*, London: Pitman.

Sunzi and Michaelson, G. (2001) *Sun Tzu's* The Art of War *for Managers: 50 Strategic Rules*, New York: Adams Media.

Thompson, J. D. (1967) *Organizations in Action: Social Science Bases of Administrative Theory*, New York: McGraw-Hill.

Wajcman, J. (1998) *Managing Like a Man: Men and Women in Corporate Management*, Cambridge: Polity Press.

Winch, P. (1958) *The Idea of a Social Science and Its Relation to Philosophy*, London: Routledge & Kegan Paul; New York: Humanities Press.

Part I
Representing organization

2 Back to the roots of the linguistic turn

Arguments against causal social research reconsidered[1]

Marja-Liisa Kakkuri-Knuuttila and Eero Vaara

Introduction

One crucial dividing line within present social and organizational research can be found in the approach to causation. While the search for causal factors of relevant phenomena such as performance constitutes the main type of research within the 'traditional' paradigms, more or less explicit rejection of the cause–effect form of knowledge characterizes the 'new' interpretive paradigms. Such a divided picture of social research is not a recent innovation and reflects philosophical disputes between *verstehende Geisteswissenschaften* and *erklärende Naturwissenschaften* that can be traced back to the late nineteenth century. Debates between 'humanistic' and 'naturalistic' modes of understanding social phenomena tend to reappear, and for the past twenty years or so these issues have pervaded organizational research (Burrell and Morgan 1979; Morgan 1997; Morgan and Smircich 1980).

The recent inspirations for the interpretive mode of social studies derive mainly from three philosophical issues, one centred on the phenomenology of Edmund Husserl and his followers, another on the hermeneutic tradition, recently represented by Hans Georg Gadamer, and the third on Ludwig Wittgenstein's later period. Applied to empirical research, each amounts to roughly the same basic perspective, characteristic of the linguistic turn in the social sciences. According to this view, the exposition of causal relations forms the main goal of the natural sciences, but interpretation is the chief task of the social sciences. Furthermore, the conceptual frameworks required are *mutually incompatible*; the models of explanation, prediction and causation typical of natural science exclude the notions relevant for interpretation and understanding (Fay 2003; Roth 2003).

Our starting point is that this division should be viewed critically and taken as a major challenge (Fay and Moon 1996). Hence, instead of being satisfied with two distinct philosophical conceptions of social reality, the 'naturalistic' and the 'humanistic', we need to develop an understanding of how the 'causal' and 'interpretive' aspects of social reality interconnect. Our focus here will be on the concepts of causation, our main aim being to offer replies to the two most challenging arguments for this dualistic picture.

We have chosen to deal with these arguments as presented by Peter Winch in his small classic *The Idea of a Social Science and Its Relation to Philosophy* (1958), because of its clarity and clear argumentation, and because it neatly represents the way of thinking shared by the hermeneutic and the phenomenological traditions. The work itself was inspired by Wittgenstein's later philosophy as represented in his *Philosophical Investigations* (1953). Winch presents the Wittgensteinian emphasis on rules by way of philosophical argument against the then dominant *reductivist, naturalist* ideal of social science based on the *nomothetic, causal* understanding of natural science.

The first argument to be dealt with here rejects causal relations and causal knowledge of social reality on the basis of the difficulty or impossibility of achieving knowledge of regularities. The stronger argument, also implicitly or explicitly shared by most interpretive and constructionist scholars, focuses on the ontological distinction between two kinds of relation, namely, *external* and *internal* ones. In brief, Winch argues that while natural sciences deal with external relations, social studies focus on internal relations. While the former concentrate on causal relationships manifested in general laws, for the latter causation is a non-issue.

Our critical scrutiny of Winch's standpoint reveals that his argument is not as flawless as might at first appear. First, in rejecting them he is somewhat inconsistent in conceding some role to social regularities. Second, our analytical scrutiny of the concepts of 'internal' and 'external' relations reveals that they do not yield the intended kind of separation between the natural and the social sphere and, likewise, between the natural and social sciences. Instead, being internally related is not a specific feature of the social realm, since both internal and external relations can be found in both the natural and social spheres. As Winch himself notes in the preface to the second edition of his treatise (1990: xi–xii), the weak point in his position is his reliance on the traditional empiricist notion of causation dating back to David Hume. As we can see, he is relying on two Humean conditions, according to which, causal relations essentially involve *regularities* between so-called *Humean causes*: that is, factors *externally related* to each other.

Our constructive suggestion for an alternative notion of causation proceeds in two steps. We will first introduce the notion of causation and causal explanation with the help of the idea of the counterfactual conditional, not previously introduced to organizational research, but widely accepted by philosophers today. Its merit lies in allowing for *token* causation by loosening the ties with the traditional empiricist regularity view. To our mind, this does not, however, yield a sufficient reply to Winch's second argument, since it has nothing to say about internal relations or other particular features of social reality. In our endeavour to find elements for a sufficient ontology of causation to satisfy the Winchian demands, we shall go all the way back to Aristotle's *Metaphysics* and *Physics*, which include a very articulate treatment of causation as causal powers and capacities (*dunamis*). Our suggestion, not previously offered in philosophical or methodological discussions, is based on the observation that the ancient Stagirite's ontological distinctions yield an alternative conception of causation that satisfies the demand by interpretive scholars for contextualism. In fact, for Aristotle a complete power/capacity consists of two partial powers/capacities internally related to each other. We shall show how this allows one to deal with some of Winch's examples of internal social relations in a manner that allows scope for both internal relations and external causal relations. It also turns out that the other Aristotelian distinctions on powers can be applied to explicate Winchian distinctions between natural dispositions and human skills. This ontology allows human skills and social causation in general to be grasped through the same basic categories as the realm of nature by adding more subtle distinctions.

Our reflective exercise hence paves the way for a deeper understanding of the important differences and similarities in the goals and methodologies of natural and human sciences. We also gain new insights into why the traditional 'naturalistic' and interpretive 'humanistic' modes of social research need not be seen as incompatible, but rather are complementary modes of investigating social reality. After all, naturalistic theories cannot do without understanding and knowledge of internal social relations, while a great many interpretive studies involve causal explanations of singular causal events.

The naturalistic and interpretive modes of social research

To begin our analysis, consider the following example:

> A sergeant standing in front of a group of men on a field calls: 'Eyes right'. The men turn their eyes to the right. A by-passer remarks to her companion: 'The privates always turn their eyes right when the sergeant tells them to.'
>
> (Modified from Winch 1958: 124–125)

It is possible to read this in two ways. The traditional reading, criticized by Winch in his treatise *The Idea of a Social Science*, the men on the field turn their eyes to the right *because* of the command issued. The command *causes* the action of the men. The whole incident *causes* the by-passer to remember having observed similar events, and as a result to express her experiences to her companion. Her statement can be taken as providing the universal generalization needed for causal explanation of the action of the soldiers in accordance with the Hempel–Oppenheim covering-law model. Her own statement will be causally explained if a suitable generalization can be supplied. The actions of others, as well as one's own reasons for acting, are here taken as causal factors influencing actions.

According to Winch, such a reading is false because it fails to consider the social meaning and embeddedness of these particular actions. He would prefer a reading whereby the soldiers' turning their eyes to the right is described as 'obeying a command'. Issuing and obeying commands are social actions, characterized in terms of the beliefs and desires involved, each defined by social rules existing only by virtue of agreement between human beings. Individual actions in general are embedded in the social contexts of practices, partly constituted by concepts the individuals themselves apply to understand their own actions. This approach leads to *interpretive social studies* with the aim of explicating intentional actions and the social rules involved in them. Causal relations are typically taken to be irrelevant to these concerns.

The primacy of language in social reality

The main contribution of *The Idea of a Social Science* is the formulation of the relevance of Ludwig Wittgenstein's later philosophical thinking in his *Philosophical Investigations* (1953), in particular its relevance to social sciences.[2] *The Idea of a Social Science* represents a hallmark of the *linguistic turn* in social research, characterized by an understanding of language and meaning as the paradigm for studying social relations, institutions and individual action. The work soon came to be considered one of the classics of *interpretive sociology*, along with the phenomenologically oriented works by Alfred Schutz, for instance (Heritage 1984).

The epistemological basis for Wittgenstein is presented by Winch as follows: what is *given* to us, as members of a society, is *a form of life* we share with other members of that society (Winch 1958: 35, 40, 44, 57). This position is in contrast to the logical empiricist epistemology according to which the given consists of atomistic – that is, mutually independent – observations made by individual people. In general, it opposes various empiricist and rationalist forms of foundationalism, which assume a foundation of knowledge not requiring any justification at all, and on which the justification of all other knowledge claims is to be based (Alston 1989; Lehrer 1990). In contrast to a set of foundational beliefs and their counterparts in reality, a form of life is a complex being consisting of various types of action, social relations and other institutions of various kinds, including language. Each of these aspects is available to us only through interpretation, and none of them can be taken as a foundation of knowledge, at least not in any absolute sense of the term. This involves a holistic conception of social reality in which parts are not taken to be independent of each other.

According to Winch, such an attitude is typical of Wittgenstein both in his early *Tractatus Logico-philosophicus* (1922) and in his later period (Winch 1958: 13–15). He illustrates this as follows:

> [I]n discussing language philosophically we are in fact discussing *what counts as belonging to the world*. Our idea of what belongs to the realm of

reality is given for us in the language that we use. The concepts we have settle for us the form of the experience we have of the world.

(Winch 1958: 15)

The whole Wittgensteinian philosophical programme arises from the idea that by investigating language we gain knowledge of reality. Language and epistemology are thus the ways to ontology.

Winch adopts language as the paradigm case through which to explicate the basic features of social reality. He begins with the description of linguistic meaning. We may learn the meaning of expressions such as 'Mount Everest' or 'mountain' by ostension – that is, by the thing being pointed out to us – or by verbal explication. What Wittgenstein was interested in was the question of what is involved in saying that the ostensive or the verbal definition determines the meaning of the term. Both kinds of definition rely on social rules, but what does 'following a rule' consist of? If it means doing the same thing again in new circumstances, what is this 'doing the same thing'? The answer we learn from Winch is simply that 'given a certain sort of training everybody does, as a matter of course, continue to use these words in the same way as would everybody else' (1958: 31). In addition to its collectivist emphasis, this implies that the application of rules involves not only conceptual knowledge of rules, but a skill type of knowledge as well, including the capacity to apply rules to new situations, even though Winch does not deal with this issue in any depth (ibid.: 55–57).

The primacy of language is only partial, however, since linguistic meaning is based on and presupposes social relations: 'those very categories of meaning, etc., are *logically* dependent for their sense on social interaction between men' (ibid.: 44). For instance, explaining someone as voting in a national election presupposes, first, the existence of certain political institutions: a parliament and a government constituted in certain ways (ibid.: 50–51). Furthermore, the reasons for action – for instance, voting for a certain person or a certain party – are social constructions, implying that they need to be understood in terms of accepted standards of reasonable action for that type of action in the given society (ibid.: 116–117; Kusch 2003).

Since social relations and ideas involved in them are, for Winch, two sides of the same coin, being different aspects of the same system of rules, a change in the meaning of terms referring to social relations involves a change in the social relations themselves. For instance, the double tasks of a social worker to establish a relationship of friendship with her clients and at the same time to accept as her first obligation to be loyal to her employer imply a change in the notion of friendship as well as in the social relations involved (Winch 1958: 123). In discussing the example we started with, he states, for instance, that it hardly makes sense to suppose that issuing commands and obeying them existed before having the concepts of command and obedience themselves (ibid.: 125).

Social science as an investigation of internal relations

In addition to language and social rules, another key concept Winch uses to describe social ontology is *internal relation*. He clarifies this notion in connection with an idea being internally related to its context: 'The idea gets its sense from the role it plays in the system' (1958: 107). Conversely, an idea that has a sense independent of a certain system can be said to be *external* to that system. Under this formulation, *contextualism* and internal relations amount to the same thing, if by contextualism we mean simply that a phenomenon is not independent of its context.[3]

We need, however, a more general definition of internal relations applicable not only to linguistic entities, but to various kinds of *relata*, not least in order to assess whether internal–external relations form the dividing line between social and natural phenomena. By replacing the term *sense* by the term *identity*, the above formulation can be generalized as follows: a thing is *internally related to its context* if its identity depends on the context and its role in it.

A more general way of expressing what internal relations amount to is saying that a thing is internally related to another if *the relation changes the identity of the former*. For instance, getting a (first) child and thus becoming a parent changes one's social as well as psychological identity. Without the child you cannot be a parent. Likewise with the institution of commanding and obeying: there cannot be commands if there is no institution of obeying. Social roles in general form a good case of internal relations as well. In addition to the master and slave example to be found in Aristotle, others include teacher and student, boss and employee, or sergeant and private.

In more formal terms, the notion of internal relation is commonly expressed thus (Bhaskar 1979; Dunn 1990; Pettit 1998): 'A thing *a* bears an *internal relation*, R, to another thing *b* provided *a*'s standing in relation R to *b* is an essential property of *a*.' The relation R of *a* to *b* changes the *identity* of *a*: *a* is not the same inside and outside its relation R to *b*. If relation R also modifies *b*'s identity, the relation R is *symmetrical*, and if only one of the relata is modified, it is *asymmetrical*. Conversely, a relation is called *external* if being in the relation in no way changes the identity of the relata, which hence remain the same outside and inside the relation.

The distinction between internal and external relations is thus a neat way of expressing the contrast between holism and atomism. An advocate of atomistic ontology accepts that things are externally related, while the proponent of holistic ontology sees things as internally related. Winch thus represents a holistic way of thinking as far as social reality is concerned, and claims that atomism is a proper way of thinking about nature.

He argues that since language is a constitutive factor of social relations, the property of being internally related characterizes social relations in general. Since social relations and institutions involve the beliefs of those participating in them, these relations and institutions involve internal relations as well: 'If social relations between men exist only in and through their ideas, then, since the relations between ideas are internal relations, social relations must be a species of internal relation too' (Winch 1958: 123). Likewise, a particular action can be understood in the given context only, which implies that it is internally related to its context (ibid.: 85). For instance, the point of a remark, a pause in a conversation, or the meaning of an interchange of glances depends on the larger situation (ibid.: 130).

A natural implication of the Winchian type of social ontology is that social research needs to take internal relations and contextualism seriously. This means that instead of seeking generalizations and cause-and-effect relations (which need to be external), the primary task of a social scientist is to investigate internal relations. This leads to the famous conception of two levels of rules in social studies, one belonging to the object of research and the other being a constitutive part of the research community (Winch 1958: 83–89, 107, 115). Along with the phenomenologists such as Schutz, Winch adopts this as a further argument for a distinctive difference between natural and social science (Heritage 1992). To illustrate, explaining what takes place in a chemical reaction only requires knowing the relevant chemical theory, but, in contrast, no logical theory helps one to understand a piece of reasoning if he or she is not already familiar with the language used in the reasoning and the logical connections within it (Winch 1958: 134).

Two arguments against causal knowledge about society

Along with several other proponents of interpretive social research, Winch opposes the nomothetic view supported by the empiricists according to which scientific knowledge claims are universal or general law-like statements (Nagel 1961). A part of this view is the regularity notion of causation, a concomitant of the empiricist conception of science since David Hume (Hume 1975; Baier 1991; Beauchamp and Rosenberg 1981).[4] This notion of causation adopted, as Winch later points out, from John Stuart Mill forms one of his main reasons for rejecting the possibility of causal knowledge of social reality (Winch 1990: xi–xii).

The empiricist project fails, according to him, because it pays too little attention to the role of ideas and their development in human history and, even more important, to the contextuality of ideas. The basic reason for Winch to be suspicious about the nomothetic ideal is that a generalization reports the constant recurrence of at least two events of the same kind. The formulation of a generalization presupposes judgements of similarity relying on social rules in order to identify similar items from apparently dissimilar ones, and dissimilar ones from apparently similar ones. If regularities of the social reality are difficult or, perhaps, even impossible to achieve, this leads to difficulty in causal knowledge under the empiricist notion of causation.

The stronger argument against causal knowledge is based on the dominance of internal relations in the social realm, since one of the standard requirements of causal relations is that the cause-and-effect factors need to be what are often called *Humean causes and effects*, meaning that they are *externally related* (von Wright 1971; Harré 2000). The point of this requirement is clearly that causation is meant to involve empirical rather than conceptual relations.

It is this latter argument that gives rise to the strong formulation of the mutually exclusive nature of explanatory and interpretive linguistic frameworks and modes of research, which we could call Winch's *incompatibility thesis*: '[T]he notion of a human society involves a scheme of concepts which is logically incompatible with the kinds of explanation offered in the natural sciences' (Winch 1958: 72; see also pp. 94, 95, 110). This thesis implies a clear distinction between natural and social research by dividing reality into two mutually exclusive spheres. If natural phenomena are characterized by external relations, as Winch presumes, and social phenomena by rules and internal relations, such an ontological distinction can be expected to meet with parallel epistemological and methodological differences. Social studies should give up research strategies, concepts and methods typical of natural science and replace them by non-causal research strategies, concepts and methods.

The most radical consequence of this line of argument is that interpretive researchers no longer need care about causal factors or methods of studying them, not to mention a philosophical concept of causation. They may ignore the whole causal approach as a mistaken way of thinking about social reality (Fay and Moon 1996: 24). This seems to be a widely shared conception among organization scholars as well, sometimes more explicitly (Morgan and Smircich 1980; Burrell and Morgan 1979), but often more implicitly (Morgan 1997; Burrell 1996).

The subordinate role of naturalistic social research

One might expect Winch to reject the role of generalizations in social sciences altogether. In fact, in addition to seeing them as difficult to achieve, he regards generalizations as unsatisfactory vehicles of historical understanding: 'Historical explanation is not the application of generalizations and theories to particular instances: it is the tracing of internal relations' (1958: 133). In the last two pages of his book, however, he allows some role for generalizations and nomothetic research. As an example, he discusses a generalization taken from Georg Simmel's treatment of the relations between Roman and Old Catholicism in his book *Conflict*: 'The degeneration of a difference in convictions into hatred and fight occurs only when there were essential, original similarities between the parties' (Simmel 1955: 31 quoted in Winch 1958: 135). Winch does not discuss whether the generalization can be taken as a causal one, but he is careful to point out that it is not the generalization itself that yields understanding concerning the relation between the two forms of Catholicism, arguing that their relationship can be understood only to the extent that one already is familiar with the two religious systems themselves and their historical relationships. And yet, generalization itself may have some epistemic role: 'The "sociological law" may be helpful in calling one's attention to features of historical situations which one might otherwise have overlooked and in suggesting useful analogies' (ibid.: 135).

By challenging the empiricist view on regularities, Winch's conception of social science does not, however, leave the naturalistic mode of social science untouched. Knowledge of social regularities involving two levels of rules clearly differs from knowledge of physical regularities. In order to formulate generalizations, a social scientist needs first to be familiar with the form of life and the social rules of similarity and difference it consists of. The nomothetic researcher is thus reminded that special investigations are required if he or she is not provided with this knowledge to begin with.

Towards an alternative conception of causation

It appears that Winch, like others who reject the possibility of causation and causal knowledge in the social realm, has not followed the most absurd implications of this claim. Without social causal relations we could not plan our lives, nor could we influence each other's actions. All organized life would be impossible. An adequate conception of causation for the social realm is thus urgently needed.

It seems, moreover, that interpretive studies often involve causal relations as well (Roth and Mehta 2002). This may easily go unnoticed, since we are not used to identifying the causal connotations of our everyday terminology.[5] For example, verbs denoting some productive activity, such as 'produce', 'construct', 'generate', 'create', 'enact', 'destroy', etc., often include a causal component. Similarly, singling out actors or agents in different social arenas such as organizations usually involves an understanding of causal powers related to their identities, roles and positions.

Consequently, a more adequate conception of social reality is required to allow interpretive studies to deal with causation. Even though Winch notes in the preface to the second edition of his treatise that a non-Humean notion of causation is necessary, he offers no suggestion on how to proceed in this matter. We shall thus take a closer look at how to rebut his two arguments against the possibility of causal relations in the social realm.

In our positive suggestion for an alternative notion of causation, we shall proceed in two steps. First, the counterfactual conditional view of causation and causal explanation, widely accepted today, offers an alternative to the regularity view. It suits the purposes of interpretive research by allowing singular causation. Since it has nothing to say about social ontology, we need to go more deeply into the nature of social causal relations. To our mind, the best way to proceed here is to take a look at the Aristotelian distinctions between causal powers and capacities. This does not imply refuting the second Humean condition that cause and effect be externally related. We shall argue, instead, that the social realm has room for both internal and external relations, and that, after all, this distinction does not form a dividing line within naturalistic and interpretive studies.

The counterfactual condition to replace the regularity condition

We shall begin with the weaker argument against causal knowledge relying on the regularity concept of causation. A notion of causation with a loose connection with regularities is required for interpretive research, which is *idiographic*, focusing on unique events, processes and the cultural schemes underlying them. Understanding these cannot rely on knowledge of regularities.

Causation need not be tied to regularities, as presumed by the empiricists. Instead, we have causal knowledge of singular incidents, not only through scientific research, but in our daily practices as well, as agreed by a large number of philosophers today (Anscombe 1975; Ellis 2000; Ylikoski 2001). This observation forms one of the insights in William Dray's work *Laws and Explanation in History*, which appeared just a year (1957) before Winch's study and includes a famous criticism of the empiricist covering-law model of causal explanation. In contrast to Winch, Dray poses the problem of causation in historical, interpretive research by starting from the historian's actual practice of using the notion of 'cause' differently from that of the natural scientist. The historian does not seek necessary and sufficient conditions, but attempts to 'draw attention to some necessary condition which, for one reason or another, is considered important in the context of writing' (Dray 1957: 112). Instead of generalizations, Dray (1957) suggests connecting causation to the notion of what nowadays is called the *counterfactual conditional*. This idea can be formulated as 'Event A is the cause of event B if B would not have happened if A had not happened.' This principle, now widely accepted among philosophers as a key feature of causal relations, yields a criterion by which to assess whether A is a cause of B. To repeat, A is not a cause of B in the particular case if B would have happened without A taking place. We cannot, obviously, empirically observe whether the counterfactual condition holds in the case in question. Neither can the assessment rely merely on the available data on the matter and their interpretation, since background knowledge available from the relevant research and everyday experience is required. The latter needs to include knowledge about causal relations, since, as the famous saying of Nancy Cartwright goes, 'no causes in, no causes out' (Cartwright 1989).

Even though often related to the regularity view (Mackie 1974; von Wright 1971; Woodward 2000), the counterfactual condition applies well to singular events (Ylikoski 2001; Ruben 2003). It is important for our purposes precisely because it allows us to dissolve the connection between causation and regularities, and hence makes it possible to develop a non-Humean notion of causation.

Assessing internal relations

Let us next take up Winch's second argument against causation, turning on the issue of internal and external relations. This is the stronger one, since it supports the logical incompatibility thesis to be found within the hermeneutic and phenomenological tradition as well. We argue that this attempt to distinguish the natural and the social realm fails, not as a result of an emphasis on internal relations, but simply because of an *overemphasis* on the role of internal relations in social ontology. Since we believe that the existence of internal relations need not rule out the possibility of external relations necessary to causation, we need to find a way to allow both for internal relations and for external causal relations in the social realm.

We shall first clarify why internal relations are considered so dangerous for causation. The answer can be traced to Hume's criticism of the rationalist notion of powers. The rationalists of the early modern period such as Malebranche argued that powers as causes were to be conceptualized so as to include their effects. Likewise, effects were to be conceptualized so as to include their causes. This forms one of the core assumptions of the deductive-axiomatic model of knowledge favoured by the rationalists (Craig 1987; Hacking 1975; Strawson 1989).

Hume attacked this conception of causation, arguing strongly, as is well known, on strict empiricist grounds. Accepting such a notion of power implies that from the mere existence of a power or a cause, one could infer the existence of another thing, namely, its effect, with logical – that is, conceptual – necessity. We get a sense of this in his famous discussion of the movement of billiard balls in his *A Treatise of Human Nature*:

> Were a man, such as *Adam*, created in the full vigour of understanding, without experience, he would never be able to infer motion in the second ball from the motion and impulse of the first. It is not any thing that reason sees in the cause, which makes us *infer* the effect. Such an inference, were it possible, would amount to a demonstration as being founded merely on the comparison of ideas.
>
> (Hume 1975: 342)

Hume argues that since we can without contradiction imagine that cause–effect relations are different from what they in fact are, we are not in possession of demonstrative knowledge of causal relations: that is, deductively valid knowledge on conceptual grounds. Furthermore, no such causes or powers are to be perceived (Hume 1975).

Hume and his followers seem to have taken this as a refutation of any notion of power, which can be shown to be an eminent fallacy (Kakkuri-Knuuttila 2003). Nevertheless, the Humean condition that causes and effects are externally and not internally related holds good. As the rationalists themselves saw, adopting their understanding of power would make empirical knowledge of causal relations impossible (Bell 2000).

Since we want to allow both for internal relations and external causal relations in the social realm, we need to ask how these could be combined. Do internal social relations imply the impossibility of external relations between interacting human agents, for instance? Cannot the sergeant's command be a causal factor for the soldiers' behaviour, or their belief that it is wise to obey the command at that moment? After much reflection on the matter (Anscombe 1958; von Wright 1971; Mele 1992; Stoutland 2002; Ruben 2003), philosophers today widely accept an affirmative answer to these questions. One influential view here has been Davidson's insight (1963) distinguishing *descriptions of causal events* and the *causal events* themselves. It is also useful to distinguish *reasons* and *actions* as general social institutions and *someone having these reasons* and *acting* in certain ways (Fay and Moon 1996).

Before taking up the example with the sergeant and his men, we should note another grave weakness in Winch's line of argument. It appears that since internal and external relations can be found in the natural as well as the social realm, Winch's attempt to separate these realms through this distinction is bound to fail. Locations in space are considered as typical cases of external relations, as are comparisons of size, weight or biological age (Hume 1975: 115). A mechanical mixture does not yield new properties for the parts of the mixture, whereas a chemical compound involves an internal relation, as the compound itself or its atomic parts have some novel – that is, emerging – properties (not possessed by the pure elements). Organic nature offers even clearer examples, since parts of organic bodies are internally related to each other. Their identity changes if separated from the body: a limb is no longer a living, functioning limb if removed from a living body.

Now back to our example of the military training. We may now formulate Winch's insightful observation concerning social relations in more explicit terms: as social institutions, commanding and obeying commands are internally related. The institution of commanding exists only in relation to the institution of obeying (Winch 1958: 125). The relation at the *type* level hence is *symmetrical*, since the same holds conversely, the institution of obeying presupposing the institution of commanding. Clearly, there is no causal relation between the institutions of commanding and obeying. The institution of commanding cannot cause the institution of obeying, because they presuppose each other.

Applying the notions of symmetrical and asymmetrical internal relations at the *token* level of commanding and obeying shows the fallacious step in the Winchian argument. Even though, as a social institution, commanding presupposes obeying, a token of commanding – that is, a particular utterance satisfying the necessary authority and other requirements for commands in the particular context – does not presuppose that it is obeyed by anyone in that unique context. If no one ever obeys commands, then the institution of commanding and obeying clearly disappears (Bloor 1997; Kusch 2002). But obeying is not presupposed in every case (Bloor 1997; Kusch 2002). Winch is quite right in saying that a command token is *internally* related to its *context*, but mistaken to think that it is internally related to the action tokens of those commanded.[6] The person commanded need not obey either because he or she has not yet learned how to do so, or because he or she simply refuses to do so for some reason. Following Fay and Moon (1996), we may note that a command token is not a kind of power described by the rationalists, but is *externally* related to the token of obeying or the refusal to obey, or whatever the actions of those commanded happen to be.

A contextualist notion of social causation

Our next task is to explicate the conceptual basis for an ontology of social causation which is in harmony with the prevalence of internal relations. Such a notion of causation thus forms part of a non-individualistic, holistic social ontology. Attempting to avoid the trap of a Platonistic ontology in which cultural schemes, organizational forms, ideological systems or political power are taken to be causally influential factors as such, we need to include in our ontology – in addition to natural beings and artefacts – merely individual human agents who have internalized such cultural codes in their socialization processes.

Since such a notion of causation can be found in the ontology of powers and capacities, it needs to be repeated that the empiricists are mistaken in believing that Hume succeeded in criticizing all notions of powers. The empiricists, like Hume himself, have tried in vain to deal with causation without powers or 'thick connections' between cause and effect factors (Cartwright 1998; Kakkuri-Knuuttila 2003). As well as in Foucault (1978) and some other Continental authors, important elements for such a notion can be found in the work of several authors in the analytic philosophy of science dealing with causation in terms of 'capacity' and 'power' (Cartwright 1983, 1989; Bhaskar 1979; Ellis 2000, 2001; Harré and Madden 1975; Harré 2000; Lawson 1997, 1999; Mäki 1992; Tsoukas 1989). We prefer, however, to go directly to Aristotle's notion of *dunamis* (often translated as power, capacity and potentiality) as explicated in his *Physics* and *Metaphysics*, and neatly elaborated in recent Aristotle scholarship (Waterlow 1982; Witt 2003). For our purposes, Aristotle's discussions seem to offer the most articulate treatment of these issues available. Even though we can take merely preliminary steps in clarifying these problems, we hope to vindicate the applicability of these ancient ontological distinctions for social causation more generally.

The ground for developing a contextualist and holistic understanding of causal factors lies in one of Aristotle's basic ontological insights, the idea that a capacity is typically not a property of a single thing; rather, a full capacity consists of two *mutually complementary* factors, called *passive* or *patient*, and *active* or *agent* capacity. As illustrations he offers examples from both natural and human capacities. As cases of active capacities he cites that which will heat, build, see and teach, and as corresponding passive capacities that which can be heated, built, seen and taught (Aristotle, *Metaphysics*, book IX, chapter 1, lines 1046a19–22; *Physics*, book I, chapter 5, lines 188a31–34; Waterlow 1982, Witt 2003).[7]

The active and passive powers themselves are thus *internally* related. For something to be an active power, it needs to be related to some corresponding passive power, and vice versa (Witt 2003). Nothing can heat if there is nothing that could be heated; the perceiving capacity does not perceive if there is nothing to be perceived; no one can teach if there is no one to be taught. To continue with our previous example, no one can command – that is, there is no institution of commanding – if no one can obey – that is, there is no institution of obeying commands. Furthermore, it needs to be emphasized that the internal relation is not between the cause-and-effect factor but between the partial capacities, which together may constitute the effective cause (Waterlow 1982). Hence, this contextualist notion of causation in no way breaks the Humean requirement that cause and effect have to be externally related.

This yields a holistic picture of reality, since the capacity to command cannot be adequately explained as a capacity of one individual only. The sergeant is capable of commanding only if the soldiers are capable of obeying him. His attempt to command remains a mere attempt if the soldiers present do not recognize his authority, or are not acquainted with the institution of commanding and obeying, or, worse, if none of them understands the language in which the intended command is expressed. Were such contextual factors requiring understanding of social rules not necessary, we could equally command stones or stars in the sky. We can combine causation with the Winchian view of contextualism and interpretation in the social sphere: identifying something as a cause of action in a particular context requires *interpretation* of the relevant social rules constituting the *context*.[8]

Since Aristotle draws the distinction between active and passive powers equally for the natural and the social realm, a similar point can also be made so far as causal relations in nature are concerned. The key point is that in order to identify something as a *cause* or part of a cause at all, it needs to be considered in the relevant context. To take Hume's example of the moving billiard ball, we may note that taken alone it is not a cause of anything under the Aristotelian ontology of causes. The moving ball has the capacity to make another ball move, but only on the condition that the other ball has the passive capacity to be moved – that it is not, for instance, nailed or glued to the table. As such, neither of the balls is a cause of anything; the cause arises as the result of the meeting of these two capacities. When the moving and the resting balls meet, the effect will be realized by necessity if there are no hindrances, according to Aristotle: '[W]hen the agent and the patient meet in the way appropriate to the potency in question, the one must act and the other be acted on' (*Metaphysics*, IX, 5, 1048a6–7).

This does not hold for human capacities or for the social realm, as pointed out in connection with our military example. So far, we have reached merely the first step in our attempts to combine interpretation and causation in the same ontological perspective. In the case of human skills, the meeting of the active capacity and the corresponding passive capacity does not necessarily lead to action. Nevertheless, we shall see that Aristotle developed further distinctions within his *dunamis* concepts to allow room for human capacities.

Further conceptual distinctions for social causation

Continuing with Winch's position that participating in social activity is based on social skills, we intend to inquire more deeply about the nature of these skills. Winch himself argues against Michael Oakeshott and Gilbert Ryle that human skill in following rules cannot be adequately understood within the framework of the behaviouristic stimulus–response model developed to describe the reactions of, for example, dogs. Since (human) social activity concerns the following of rules, it involves an 'understanding of what is meant by "doing the same thing on the same kind of occasion"' (Winch 1958: 61).

Winch claims that the possibility of *understanding* and *reflecting* upon social rules constitutes the essential difference from dispositions understood in the behaviourist sense. In the case of the stimulus–response model, we have 'just a causal influence', while in the case of human social activity we may say that

> I continue in a certain way because of my past training. The phrase 'because of', however, is used differently of these two situations: the dog has been *conditioned* to respond in a certain way, whereas I *know* the right way to go on *on the basis of* what I have been taught.
>
> (Winch 1958: 62)

This is where the further conceptual distinctions Aristotle draws in connection with his notion of *dunamis* are most useful. In the following, we shall briefly elaborate four of these altogether. One characteristic that the behaviourist notion of disposition cannot sufficiently deal with is the distinction between innate and learned capacities, whether they concern dogs or humans (*Metaphysics* 1047b31–35). Aristotle here applies his conception of a hierarchy of skills. He calls those allowing one to use a language – English or Finnish, for instance – *first capacities*. The same idea can be applied to the mastery of any social rule. With respect to the first capacities, that of being able to learn a human language or a rule is called a *second capacity*. It is the latter kind that we possess at birth, while the former are learned on the basis of the second capacities.

Two further distinctions help us to conceptualize human action in contrast to the dispositions of nature. Using an example from his favourite field, medicine, Aristotle remarks that a doctor is capable of healing his patient, but the same capacity makes him capable of killing his patient. Human skills hence differ from natural dispositions, for clearly salt cannot choose whether to dissolve in water or not; this is determined by its properties and by those of water. Neither can glass decide whether to break or not when hit by a stone. For this distinction, Aristotle uses the terms *rational* (*meta logon*) and *non-rational* (*alogon*) capacities (*Metaphysics*, IX, 2).

Which of these possibilities the doctor chooses to realize is hence not determined by his capacity alone. The choice depends on his goals: what he desires to do. Human action is thus preceded by two causal components, the *capacity* and the *desire*. To give some further examples, a builder can choose whether to build or destroy; the sergeant can choose whether to continue with his commands or let the soldiers go to dinner; and the soldier can choose whether to obey the command or protest.

Following Aristotle, the contemporary theory of action expresses this idea in the *belief–desire* model of practical reasoning with the two premises: desire for the goal and belief concerning the means (Charles 1984; Cooper 1975; von Wright 1971; Stoutland 2002). Aristotle expresses the causal relation involved thus: '[E]very agent, which has a rational power, when it desires that for which it has a power, and in the circumstances in which it has the power, *must* do this' (*Metaphysics*, IX, 5, 1048a13–15).

In order to achieve a full picture of Aristotle's understanding of causation, one more distinction should be discussed. In her recent work *Ways of Being: Potentiality and Actuality in Aristotle's Metaphysics* (2003), Charlotte Witt argues that the above conceptual resources are not yet sufficient to explain change, according to Aristotle. The most important ontological distinction for that purpose is the one between *potentiality* and *actuality*. The notion of potentiality was explicitly rejected by Hume (1975), and empiricist thinking has since been *actualist* – existence referring only to actual being. This pair of concepts is worth particular emphasis, since the empiricist actualist thinking appears still to have a strong hold.

According to Witt, potentiality and actuality are two different *ways of being* and hence add no new categories to the Aristotelian list including substance, quality, quantity, relation, etc., but cut across all categories. This means that the same powers are *inactive* and *active* at different moments of time; that is, exercised and unexercised. To turn to the previous examples, a thing's capacity to heat exists even though it is not exercised; the capacity to see exists even when eyes are closed; the builder's capacity to build exists when he or she is on holiday; and likewise with our sergeant's capacity to give commands and the soldiers' capacity to obey them.

Because of not distinguishing potentiality and actuality, Hume's version of the regularity conception of causation denies all 'real' or 'thick' connections in the world underlying the causal regularities. Therefore, for him anything may cause anything, and anything may be the result of anything (Hume 1975). In our alternative notion of causation, the 'real' connections are constituted by the capacities and skills which simultaneously restrict the possibilities of change and form its basis. No more mystical or metaphysical assumptions are needed here except the idea that the capacities and the properties responsible for them also exist when they are not exercised. This argument, originally used by Aristotle against the Megarians, who, he asserts, expound an actualist ontology, can be turned against all versions of actualism (*Metaphysics*, IX, 3, 1046b29–1047a11; *Physics*, III, 1, 200b26–201a9; Waterlow 1982; Witt 2003).

The relevance of potentiality for social ontology may be illustrated by the following passage, describing the performative conception of social rules:

> The rule R, as an institution, exists only in and through references to R, citing R, describing actions as instances of R, or as being instances of R, or as attempts to follow R, or as failures to follow R, and so forth through the entire gamut of possible glosses.
>
> (Bloor 1996: 17 quoted in Kusch 2003: 343)

Without intending to describe Bloor's ontological position in full, we may note that, taken as such, this passage conveys an actualist position because rule R is said to exist only at those moments it is enacted. We may now ask, along with Aristotle, how the performative theorist explains how the occurrences of R originate and how they cease to exist. If the rule exists only when it is actual, how does it ever become actual? How is it possible that human beings can understand each other, that we are capable of using terms in the same sense, or interacting with each other, often in a fairly coordinated manner, and that we may negotiate about meanings and change them where the rules have no potential being?

Conclusion

Social sciences in general and organization studies in particular are characterized by distinctive paradigms often seen as incompatible with each other. This is unfortunate, since it reduces the scholar's ability to make use of ideas developed outside his or her own favourite paradigm. Since the linguistic turn, as a result of arguments like those of Winch in particular, methodological literature on interpretive studies has formed a methodological paradigm that leaves little or no room for causation in social studies dealing with meanings, rules and institutions. In our analysis, we have, however, shown that this rejection rests mainly on the Humean regularity view of causation, and on a problematic understanding of internal and external relations. We have argued that the notion of counterfactual conditional, by developing an alternative contextualist capacity ontology of social causation, assists in bringing causation back to interpretive studies without rejecting any important insight of its proponents and thus developing bridges between seemingly incompatible paradigms.

It should be emphasized that while we have sketched the rudiments of an alternative notion of causation, this conceptual framework is not by any means complete. In fact, what we have done is to show how a counterfactual basis for causation and age-old Aristotelian ideas concerning active and passive powers, potentiality and actuality, together with some further distinctions to distinguish between human and non-human capacities, provide means to overcome the deficiencies in the Humean regularity conception of causation. However, these Aristotelian conceptions, even when developed to fit with the current understanding of social reality, are obviously not enough to create a satisfactory social ontology beyond the immediate questions concerning human skills, learning and the capacity to act or refuse to act according to specific rules in particular situations. Further development of this alternative causal basis of social ontology can thus be seen as a specific challenge for future studies. Particularly important questions are sociological and organizational analyses of power, the constitutive role of social structures and discourses, and the kind of 'causal power' that they have over individuals. While we have here picked up the works of a few significant authors essential for our arguments, it is clear that a more focused discussion of these topics would require a more thorough analysis of specific treatments in the philosophical literature on these issues.

At another level, our study reveals how superficial incompatibilities at the conceptual level are often historical constructions. In this case, the Humean conception of causation and the Winchian overemphasis on internal relations did not seem to allow for meaningful 'causal analyses' in interpretive social studies. Going all the way back to pre-modern Aristotelian notions, among other things, provided us with the resources to develop an alternative view. Although this is just one example, it seems that unravelling and reformulation of specific concepts can be an effective means of clarifying the relations between seemingly incompatible paradigms.

In all, we can thus certainly approve of causal vocabulary in interpretative social and organizational studies – something that has probably always been there.

Notes

1 We should like to thank the following colleagues for discussions and comments on earlier drafts of the paper: Alessia Contu, Bogdan Costea, Lars Hertzberg, Kaisa Heinlahti, Lucas Introna, Jaakko Kuorikoski, Martin Kusch, Susan Meriläinen, Johanna Moisander, Jukka Mäkinen, Maria Lasonen-Aarnio, John Sillince, Kristina Rolin, Tuula Tanska, Raimo Tuomela and Petri Ylikoski, as well as other participants of the philosophy Stream at the Seventeenth EGOS Conference and the philosophical lunch seminars at the Helsinki School of Economics.

2 For discussions on Winch and the debates roused by his treatise, see Bernstein (1976), Fay (2000), Henderson (1987), Hertzberg (1994) and Wilson (1970).

3 This way of characterizing internal relations coincides with the principle of the *hermeneutic circle*, which means that a part, such as a word, has to be understood in terms of its context, and vice versa (Burrell and Morgan 1979).

4 For treatments on causation in Hume, see Bell (2000), Blackburn (2000), Broackes (1993), Craig (1987, 2002) and Strawson (1989, 2000).

5 Winch also points out that explanation and prediction of social phenomena are sometimes possible (1958: 89–90, 93), which seems to contradict the incompatibility thesis. The following is one of the few instances with causally laden terminology that we have been able to identify in his own treatise. In commenting on the role of intentional action in historical trends, he remarks that 'such trends are in part the *result* of intentions and decisions of their participants' (1958: 93). We take it that 'result' is to be understood as an effect of some influencing factor: that is, a causal effect of some kind.

6 An amusing parallel can be found in Hume himself. In his criticism of the general principle of causation, he points out that some of the arguments for it are based on the fact that 'cause' and 'effect' are relational terms. Such arguments he considers fallacious:

> They are still more frivolous who say, that every effect must have a cause, because it is implied in the very idea of effect. Every effect necessarily presupposes a cause; effect being a relative term, of which cause is the correlative. But this does not prove that everything must be preceded by a cause; no more than it follows, because every husband must have a wife, that therefore every man must be married.
>
> (Hume 1975: 128)

Here Hume allows the simultaneity of internal and external relations, the internal relation prevailing between the general terms 'cause' and 'effect', while the external relation holds between the particular things causally related.

7 In recent discussions of powers and capacities, this idea has, somewhat perplexingly, been largely ignored, Ellis (2000, 2001) being one notable exception. Some others distinguish powers as to their degree of activity, calling the more active ones 'powers' and the more passive ones 'liabilities' (Harré and Madden 1975), or 'active' and 'passive' (Woodward 2000), without taking these as forming mutually complementary pairs in the Aristotelian sense. One possible reason to this may be Hume's great influence on the discussions of causation in general. Interestingly, the distinction between active and passive powers was a standard distinction in the medieval discussions of causation (Knuuttila 1999, 2000). It did, however, survive until Locke, who in fact is one of Hume's sources (Locke 1894; Kakkuri-Knuuttila 2003).

8 The main aim of an interpretive study may be to identify causes of a unique event, such as the causes of the First World War, or shootings in American schools. For an interesting argument concerning how the investigation of causes of a singular event requires complex moves of interpretation, see Roth and Mehta (2002). We find their distinction between positivism and interpretation somewhat perplexing, however.

References

Alston, W. P. (1989) *Epistemic Justification: Essays in the Theory of Knowledge*, Ithaca, NY: Cornell University Press.

Anscombe, G. E. M. (1958) *Intention*, Oxford: A. T. Broome.

Anscombe, G. E. M. (1975) 'Causality and determination', in E. Sosa (ed.) *Causation and Conditionals*, Oxford: Oxford University Press.

Aristotle (1984) *The Complete Works of Aristotle: The Revised Oxford Translation*, 2 vols, Bollingen series LXXI 2, ed. J. Barnes, Princeton, NJ: Princeton University Press.

Baier, A. C. (1991) *A Progress of Sentiments: Reflections on Hume's 'Treatise'*, Cambridge, MA: Harvard University Press.

Beauchamp, T. L. and Rosenberg, A. (1981) *Hume and the Problem of Causation*, New York: Oxford University Press.

Bell, M. (2000) 'Sceptical doubts concerning Hume's causal realism', in R. Read and K. A. Richman (eds) *The New Hume Debate*, London: Routledge.

Bernstein, R. (1976) *The Restructuring of Social and Political Theory*, Philadelphia, PA: University of Pennsylvania Press.

Bhaskar, R. (1979) *The Possibility of Naturalism: A Philosophical Critique of the Contemporary Human Sciences*, Brighton: Harvester Press.

Blackburn, S. (2000) 'Hume and thick connexions', in R. Read and K. A. Richman (eds) *The New Hume Debate*, London: Routledge.

Bloor, D. (1996) 'Wittgenstein and the priority of practice', manuscript cited in M. Kusch (2003) 'Explanation and Understanding', in L. Haaparanta and I. Niiniluoto (eds) *Analytic Philosophy in Finland*, Amsterdam: Rodopi.

Bloor, D. (1997) *Wittgenstein: Rules and Institutions*, London: Routledge.

Broackes, J. (1993) 'Did Hume hold a regularity theory of causation?', *British Journal for the History of Philosophy* 1: 99–114.

Burrell, G. (1996) 'Normal science, paradigms, metaphors, discourses and genealogies of analysis', in S. R. Clegg, C. Hardy and W. R. Nord (eds) *Handbook of Organization Studies*, London: Sage.

Burrell, G. and Morgan, G. (1979) *Sociological Paradigms and Organizational Analysis*, London: Heinemann.

Cartwright, N. (1983) *How the Laws of Physics Lie*, Oxford: Clarendon Press.

Cartwright, N. (1989) *Nature's Capacities and Their Measurement*, Oxford: Clarendon Press.

Cartwright, N. (1998) 'Causation', in *Routledge Encyclopedia of Philosophy*, London: Routledge.

Charles, D. (1984) *Aristotle's Philosophy of Action*, London: Duckworth.

Cooper, J. (1975) *Reason and Human Good in Aristotle*, Cambridge, MA: Harvard University Press.

Craig, E. (1987) *The Mind of God and the Works of Man*, Oxford: Clarendon Press.

Craig, E. (2002) 'The Idea of Necessary Connection', in P. Millican (ed.) *Reading Hume on Human Understanding*, Oxford: Clarendon Press.

Davidson, D. (1963) 'Actions, reasons and causes', *Journal of Philosophy* 60.

Dray, W. (1957) *Laws and Explanation in History*, London: Oxford University Press.

Dunn, J. M. (1990) 'Relevant predication 2: Intrinsic properties and internal relations', *Philosophical Studies* 60: 177–206.

Ellis, B. (2000) 'Causal laws and singular causation', *Philosophy and Phenomenological Research* 61: 1–23.

Ellis, B. (2001) *Scientific Essentialism*, Cambridge: Cambridge University Press.

Fay, B. (2000) 'Winch's philosophical bearings', *History of the Human Sciences* 13: 50–62.

Fay, B. (2003) 'Phenomenology and social inquiry: from consciousness to culture and critique', in S. P. Turner and P. A. Roth (eds) *The Blackwell Guide to the Philosophy of the Social Sciences*, Oxford: Blackwell.

Fay, B. and Moon, J. D. (1996) 'What would an adequate philosophy of social science look like?', in M. Martin and L. C. McIntyre (eds) *Readings in the Philosophy of Social Science*, Cambridge, MA: MIT Press; London: A Bradford Book.

Foucault, M. (1978) *The History of Sexuality*, vol. I, *Introduction*, trans. R. Hurley, New York: Pantheon.

Hacking, I. (1975) *Emergence of Probability: A Philosophical Study of Early Ideas About Probability, Induction and Statistical Inference*, London: Cambridge University Press.

Harré, R. (2000) 'Dispositions and powers', in W. H. Newton-Smith (ed.) *A Companion to the Philosophy of Science*, Blackwell Companions to Philosophy, Oxford: Blackwell.

Harré, R. and Madden, E. H. (1975) *Causal Powers: A Theory of Natural Necessity*, Oxford: Basil Blackwell.

Henderson, D. K. (1987) 'Winch and the constraints on interpretation: versions of the principle of charity', *Southern Journal of Philosophy* 25: 153–173.

Heritage, J. (1984) *Garfinkel and Ethnomethodology*, Cambridge: Polity Press.

Heritage, J. (1992) *Garfinkel and Ethnomethodology*, Cambridge: Polity Press.

Hertzberg, L. (1994) *The Limits of Experience*, Acta Philosophica Fennica 61.

Hume, D. (1739/1975) *A Treatise of Human Nature*, book 1, ed. D. G. C. MacNabb, Glasgow: Fontana/Collins.

Kakkuri-Knuuttila, M.-L. (2003): 'Voima ja mielenliikkeet', in S. Heinämaa, M. Reuter and M. Yrjönsuuri (eds) *Spiritus Animalis: Kirjoituksia Filosofian Historiasta*, Helsinki: Gaudeamus. The English version, entitled 'Assessing Hume's arguments against "powers": a new argument for realism', was presented at the Hume Conference in Helsinki, 6–10 August 2002.

Knuuttila, S. (1999) 'Medieval theories of modality', in E. N. Zalta (ed.) *Stanford Encyclopedia of Philosophy* [Online] http://plato.stanford.edu/archives/fall1999/.

Knuuttila, S. (2000) 'Necessities in Buridan's natural philosophy', in J. M. M. H. Thijssen and J. Zupko (eds) *Medieval and Early Modern Science*, vol. 2, Leiden: Brill.

Kusch, M. (2002) *Knowledge by Agreement: The Programme of Communitarian Epistemology*, Oxford: Oxford University Press.

Kusch, M. (2003) 'Explanation and understanding: the debate over von Wright's philosophy of action explanation revisited', in L. Haaparanta and I. Niiniluoto (eds) *Analytic Philosophy in Finland*, Poznan Studies in the Philosophy of the Sciences and the Humanities 80, Amsterdam: Rodopi.

Lawson, T. (1997) *Economics and Reality*, London: Routledge.

Lawson, T. (1999) 'Feminism, realism, and universalism', *Feminist Economics* 5 (2): 25–59.

Lehrer, K. (1974) *Theory of Knowledge*, London: Routledge.

Locke, J. (1894) *An Essay concerning Human Understanding*, Oxford: Clarendon Press.

Mackie, J. L. (1974) *The Cement of the Universe*, Oxford: Clarendon Press.

Mäki, U. (1992) 'The market as an isolated causal process: a metaphysical ground for relation', in B. Caldwell and S. Boehm (eds) *Austrian Economics: Tensions and New Developments*, Boston: Kluwer.

Mele, A. (1992) *Springs of Action*, New York: Oxford University Press.

Morgan, G. (1997) *Images of Organization*, 2nd edn, London: Sage.

Morgan, G. and Smircich, L. (1980) 'The case for qualitative research', *Academy of Management Review* 5: 491–500.

Nagel, E. (1961) *The Structure of Science: Problems in the Logic of Scientific Explanation*, London: Routledge & Kegan Paul.

Pettit, P. (1998) 'Defining and defending social holism', *Philosophical Explorations* 3: 169–184.

Roth, P. A. (2003) 'Beyond understanding: the career of the concept of understanding in the human sciences', in S. P. Turner and P. A. Roth (eds) *The Blackwell Guide to the Philosophy of the Social Sciences*, Malden, MA: Blackwell.

Roth, W. D. and Mehta, J. D. (2002) 'The *Rashomon* effect: combining positivist and interpretivist approaches in the analysis of contested events', *Sociological Methods and Research* 31: 131–173.

Ruben, D.-H. (2003) *Action and Its Explanation*, Oxford: Clarendon Press.

Simmel, G. (1955) *Conflict*, Glencoe, IL: Free Press.

Stoutland, F. (2002) *The Belief–Desire Model of Reasons for Action*, Uppsala Prints and Preprints in Philosophy 4.

Strawson, G. (1989) *The Secret Connection: Causation, Realism, and David Hume*, Oxford: Clarendon Press.

Strawson, G. (2000) 'David Hume: objects and power', in R. Read and K. A. Richman (eds) *The New Hume Debate*, London: Routledge.

Tsoukas, H. (1989) 'The validity of idiographic research explanations', *Academy of Management Review* 14: 551–561.

Waterlow, S. (1982) *Nature, Agency and Change in Aristotle*, Oxford: Clarendon Press.

Wilson, B. R. (1970) *Rationality*, New York: Harper & Row.

Winch, P. (1958) *The Idea of a Social Science and its Relation to Philosophy*, London: Routledge & Kegan Paul: London; New York: Humanities Press.

Winch, P. (1990) *The Idea of a Social Science and Its Relation to Philosophy*, 2nd edn, London: Routledge; New York: Humanities Press.

Witt, C. (2003) *Ways of Being: Potentiality and Actuality in Aristotle's Metaphysics*, Ithaca, NY: Cornell University Press.

Wittgenstein, L. (1922) *Tractatus Logico-philosophicus*, trans. C. K. Orden, London: Kegan Paul.

Wittgenstein, L. (1953) *Philosophical Investigations*, trans. G. E. M. Anscombe, Oxford: Blackwell.

Woodward, J. (2000) 'Explanation and invariance in the special sciences', *British Journal of Philosophy of Science* 51: 197–254.

von Wright, G. H. (1971) *Explanation and Understanding*, London: Routledge & Kegan Paul.

Ylikoski, P. (2001) *Understanding Interests and Causal Explanation*, Helsinki: Petri Ylikoski.

3 Language and landscape

Towards new architectures of thought[1]

Anne Wallemacq and Jean-Marie Jacques

Among the maps of peoples said to be primitive, there exists a unique group of nautical maps of the Marshall Islands in the Pacific Ocean. Constructed out of rush bound together, these maps are real models employed by the inhabitants to conserve navigating traditions. These "marine maps" are of pedagogical and mnemonic-technical use.

They represent the ocean currents of the southwestern Pacific around the Marshall Islands, with the influence of atolls (coral islets on the archipelago) on the tides, their refraction and movements. The navigator of the Marshalls does not bring these models along with him in his canoe; they first serve in his training, then function as a memory aid. He observes the movement of waters, listens to the rhythm of the waves, and with the help of these observations, chooses a route.

(George Kish, *La Carte, image des civilisations*,
Paris: Seuil, 1980, pp. 11, 188–189)

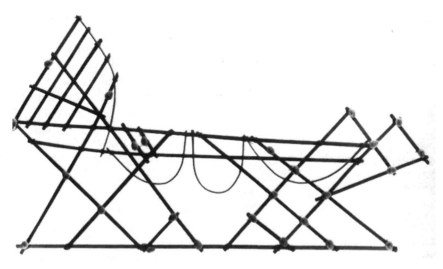

Figure 3.1 Marine map of the Marshall Islands (source: J.-F. Pirson, *La Structure et l'objet*, Liège and Brussels: Mardaga, 1984, p. 78, figure 74).

Representing language?

On the cutting edge of new interests, language analysis has left the sphere of arts departments behind. Artificial intelligence has opened the doors of computer science departments to it; statisticians and mathematicians via datamining and graph theory have allowed it to approach the concepts of abstraction and analogy in practice; geographers have offered it the cartographical metaphor as a means of representation; architects and artists have made bridges to cyberspace and virtuality. Moreover, with the Internet's development, all these disciplines have found new possibilities for exercising their talents for understanding and representing this new universe and facilitating navigation through it, for transforming data identified by means of ever more "intelligent" information-gathering search engines.

Language is now treated in many often surprising ways: it is counted, it is cut up, it is simplified, purified, structured via (hyper)links that compose it like a system of interfitting boxes, superimposed on or opening into one another. These processes are in turn associated with representational means new both as to the form and the meaning of text: maps, constellations, trees, tubes, mountains, etc.

Many programs deal with spoken language (voice recognition through more intuitive man–machine interfaces) as well as written language (orthographical and grammatical translation and word-processing verification). Classifying and analysing *relations between texts* is the very basis of the World Wide Web and Internet search engines. The organizational field of analysis is not at rest either. Many speech analysis programs have been developed on the successes of the development of discourse analysis in organizations (Putnam and Fairhurst 2000). These approaches, and the comprehensive approaches more generally, fit into the far-reaching reversal of perspective originating with Wittgenstein, through which natural language has acquired its status and legitimacy (Coulter 1991). It is no longer a matter of "purifying" language to attain formal reasoning. It is, on the contrary, one of understanding the everyday logic proper to ordinary reasoning, the patterns belonging to natural language (Grize 1984a, b, 1989, 1997; Garfinkel and Sacks 1970; Sacks 1984), because, in fact, the universe of meaning (or/and stock of knowledge – Schutz 1962) of the individual or group of individuals we study develops through this (Garfinkel 1967; Grize 1997; Weick 1995). Inside this language we reason (Grize 1984a, 1989; Apotheloz *et al.* 1984; Aqueci 1984; Sharrock and Coulter 2001) and perceive (Lévi-Strauss 1962a, b; Whorf 1958; Journet 1999) and feel (Damasio 1999). Power games are bound up in its use (Foucault 1980). It entails belonging to a group (cf. the notion of "member" in ethnomethodology (Heritage 1984; Coulon 1995)).

More particularly, in the domain of organization analysis a research field has developed that is aimed at determining the perceptions of different actors in an organization through natural language (managerial and organizational cognition – Eden and Spender 1998; Hellgren and Löwstedt 2001;

Sims 2001), making appeal to various programs of "cognitive cartography" (see, among others, Eden *et al.* 1979; Cossette 1994; Eden 1988, 1992; Eden and Spender 1998; Laukkanen 1992, 1994). Essentially, these programs want to account for what we shall call "ordinary causality": that is, the way actors in an organization link concepts and sequences of events between them and hence represent reality to themselves. It is less a matter of purifying natural language and aiming at formal causality than of taking into account the meaning system by which the individuals (and groups) evolve.

These cognitive cartography softwares rest on an interesting visualization metaphor: language is represented as "maps". As an example, let us take here one of the classic programs used in analysing organizations: Decision Explorer© (Eden *et al.* 1979, 1992), based on the theory of "personal constructs" (Kelly 1955). An analysis tool but also a tool for intervention in organizations, it is able to show how an individual or group of individuals links concepts. The concepts (ideas, things, objects referred to by the speaker) are represented by boxes. These boxes are linked to one another by traits. Thus, we are able to determine how, for a given speaker, things are linked together, by which chain of implication an event is supposed (always for a given speaker) to affect another. We can also short-cut or simplify a reasoning process, we can identify different reasoning processes within the same group of people, we can identify loop reasoning, we can tell which questions are central (strongly linked) and which are more tangential, etc. (see Figure 3.2).

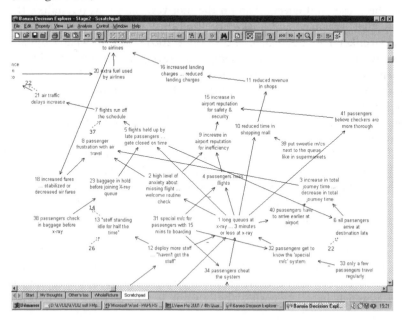

Figure 3.2 Screenshot from the program Decision Explorer (© 1991–2001 Banxia Software (www.banxia.com)).

This mode of visualization, however interesting, naturally carries its own built-in system of presuppositions. It stresses implication relationships (what acts on what) between relatively well-identified entities (the boxes). This visualization question is anything but harmless. It is, in fact, not only the use made of the analysis that affects it, but furthermore, this visualization bears its own conception of language within itself.

We too are developing a "cognitive cartography" software program, EVOQ©, which is inspired by a quite different conception of language and thus requires another visual metaphor to be represented. For our needs, we have a conception of natural language greatly inspired by structuralism (Lévi-Strauss 1962a, b; Saussure 1966; Greimas 1966; Barthes 1957, 1964a, b) and post-structuralism (Derrida 1978, 1981a, b; Deleuze 1969, 1988), but also strongly influenced by phenomenology, particularly the thought of Merleau-Ponty (1945, 1960, 1967), Schutz (1962) and Garfinkel (1967; Garfinkel and Sacks 1970).

This sort of thinking does not express itself in terms of boxes and links. In this conception, the accent is less on what language designates (what is denoted) than on what it conveys (what is connoted or evoked) (Saussure 1966; Greimas 1966; Derrida 1978, 1981b); less on the arrows (implication relations) than on the box edges: the identity/difference system constituting them (the very constitution of units, of "what we're talking about") (Lévi-Strauss 1962a, b; Greimas 1966; Derrida 1978, 1981b; Weick 1995; Apotheloz 1984; Borel 1984a; Bourdieu 1982; Durkheim and Mauss 1903), less on the causes and effects than on the motives, the forms (Gestalts), the patterns that organize and make intelligibility possible (Merleau-Ponty 1945; Garfinkel 1967; Sharrock and Coulter 2001), less on what language lets us say and rather on what it sometimes says without our knowing it, obliquely (Merleau-Ponty 1960), on the rebound (Derrida 1978, 1981b). Quite simply, this conception of language seeks less to account for a form of reasoning than to account for an undoubtedly still more elementary level: the semantic field the speaker is located in and copes with and which organizes his or her perception.

We cannot take up the program's *modus operandi* in detail here (see the EVOQ© website), but EVOQ© is based on structural analysis. A rather operational retranslation of Greimas (1966) was made by Hiernaux (1977), then taken up again by Piret *et al.* (1996). Inspired by this view, EVOQ© elicits the semantic field that accompanies the words, notwithstanding the intention of the speaker.

The *semantic field* is the whole set of associations/opposites that surround words. The meaning of words is relational. The semantic field stands for the relation system in which a word or, more largely, a text, is set. A word is defined as much by its opposites (by what it is not) as by what it means intrinsically.

The pair word/opposite is the basic unit for analysis. It makes up what we call a "*disjunction*". But the meaning of a word is also inducted (or at least "coloured") by the attributes that are linked to it, as well as by the inverted picture of the attributes that are associated with its opposite. This body of attributes makes up the evocation system, which helps with the meaning of a word. Unlike most software of its kind, which analyses the content, EVOQ© does not aim at reducing the meaning in order to make it as unequivocal as possible; on the contrary, it aims at restoring the open and plurivocal character of the meaning.

Let us illustrate what we have just said by means of an example. When I say "white", I do not merely mention the colour (denotation). If it is implicitly opposed to black within a given speech utterance, it calls up other associations: white connotes purity, neatness, virginity, light, life, as opposed to black, which suggests hell, night, darkness, evil, dirt, impurity, mourning, and so on. When I say white (as opposed to black), I evoke the whole set of these associations. The white/black disjunction and the evocation system that lies in the wake of these words are what we call a semantic field.

If now, in another speech utterance, white is opposed to red, it is given another "coloration"; it belongs to another semantic field. It becomes pallid: death as opposed to red, life, passionate character; white, the dull, the neutral; red the colourful, the flashy, but also red, ruby, warmth, fullness; white, coolness, cold, emptiness. It is worth noting that the same word, "white", in one case means life but in another means death, depending on the semantic field.

In the field of organization studies, the elicitation of these semantic fields is very illuminating since it brings to light the perceptual system specific to an individual or a group. These semantic fields are carried by language. It may be language as we mean it classically, but it may be the specific language spoken by an organization or a group. In this case, by "language" (which we call code [or argot], following the ethnomethodologists) not only do we mean new words, technical words or borrowed words that are specific to an organization, but we mean also the specific use that is made of common words in this particular context, as well as their wake of associations.

Another example, this time from Anne's experience. When first I was hired by the department of managerial sciences, I had only a relatively vague idea of what management represented as a scientific discipline. But very soon it became obvious that the point was that in this faculty, management was not economics. Independently of any intrinsic definition, management is obviously defined as much by its opposite, by what it is not – economics – as by what it is "actually".

Economics and management make up a kind of couple (a disjunction), the attributes of which are reflected in an inverted picture: I understood very quickly that economics was "scientific" ("non-scientific" management?), a "pure" science (impure management?) carried on by "fundamental" research, which gives an inverted and not so prestigious picture of management:

applied, superficial, not pure (impure, illegitimate?) non-science (the legitimacy of which can be then contested inside a university). To this vision, management gives a counter-picture: an applied discipline certainly, but, by implication, useful, something which is not limited to speech and analysis (implicitly like economics) but which acts, which is pragmatic but in the positive sense of the word. The game of counter-pictures goes on: useless economics, a speech that does not commit itself, and so on and so on.

Let us notice that if, on the other hand, I talk about economics to my grandmother, she will associate it with putting aside some money, woollen socks, saving, and for her there will be no reason for opposing economics and management: the latter is more up to date than the second, the former being more linked to private use and the latter to the business world.

How can we find a space of visualization that allows such a focus on semantic fields and which would be coherent with this underlying conception of language?

Thought and architecture: architectures of thought[2]

When we reflected on a representational space for the EVOQ© program, we wanted first of all "simply" a representational space whose properties embraced the conception of language underlying the theoretical referential we referred to. But our intention was not just to be coherent. More importantly, we had in mind the idea of proposing a type of space such that in "manipulating" it (in using it concretely, by hand), the analyst might, owing to the very characteristics of this space, *de facto* be led towards the register of structuralist and post-structuralist analysis. In other words, much more than being merely a support for perception, the space we thought of was seen as an operator: by its very characteristics it had to be able to make us access the interpretational conditions we envisaged. Thus, as we have seen, by its very existence, representation in boxes and nodes brought to our attention the relationships between the entities preconstituted. For us, it was a matter, on the contrary, of finding a representational space that would draw our attention to the wake of words, to the system of evocation (associations and oppositions) belonging to language, that the speaker conveys, sometimes unwittingly.

Yet in reading and rereading "indirect language and the voices of silence" (Merleau-Ponty 1960), in which the author deals with the structuralist Saussure's thinking on language in a personal, inspired and imaginative way, it appeared more and more clearly to us that what he was doing in this text was calling us towards a space of another type that we could eventually transpose as a adequate spatial metaphor for representing EVOQ© analysis.

But this space towards which we are led through Merleau-Ponty's text is a very strange one, a space that is not organized by conventional logic. This, which at first is very disturbing, is finally a way of penetrating a new universe of thought, a universe organized by another "architecture of thought". In this space, in this "architecture", thought – and here particularly thought on language – unfolds via other articulations, other operations and other rules than classical thought.

Let us move now towards this idea of "architecture of thought". Quite logically, we feel impelled now to use another "style" in order to better "fit" the type of thinking embedded in Merleau-Ponty's text.

Between spaces and thoughts

Assemblages, articulations, attachments . . . Lace, weave, intertwine, button, screw, implant, articulate, glue, refasten, place, encrust, print, set, bolt, pile up, heap up, interlard, sew, stick on suction cups, hook, staple, bind (a book), graft, suspend, fill, knit, crochet, harpoon, etc. Are these simple analogies? Each of them possesses a specific mode of "operation", a way of linking (concepts, ideas, words, things, materials). To intertwine is not to tie, to glue is not to button, to screw is not to bind (like a book). These are all truisms that cease to be once we reflect on our mental operations (mental? discursive?), how we tie one idea to another (causality, symbolic functioning, joining, associating), but also how we arrive at the units we talk about (a stitch is not a brick, a stake is not a tightener). On what principle of identity/difference do we "put together" what "goes together"? How do the tomatoes go with the red tablecloth and the bottles with the window in "Becassine straightens up"? How does the woodpecker "go with" the tooth in Lévi-Strauss (1962a, b), the turquoise with the blue or with the green (Corneille 1976)?

Let us now contrast three types of architecture and suggest the reader make the transposition him- or herself: to see there are not only architectures but architectures of thought, types of relationships, types of articulation, basic units that are different too and have their own "operational modes" (Pirson 1984). The first, architecture from the bottom up, works by piling things up, piling brick on brick, weight on weight. It is a sequential model, additive, divisible; the modification of a part does not alter the whole. Larger units form the lintel or the joists supporting the floorboards. A structure with main walls where the surface is built at the same time as the structure itself. Rectilinear space, rules, compasses, levels.

The second is Gaudí's threads model, a study for the church of Colonia Güell. Another type of space, other connections, another architecture of thought. One need only turn the model to see the church. A model conceived from above, lines, attachments, weights, joints, laces, knots, structure without surface: it being a sort of absence, between the lines. From a unit of one dimension, the line, the crossings and intersections make three. A model of the totality, the weights are in perpetual relation, balancing and unbalancing themselves; the basic units are already relative: to touch one is to touch the others and all of them. A model constantly more complex, of

Figure 3.3 Building a house: Aline (© 2004 Aline Bodson).

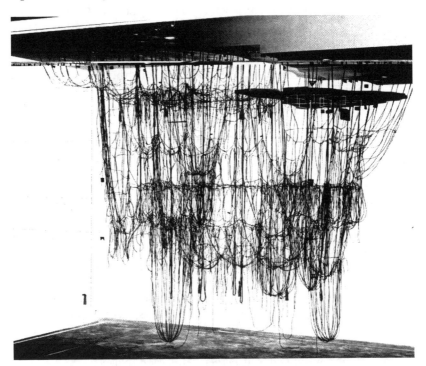

Figure 3.4 Gaudí's threads model (source: J.-F. Pirson, *La Structure et l'objet*, Liège and Brussels: Mardaga, 1984, p. 61, figure 59. © 1984 Pierre Mardaga).

Figure 3.5 Canvas surface (© 2004 Jean-Marie Jacques and Anne Wallemacq).

excrescence on excrescences, a curved space where the ceiling goes to the ground and the ground to the ceiling.

The third, a surface, a canvas, extended between (loosened and stretched) and subtended (in the proper sense) on stakes, of another nature than the canvas; the surface is given straight off. Trimming, links, stretchers, stretching and fixing, rigging. Two forces oppose one another, upward, downward, and resist in this opposition, condensation and verticality of the stake, horizontality of the canvas and extension.

Based on structuralism, EVOQ© calls for an architecture in which the main features of this theoretical frame are embedded. The architecture needed is probably closer to Gaudí's, or to the tent, than to the brick ones, since structuralism entails relational thought, a thought starting from the whole, a synchronic reasoning, where the elements are defined by their positions in relation to one another, in their differences, having no intrinsic value; where the composition of elements prevails over a simple additive principle.

Let us turn now to Merleau-Ponty's text "Indirect language and the voices of silence" (1960), which conveys us to an original architecture that is still more radically different than the ones we have just presented.

Indirect language and the voices of silence

As we will see now, with Merleau-Ponty, language is a strange object. And it is probably these specific features that call for another type of space. This "other architecture of thought" suggested by Merleau-Ponty is totally embedded in his metaphors and style. We have the impression that he really speaks from inside of it and is inviting us to come and see what we see when we adopt the proper rules of this space. This is not a purely intellectual game for Merleau-Ponty: the characteristics proper to language open this kind of space, this kind of architecture. This text is thus a very beautiful and a very interesting reflection on language too. But entering this architecture asks us to accept that we are passing to "the other side of the mirror" and to be a little disturbed in our habits of thinking (and logically, in our habits of reading).

An architecture with no outside?

> [S]peech, . . . a domain whose doors, it's thought, only open from the inside.
>
> (Merleau-Ponty 1960: 66)

To talk about language, I talk. To talk about the fact that I'm talking about language, I'm still talking. I talk about the fact that I talk about the fact that I talk about language. In short, I cannot get outside language to talk about it. I cannot talk about language from a position of exteriority. I can only talk about language from "inside", aware that I'm talking. Every time I want to talk about it from the exterior, I'm brought back to its bosom, its interior. This is the title of Ionesco's play: *Amedee, or How to Get Rid of It*, language, that sticky material I can't get free of. It's impossible to get a bird's-eye view. There is no position of exteriority possible: we are in the world, we belong to the world we describe: "no language before language" (Merleau-Ponty 1960: 69).

A bottomless pit? an architecture without foundation?

> Speech always plays on a background of speech, it is never more than a fold in the immense tissue of speaking.
>
> (Merleau-Ponty 1960: 68)

We never break through the surface of words. Beneath words there are more words. I shall never grasp the real "purity" that would be virgin of words, the one that is not inserted into language. Words are not in a simple relationship designating a real whose forms and pieces are pre-formed and that words only revive and reflect. We never get to the designated object "in itself". We shall never grasp the denoted as "pure"; it is always inserted, already set in language.

Laterals, edges, distances

Meaning is not underneath words, nor above them. The relationship between meaning and words is not a correspondence table.

This meaning nascent on the edge of signs...

As far as language goes, if it is the lateral relationship of sign to sign that makes each of them significant, then meaning only appears at the intersection and, as it were, in the intervals between words.

(Merleau-Ponty 1960: 66, 68)

Things are no longer defined in themselves, by what they might be intrinsically. They are defined by their edges, by the system of differences marking their distance from what they are not, and what, at the same time, defines them.

> [O]ne to one signs signify nothing; each of them expresses less a meaning than marks a gap in meaning between itself and the others. Since we can say this about signs, a language is made up of differences without terms or, more exactly, the terms in it are only engendered by the differences appearing between them.
>
> (ibid.: 63)

Surface thought, surfing on the surface of words: besides denoting, there is connoting, the ensemble of associations and oppositions conveyed by the use of words in a given culture. The object of the search is displaced from the "vertical" significans–signification relation (the signification under the significans, there to support and carry it; the other, the significans, being only speech on, above the object) towards the "horizontal" relation, of significans to significans, of words to words.

> [A]nd finally, words have a power, because, working next to one another, they are moved at a distance by it like the tides by the moon, and in this tumult evoke their meaning much more imperiously than if each of them brought along only a languid signification it is the indifferent and predetermined index of. Language speaks peremptorily when it renounces declaring the thing itself.
>
> (ibid.: 71)

And meaning is superadded. "Like a weaver then, the writer works backwards: he only has to do with language, and thus he suddenly finds himself surrounded by meaning" (ibid.: 72).

Surprise and upsurge, birth, meaning is not prior to language, something that language tries to translate. "A lateral or oblique meaning streams in between the words, – it's another way of shaking the apparatus of language or narrative to get a new sound out of it" (ibid.: 75).

Interlacing or foundation, horizontal or vertical

> Just because he [Saussure] is going to deny signs all but "diacritical"
> meaning, he cannot found language on a system of positive ideas.
> The unity he talks about is a unity of coexistence, like the parts of a
> vault bolstering one another. In this type of system, the parts of the lan-
> guage learned are immediately worth the whole and progress will be
> made less by addition and juxtaposition than by the internal articula-
> tion of a function already complete in its own way.... The real is a
> seamless cloth.
>
> (Merleau-Ponty 1960: 64)

It is not because it no longer relies on an objective reality (pure denotation)
that it does not hang together. For Merleau-Ponty, it is precisely because of
this tangle that it hangs together. "[T]he verbal chain's unceasingly cross-
checking itself, the undeniable emergence of a certain phonematic range
speech is visibly composed of, finally attracts the child towards the side of
those who can speak" (ibid.: 66).

The lateral liaison (systems of "differences without ends", the edge to
edge, the weaver's knot, the cloth's tangled threads, bolstering vaults) sub-
stitutes for digging foundations. "Saussure's intuition becomes clear: with
the first phonematic oppositions the child is introduced to the lateral liaison
of sign to sign as the foundation of a final relation of sign to meaning"
(ibid.: 65).

Medium or material, transparent or opaque?

> So there is an opacity to language: it nowhere stops to make room for a
> pure meaning; it is only ever limited by more language and meaning
> never appears in it unless set in words.
>
> (Merleau-Ponty 1960: 68–69)

Language is not some transparent medium, said to serve us to express ideas
that would supposedly be already established elsewhere beforehand. In the
crucible of language, meaning is formed and fused.

> For the talker no less than the listener, it [language] is indeed some-
> thing more than a ciphering or deciphering technique for ready-made
> significations: it must first of all make them exist as locatable entities,
> by installing them at the intersection of linguistic gestures as what they
> show by common accord. Our analyses of thought act as if, before
> having found its words, thought was already a sort of ideal text our
> phrases sought to translate. But the author himself has no text to
> compare his writings with, no language before language.
>
> (ibid.: 69)

Words are physical, material. This first of all means that they are opaque, that they are not simple instruments of what is signified – hence the importance of the significans as such, meaning then that they are their own "logic", their own "mode of operation" as Pirson says (1984: 51). Language has a life of its own. It is not transparent. Like the painter's (tubes, brushes and palette) painting, it is opaque, matter, texture, endowed with its own movements and connections. And the final result, the work, the meaning, is much more, and indeed something other than, the simple materialization of a project: it is the surprise of the work, created on the canvas, less like a projection on it than a dialogue.

> Much more than a means, language is something like a being.
>
> (Merleau-Ponty 1960: 69)

> To understand [speech], we needn't consult some interior lexicon of words or forms, thought to provide the pure thoughts they cover: we need only lend ourselves to its life, to its movement of differentiation and articulation, to its eloquent gesticulation. Thus there is an opacity to language.
>
> (ibid.: 68)

Outside or inside? correspondence system or whirlwind

> Speech as a whole … alone … shows how language attracts [the child learning to talk] to itself.
>
> (Merleau-Ponty 1960: 66)

We cannot get outside language. Underneath language there is more language, before language there's still more language. Speech is not a translucid and transparent medium at my disposal. It is a milieu that we bathe in, full of odours, evocations and waves carrying us back and forth, submerging us, crashing waves the speaker bathes in. We get caught up in, or else "abandon" ourselves to, its "eloquent gesticulation". "Everything said around him struck him like a whirlwind, tempted him by its internal articulations and led him almost to the point where all this noise was trying to say something" (ibid.: 65–66).

Meaning is not a projection of my mind through language; language, the associations and oppositions conveyed by speech, is the milieu that bathes and resists me and creates meaning effects beyond my will. We are in the power of words.

> At the very moment language fills our mind to the brim, without leaving the slightest place for a thought that's not caught up in its vibration, and to the very extent we abandon ourselves to it, it goes beyond "signs" toward their meaning".
>
> (Merleau-Ponty 1960: 69)

Paradoxes, regressions to the infinite, reflexivity, siphons, mirrors and labyrinths

This new "space" for thinking language suggested by Merleau-Ponty's text is not purely ludic. It is needed by the very feature of this apparently simple fact of studying language. It all takes place as if the very reflexivity of "talking about language" (talking about talking) conveyed permanent language games. And this is not limited to structuralist thought or its reinterpretation by Merleau-Ponty.

For example, the ethnomethodologist's concept of accountability (Garfinkel 1967; Coulon 1995), which points to the fact that in describing something we constitute it as thing, is paradoxical: the verb "describe" is transitive and so supposes a prerequisite – the object described – which we say is constituted in the very act of description. We can multiply the examples here: the indexicality concept (Garfinkel 1967; Coulon 1995), which refers to the fact that words refer to words which refer to words, never reaching the reality "out there", is again a particular logical figure, a regression to the infinite: to define a word I use other words. The same with reflexivity: we can only talk about language with language (Merleau-Ponty 1960), about cognition on the basis of cognition (Varela 1989). Still again, Merleau-Ponty's very formula (1945: xv), an approach that "joins extreme objectivism and extreme subjectivism", forms a real contradiction whenever the two terms are held together, which is what Merleau-Ponty recommends. Or yet again, the notion that we can no longer grasp the departure point of language. We have the same with "vision": "let's consider the case of visions: which comes first, the world or the image?" (Varela 1989: 103).

We can go on and on giving examples like this. When we plunge into the literature that takes the reflexivity of language seriously into account, we get the real impression of having slipped through to the other side of the looking glass with Alice and find ourselves caught up in a space of thought whose composition rules are different. We feel that Merleau-Ponty and Varela and, in another style, Garfinkel too keep pointing towards this place, towards this thought topology, where paradoxes, like regressions to the infinite, are not resolved but take on another meaning, happen in articulations that are no longer the perpetual enigmas of thought but rather open a different account of analysis and interpretation to it.

Whirlwinds, chasms, labyrinths, siphons and mirrors. How many stories use these images, bidding the reader to travel in strange lands: subterranean worlds, upside down, parallel domains whose logic is both strange and familiar to us, an elsewhere that's here, seething under our feet, in the folds, in a retreat from the world, forgotten, unsteady and so coherent. Strangeness, terra incognita, above, underneath and within.

Lewis Carroll, Edgar Allan Poe, Borges, all authors who have made these oddities into a genre, operate a passage from a known world to a universe ruled by another logic whose meanders we follow. A passage towards an undreamed-of and adventurous world. We turn with the whirlwind, we fall endlessly into the chasm, slowly and complaisantly, smothering in the waterspout till it spills us out towards new destinations, lost references, new births.

These language games (paradoxes, reflexivity, etc.) are not purely ludic (which does not prevent our taking a certain pleasure in them). They all take place as if we had to play with language and in some way toy with it to make it say what it cannot say classically. For ordinary language (at least the French language) is the depository of a "vertical" worldview where the real world is prior to and below our perceptions and interpretations.

But the moment we take seriously the fact that we cannot get out of language, and that we never gain access to reality "out there", but always as already set in language, we are led towards these innumerable language games. Like waterspouts, chasms and other mouseholes, these tropes are passage operators letting us say with language itself something that escapes its categories. These operators of passage towards a lateral, surface thought organize Merleau-Ponty's text.

Semantic landscapes

Coming back to our software program, we see clearly now that the simple question of the space of visualization has become a highly theoretical question. In fact, it should be a Merleau-Ponty-type space: language should be presented there as a universe I bathe in, sometimes creating meaning effects unknown to me. A universe where words refer to, associate with, oppose and clarify one another in this relationship; a universe with no below, beyond or within; yet a solid universe, where things are always already set in language. An opaque, non-transparent universe, where language never designates directly; it evokes and in its retreating generates a new meaning. It is a question of representing the very formation of "what I'm talking about", the boxes' edges and the way they are constituted on this edge, this limit, this difference.

How can we find a representational space that espouses this feature and this underlying conception of language? Moreover, this space should lead the EVOQ© user to this underlying conception of language and our special focus on the semantic fields. Thus, it is a question of our seeing the space of representation as such, as a system of analytical presuppositions which should correspond to the very conception we develop of language and its particular way of unfolding. Lévi-Strauss was fascinated by geology and the intelligibility one can read in landscape and the irregularities of land; Merleau-Ponty left us the image of cloth, of intertwining; Derrida that of the mark, the trace of the stylus engraving the matter of language like the root engraving the soil.

Finally, we have opted for an abstract landscape as a visualization metaphor: a landscape in between surface, matter and cloth, a preliminary

matter, with no beginning or end in which I am born and struggle, that sur-
passes me and includes me, shallow, lacking depth, a surface that is never
white, always already marked by opposition systems engraved by speech
and preceding what I say and giving it meaning on the rebound, partially
undecidable.

In order to see how these semantic spaces work and how they can be
illuminating for discourse analysis in the field of organization studies, let's
take an example. This example deals with the way "crisis management" is
organized at the level of the Province of Namur (Jacques *et al.* 2002). We
analyse here a small part of an interview with a fireman speaking about the
organization of crisis management at the Provincial level.

An example

Concretely, EVOQ© can work with texts of different types (interviews,
papers, discourse, etc.). Without getting into too many details here (for
a more detailed presentation, you can go to the EVOQ© website), let us
point out that the researcher enters into the software the disjunctions
(e.g. white/black) and associations (white–pure/black–impure) he or she
finds in the text. These are then stocked in a specific dictionary that can be
used (and enriched) for other analysis in the same research field or can be
exported to another field. In that case, the software identifies the system of
disjunctions–associations which can be retrieved in the text that is being
analysed.

Accordingly, an outline view is provided representing a semantic model
of the text analysed. The user can rearrange the relationships and/or go on to
a higher level of abstraction, towards another vision of the same text. The
three-dimensional representation of the model is then generated, in which
the disjunctions are represented as various edges of folds. This model is
modifiable in real time, progressively, during interactions between user and
system as well as during modification of the textual information base. The
landscape representation undulates, folds or swells depending on which part
of the text the analysis focuses on or depending on the new rapprochements
or caesurae it discovers.

Let us now turn to the interview.

> At **the crisis centre**, there's **no problem**; there, everybody comes, the
> problem arises. What happens once there's a crisis? Well, we send the
> troops into **the field**, so the firemen arrive and I'd say that just about
> everyone's there, it's a pretty **chaotic** situation.
>
> [The first] **mission** [is] to save lives if there are any left to be saved.
> Then afterwards, if possible, as soon as possible, it's to straighten things
> out discipline-wise.
>
> We've seen that there was **no one for [the] function** of delegated
> coordinator. He's called the PCO commander or the delegated coordina-

tor ... and it's an important coordination, because it's **right in the field**. And it has to be done by people who are **up to speed on what's going on** on the site then...

... "I'm not much in favour of a commander of firemen [as coordinator], I don't hide it, because I'd rather it be someone who's not involved in any one field, so he won't ... I read here, he's ... the arbiter of interdisciplinary **tactical** options. An arbiter should be neutral."

The fireman first set up the very classical disjunction between "the field" and the "crisis centre". At the crisis centre there is no problem, but in the field the situation is a bit chaotic in a crisis situation.

When we look at other interviews we made about the organization of the crisis management in the Province of Namur, this distinction between at the crisis centre and in the field is always used. It constitutes a collective reference frame in which the speakers behave. This distinction is well known in the occidental world. It is rather similar to the army "at the front"/"at the command post" disjunction and to the Taylorist distinction that opposes "conception" and "execution". Moreover, it is nourished by evocations of these two superimposed semantic systems: as a matter of fact, we find in the other interviews the semantic field according to which "in the field" "you cannot think" but only "act"; you are "emotionally kept" by the situation, while "at the crisis centre" "there is no problem" because of the fact that, being "far" from the events, you are not emotionally held and you can make "rational decisions".

It is interesting to note that this disjunction is both spatial and symbolic: to be far is to be spatially remote but also to be emotionally distant, to have distance and perspective to think. We find here one of our major cultural

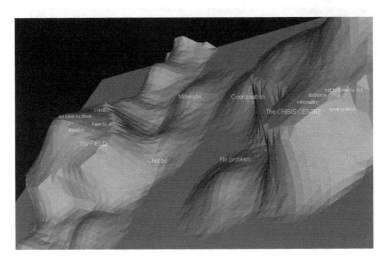

Figure 3.6 Three-dimensional representation of the text analysed.

distinctions between emotion and rationality associated with the in/out disjunction: you can think when you are out, you can feel when you are in. You cannot feel when you are out, and cannot think when you are "in".

In this concrete and semantic context, the question for the fireman (who is someone who belongs in the field) is to find a way to deal with the chaotic situation we find in the field when a crisis arrives. The problem is not that easy, since coordination is supposed to be done "at the crisis centre". To put some "coordination" into the field would mean a complete rearrangement of the common reference frame we have just elicited, and he is of course not in a sufficiently high-powered position to suggest it. Thus, he introduces another disjunction: tactical/strategic (still an army disjunction). This makes room for some coordination in the field (and no longer only at the crisis centre): at a "tactical level". Granted, this rearrangement does not reorganize in depth the basic disjunction; it is on the contrary rather coherent with it ("strategic" is on the side of rationality, decision-making, etc.).

Now, in this new place in the landscape, there is something quite difficult to combine because the "tactical coordinator" (called "PCO", "delegated coordinator") needs to be both involved (you are in the field) and not involved (otherwise you are emotionally held), close and far, in and out ... quite hard to find: "there was no one for this function". He is not in favour of someone from the field, who would belong to one of the "disciplines" at stake in the situation and thus not be "neutral" (in). Should it be someone from the crisis centre (out)? Even if we do not have the rest of the text, we now know enough of his semantic landscape to guess the different possibilities he will investigate and the pros and the cons of each of them.

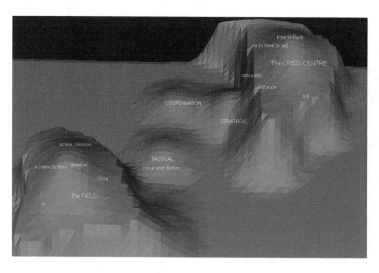

Figure 3.7 Another three-dimensional representation.

EVOQations in organizational life

From the first steps in the program's development, its name, EVOQ©, seemed obvious to us. This label condensed the level of analysis it pointed towards: the level of evocations more than of denotations; the level of significans more than of signification; the lateral level, where the words take on meaning in relation to one another, more in what they convey than in what they actually designate; the multi-vocal character of words rather than their univocity; less the level of what the speaker "wants to say" than that of the talk his or her speech fits into, producing a meaning that partially escapes the speaker.

This level and, more generally, this analytic perspective seem to us particularly useful in studying the life of organizations. In fact, from a strictly theoretical point of view first, the program is rooted in an "interpretive" approach to organizations (Hatch 1997). Rather than seeing the organization as a system of rules organizing the conformity of behaviours and their coordination, in an interpretive paradigm the latter are obtained by the fact that the members talk the same "talk", use the same code, the same interpretation system. This interpretation system only rarely being explicit, it is constantly presupposed by the various organization members. As Garfinkel said (Heritage 1984), for that matter, it is this speech that founds the group. We do not first have the group, then the speech. It is sharing (or rather, the reciprocal presupposition of sharing) the same code that creates "membership".

The program brings to light this very basic level of the system of reciprocal presuppositions. Thus, it lets us put a finger on a certain number of interesting phenomena: structural misunderstandings (two systems of different presuppositions that cross without meeting) (Wallemacq 1994); anomic situations (Hilbert 1992) where the code is lost and behaviours can be interpreted in a thousand different ways without any one standing out as the "natural interpretation" (Wallemacq and Sims 1997); but also the almost ritual interaction sequences in which one has the impression of knowing all the replies before they are uttered (these are merely due to the fact of replaying the same code). Similarly, it helps us understand how meaning-effects, sometimes (often) beyond our ken, are created: a distortion between what we "wanted to say" and the way things have been understood, interpreted, this interpretation catching us on the rebound and constituting, like an aftereffect, what we "really" said (that is, what is taken for real, intersubjectively). EVOQ© is also a tool that helps elicit the power games between semantic fields: which language invades another, which semantic field is borrowed from another field, for what purpose, etc.

In organizational analysis, it also seems important to us to see that language is not simply a register of interpretation; it concretely organizes perception (sense-making), collective facts, world visions and individual practices in situations. The program brings to light the fundamental distinctions around which an individual's, or a group of individuals', perception is organized – how he/she/they classifies/y people, phenomena, things, and how these distinctions (these systems of differences) are "enacted" (Weick 1995) in the organization's practical, material and tangible distinctions.

For analysts and interveners in an organization, the software program and the perspective animating it are also particularly useful, because by the very fact of aiming at the speech level, they aim at the collective plane: speech only ever assumes meaning in relation to a collective code. Thus, the code always partially eludes the individual, who nonetheless contributes to constituting it in using it. But the collective aimed at here is obviously neither a sum nor a composition of individual interpretation systems. The code is *forthwith* collective to the extent that it amounts to a reciprocal presupposition system with regard to the meaning of behaviours and words. For that matter, in the case studies we have carried out we have been quite surprised to observe the extent to which, when we are dealing with different interveners, formed in different disciplines, the conflicts opposing them take place *within* relatively well-unified reference terms. The conflicts and power plays dealing with the very definition of code, *on* these very terms of reference, would obviously be well worth analysing.

Finally, quite simply, the level of analysis the software brings to light is as interesting for the professional as for the analyst, basically because it works on the level of the system of obvious facts the organization builds up (e.g. in the field/at the crisis centre). Hence, it gets us out of the framework of these obvious facts and opens up the possibility of proposing other kinds of action and intervention (e.g. what are the pros and the cons of a crisis management system based on the "in the field"/"at the crisis centre" disjunction? Around which other system of disjunctions might one conceive another way of organizing?).

Notes

1 This research was supported by the University of Namur under a FSR grant.
2 This parallelism, or, more fundamentally, this idea of eliciting the echo of a space, of a certain architecture and way of thinking, is not new. We recall Panofsky's brilliant demonstration (1967). Panofsky in fact showed how Gothic architecture and scholastic thinking use the same operations, the same articulations, the same liaisons, so much so that they can be treated as homologues.

References and further reading

Apotheloz, D. (1984) "Logique naturelle, des objets de discours: propriétés, relations d'appartenance", in F. Aqueci "La Logique naturelle de Jean-Blaise Grize", *Cahiers Vilfredo Pareto* 67: 179–200.
Apotheloz, D., Borel, M.-J. and Pequegnat, C. (1984) "Discours et raisonnement", in J.-B. Grize (ed.) *Sémiologie du raisonnement*, Berne: Peter Lang.
Aqueci, F. (1984) "La Logique naturelle de Jean-Blaise Grize", *Cahiers Vilfredo Pareto* 67: 179–200.

Atkinson, J. M. and Heritage, J. (eds) (1984) *Structures of Social Action: Studies in Conversation Analysis*, Paris: Maison des Sciences de l'Homme; Cambridge: Cambridge University Press.

Barthes, R. (1957) *Mythologies*, Paris: Seuil.

Barthes, R. (1964a) "Recherches sémiologiques", *Communications* 4: 1–3.

Barthes, R. (1964b) "Éléments de sémiologie", *Communications* 4: 91–135.

Berger, P. and Luckmann, T. (1967) *The Social Construction of Reality*, London: Allen Lane.

Borel, M.-J. (1984a) "Objets, signe, classe-objet", in J.-B. Grize (ed.) *Sémiologie du raisonnement*, Berne: Peter Lang.

Borel, M.-J. (1984b) "Dimensions du raisonnement non formel et logique-calcul", in J.-B. Grize (ed.) *Sémiologie du raisonnement*, Berne: Peter Lang.

Bourdieu, P. (1982) *La Distinction: critique sociale du jugement*, Paris: Minuit.

Cassirer, E. (1933) "Le Langage et la construction du monde des objets", *Journal de Psychologie Normale et Pathologique* 30: 18–44.

Cooper, R. (1989) "Modernism, post modernism and organizational analysis 3: The contribution of Jacques Derrida", *Organization Studies*, 10 (4): 479–502.

Corneille, J.-P. (1976) *La Linguistique structurale, sa portée, ses limites*, Paris: Larousse Université.

Cossette, P. (ed.) (1994) *Cartes cognitives et organisation*, Quebec: Presses de L'université Laval and Les Éditions ESKA.

Coulon, A. (1995) *Ethnomethodology*, Qualitative Research Method Series 36, Thousand Oaks, CA: Sage.

Coulter, J. (1991) "Logic: ethnomethodology and the logic of language", in G. Button (ed.) *Ethnomethodology and the Human Sciences*, Cambridge: Cambridge University Press.

Cressant, P. (1970) *Lévi-Strauss*, Paris: Éditions Universitaires.

Damasio, A. R. (1999) *The Feeling of What Happens*, New York: Harcourt.

Deleuze, G. (1969) *Logique du sens*, Paris: Minuit.

Deleuze, G. (1986) *Foucault*, Paris: Minuit.

Deleuze, G. (1988) *Le Pli: Leibniz et le baroque*, Paris: Minuit.

Derrida, J. (1978) *Writing and Difference*, London: Routledge & Kegan Paul.

Derrida, J. (1981a) *Positions*, Chicago: University of Chicago Press.

Derrida, J. (1981b) *Dissemination*, London: Athlone Press.

Durkheim, E. and Mauss, M. (1903) "De quelques formes primitives de classification", in M. Mauss (1971) *Essais de sociologie*, Paris: Seuil.

Eden, C. (1988) "Cognitive Mapping", *European Journal of Operational Research* 36: 1–13.

Eden, C. (1992) Special Issue on the Nature of Cognitive Maps, *Journal of Management Studies* 29.

Eden, C. and Spender, J.-C. (eds) (1998) *Managerial and Organizational Cognition: Theory, Methods and Research*, London: Sage.

Eden, C., Ackerman, F. and Cropper, S. (1992) "The analysis of cause maps", *Journal of Management Studies* 29 (3): 309–324.

Eden, C., Jones, S. and Sims, D. (1979) *Thinking in Organizations*, London: Macmillan.

Foucault, M. (1980) *Power/Knowledge*, New York: Pantheon.

Garfinkel, H. (1967) *Studies in Ethnomethodology*, Englewood Cliffs, NJ: Prentice Hall.

Garfinkel, H. and Sacks, H. (1970) "On formal structures of practical action", in J. C. McKinney and E. A. Tiryakian (eds) *Theoretical Sociology*, New York: Appleton Century Crofts.

Greimas, A. J. (1966) *Sémantique structurale: recherche de méthode*, Paris: Larousse.

Grize, J.-B. (ed.) (1984a) *Sémiologie du raisonnement*, Berne: Peter Lang.

Grize, J.-B. (1984b) "Langues naturelles et langages formels", *Cahiers Vilfredo Pareto* 67: 231–286.

Grize, J.-B. (1989) "Logique naturelle et représentations sociales", in D. Jodelet (ed.) *Les Représentations sociales*, Paris: Presses Universitaires de France.

Grize, J.-B. (1997) *Construire le sens*, Berne: Peter Lang.

Harland, R. (1987) *Superstructuralism: The Philosophy of Structuralism*, London: Methuen.

Hassard, J. (1993) "Postmodernism and organizational analysis: an overview", in J. Hassard and M. Parker (eds) *Postmodernism and Organizations*, London: Sage.

Hatch, M. J. (1997) *Organization Theory: Modern, Symbolic and Post-modern Perspectives*, Oxford: Oxford University Press.

Hellgren, B. and Löwstedt, J. (eds) (2001) *Management in the Thought-Full Enterprise: European Ideas on Organizing*, Bergen: Fagbokforlaget.

Heritage, J. (1984) *Garfinkel and Ethnomethodology*, Cambridge: Polity Press.

Hiernaux, J. P. (1977) *L'institution culturelle II: Méthode de description structurale*, Louvain-la-Neuve: Presses Universitaires de Louvain (UCL).

Hilbert, A. (1992) *The Classical Roots of Ethnomethodology: Durkheim, Weber and Garfinkel*, Chapel Hill: University of North Carolina Press.

Jacques, J.-M. and Gatot, L. (1998) "Environmental and industrial risk and crisis assessment: a cognitive approach", *Proceedings of the Society for Risk Analysis 1998 Annual Conference: Risk Analysis: Opening the Process*, Paris, 11–14 October.

Jacques, J.-M., Gatot, L. and Wallemacq, A. (2002) "Risk perception and crisis management: landscape of mind, landscape of action", in K. Fabri and M. Yeroyanni (eds) Proceedings of the EU-MEDIN Workshop on Natural and Technological Hazards, Conference 2000, Luxembourg: Office for Official Publications of the European Communities.

Journet, N. (1999) "L'Hypothèse Sapir–Worf, les langues donnent elles forme à la pensée?", *Sciences Humaines* 95: 38–40.

Kelly, G. A. (1955) *The Psychology of Personal Constructs*, New York: W. W. Norton.

Laukkanen, M. (1992) *Comparative Cause Mapping of Management Cognition: A Computer Data Base Method for Natural Data*, Helsinki: Helsinki School of Economics and Business Administration Publications, D-154.

Laukkanen, M. (1994) "Comparative cause mapping of organizational cognitions", *Organization Science* 5 (3): 322–343.

Lévi-Strauss, C. (1962a) *Le Totémisme aujourd'hui*, Paris: Presses Universitaires de France.

Lévi-Strauss, C. (1962b) *La Pensée sauvage*, Paris: Plon.

Linstead, S. (1993) "Deconstruction in the study of organizations", in J. Hassard and M. Parker (eds) *Postmodernism and Organizations*, London: Sage.

Merleau-Ponty, M. (1945) *Phénoménologie de la perception*, Paris: Gallimard (NRF).

Merleau-Ponty, M. (1960) *Signes*, Paris: Gallimard (NRF).

Merleau-Ponty, M. (1967) *L'Œil et l'esprit*, Paris: Gallimard (NRF).

Panofsky, E. (1967) *Architecture gothique et pensée scolastique*, Paris: Minuit.

Panofsky, E. (1975) *La Perspective comme forme symbolique*, Paris: Minuit.

Piret, A., Nizet, J. and Bourgeois, E. (1996) *L'Analyse structurale: une méthode d'analyse de contenu pour les sciences humaines*, Paris and Brussels: De Boeck & Larcier.

Pirson, J.-F. (1984) *La structure et l'objet: essais, expériences et rapprochements*, Liège and Brussels: Mardaga.

Putnam, L. L. and Fairhurst, G. T. (2000) "Discourse analysis in organizations: issues and concerns", in F. M. Jablin and L. L. Putnam (eds) *The New Handbook of Organizational Communication: Advances in Theory, Research and Methods*, Thousand Oaks, CA: Sage.

Sacks, H. (1984) "Notes on methodology 1965–71", in J. M. Atkinson and J. Heritage (eds) *Structures of Social Action: Studies in Conversation Analysis*, Paris: Maison des Sciences de l'Homme; Cambridge: Cambridge University Press.

Saussure, F. de (1966) *Cours de linguistique générale*, Bibliothèque scientifique, Paris: Payot.

Schutz, A. (1962) *Collected Papers I: The Problem of Social Reality*, The Hague: Martinus Nijhoff.

Sharrock, W. and Coulter, J. (2001) "Réflexions sur le raisonnement: Wittgenstein et Garfinkel contre la théorie et la méthode", in Colloque de Cerisy (sous la direction De Fornel M., Ogien A., Quere L.), *L'Ethnométhodologie*, Paris: La Découverte.

Sims, D. (2001) "From thinking in organizations to management in the 'thoughtfull enterprise': an Historical Projection", in B. Hellgren and J. Löwstedt (eds) *Management in the Thought-Full Enterprise: European Ideas on Organizing*, Bergen: Fagbokforlaget.

Sims, H. P. and Gioia, D. A. (1986) *The Thinking Organization*, San Francisco: Jossey-Bass.

Varela, F. (1989) *Connaître: les sciences cognitives, tendances et perspectives*, Paris: Seuil.

Wallemacq, A. (1994) "Is non sense meaningful? An empirical approach to an anomical situation", *Actes du Workshop on Managerial and Organizational Cognition*, Brussels, 26–27 May 1994, European Institute for Advanced Studies in Management.

Wallemacq, A. and Jacques, J.-M. (2001) "Semantic landscapes", paper presented at the 17th Egos Conference Standing Working Group on the Philosophy of Organization, Lyon.

Wallemacq, A. and Sims, D. (1997) "The struggle with sense", in D. Grant, T. Keenoy and C. Oswick (eds) *Discourse and Organization*, Thousand Oaks, CA: Sage.

Wallemacq, A., Jacques, J.-M. and Gatot, L. (2000) "Space of thought: spatial metaphors in cognition", paper presented at the Seventh International Workshop on Managerial and Organizational Cognition (EIASM), University of Esade, Barcelona, 6–9 June 2000.

Weick, K. E. and Bougon, M. G. (1986) "Organizations as cognitive maps: charting ways to success and failure", in H. P. Sims and D. A. Gioia (eds) *The Thinking Organization*, San Francisco: Jossey-Bass.

Weick, K. E. (1969) *The Social Psychology of Organizing*, Reading, MA: Addison-Wesley.

Weick, K. E. (1995) *Sensemaking in Organizations*, Thousand Oaks, CA: Sage.

Whorf, B. L. (1958) *Language, Thought and Reality*, New York: Wiley.

4 *Glissement*

Gaming with(out) the matrix

Hugo Letiche and Joachim Maier

Introduction: four definitions of *glissement*

(*i*) Glissement *as defined in games*

> Déplacement d'une pièce d'un endroit à un autre, qui se fait sans soulever ni retourner celle-ci. La pièce peut ainsi être déplacée de la case où elle se trouve à une case voisine libre, orthogonalement ou obliquement. Si la case n'est pas libre, généralement la pièce qui occupe cette position est retirée. Dans la plupart des jeux et des récréations, les pièces se déplacent par glissement ou par saut.[1]
>
> (*Dictionnaire de mathématiques récréatives*, www.recreomath.qc.ca)

Thus, *glissement* has to do with the repositioning of a piece (or token) in a game without lifting it from the surface of the game. *Glissement* is movement enclosed in context; a shift of position governed by strict rules and by small steps, but capable of making a difference. *Glissement* rotates around the 'differences that make and mark a difference' (Bateson 1972). It describes movement that is permitted within the rules of a game, and within the boundaries of a 'system' – it defines some sort of change, while opening up options for next moves. Some change is so disruptive that it destroys the system (i.e. game). Some change is so minor that it is imperceptible to the system (or game). *Glissement* is change the system can accept – every gaming system is *robust* enough to sustain (some) choices. The epistemic problem is, how can one know what change the system can or cannot accept? Or, with respect to organizations, 'Who is in the position to decide (and/or block) relevant moves? What if the system becomes seriously playful? After all, *glissement* has to do with self-generating and self-defining systems: the game only continues as long as it produces further moves out of the state into which it has put itself. Movement along the game board is at least twofold: the 'game' plays the participants at least as much as the participants play the game. 'A game is a machine that can get into action only if the players consent to become puppets for a time' (McLuhan 1965: 237–238) – but if the players become machines, they are unable to make a difference. Then the game gets caught in an endless loop and is virtually dead. If the participants remain outside the game – that is, remain 'observers' – then they do not play. From within the game, one accepts the rules of the game and one plays. From the inside, the rules are self-constituting. Only by stopping or significantly irritating the game can the 'rules' be (re)negotiated. But if one stops the *glissement* of the game – that is, the action or movement inherent to the 'game' – one cannot be sure whether the 'game' will be restarted or restartable. Ending the game can always turn out to be the endgame.

Glissement is only half observable – one can see the moves, but not at the same time 'observe' the environment through which the moves move. Either one submits and responds to the game, or one remains an observing consciousness outside the game. Players reenter the game through their moves – via their ability to make a difference on the game board. Games open to the players' moves by operationally closing themselves. This 'operational closure' is a precondition to the game's autonomy and self-referentiality. A game can be observed only from inside its set of meanings. As long as a game is ongoing, it (re)creates its own patterns and logics of 'sense'. To participate in a game, one has to 'play'. Every move in the 'game' makes sense in its logic of play. Inside play, one makes 'moves' and these are received, accepted and 'understood'. Moves evoke new (counter-) moves. A game is a pattern of action–comprehension–response–comprehension–action, etc. The pattern only exists if enacted – someone either does or doesn't play the game. One can only observe the *dialogic process* of the 'game' from the inside. One can observe a game as an outsider, but then one is not a part of the (inter)action that is the game. One sees the players and their behavior, but one does not see the 'game'. *Glissement* is the movement with and within the game.

(ii) Glissements progressifs du plaisir

Accelerative Slippages of Pleasure (1974) is a film by Alain Robbe-Grillet. It is film as 'game'. It mixes 'realism' and psychological fantasy. Grotesque situations are followed by visualizations of fetishism and obsession. The sound track is a collage unto itself. It is film as an invitation to play with film. The pretense for the 'plot' – Alice killed her friend Nora and cut out her heart with a pair of scissors – is deconstructed by playing with the 'filmatic' and experimenting with psychological fascination(s). A 'true' history of the 'self' is unavailable. Who or what could define such a 'truth'? The living person knows a range of 'selves' bounded by situations, circumstances and constructs. In experience, the singularity of reference shifts and turns. In the film, the signature of the 'self' is throughout the 'text' – it is the experienced, the events, the stream of activity. Attributing a fixed point of reference to someone, or even to oneself, denies the constant interaction of self and other, communication and system, organization and circumstance (Havercroft 1994). Identity flows and shifts – it is in everything, but cannot be identified with anyone or anything. Identity is floating and characterized by its fissures. It is the *glissement* of experience.

> I realize fully that the *parole*, the speech, the 'word' of a writer such as myself, has something strange and even contradictory about it, even within its own creator. At the moment when I write, let us say, *La Jalousie* or *Glissements progressifs du plaisir*, what I propose is improbable and consequently unacceptable; that is, my *parole* as a writer or as a cineaste in my novels or in my films is abrupt, inexplicable, nonrecuperable for any correctly organized discourse. Nevertheless, you have noticed that I speak with the same clarity as any professor, and this constitutes an extremely interesting contradiction because it goes to the very heart of the debate; order and disorder never cease to interact, to contaminate each other, to practice a sort of mutual recuperation. If, having written a novel of disorder, I don't find someone – for example, Bruce Morrissette, about *La Jalousie* – to prove that it has order, I'll do it myself. The principle of order is so crucial that I wish to prove that the disorder which I've created I can myself transform into order. But, as soon as I have shown that it has its order, from that moment on I've destroyed the interest of my work. I have brought about within an organized discourse, organized according to the normal logic of Cartesianism, the recuperation of something which was in fact a machine of war against order. I often run into people who say to me after a film, 'Ah, it's a pity that you didn't come to explain all of that before the film. We didn't understand a thing, and it is such a fine thing that you have explained it.' And I reply, 'Yes, but don't trust that too much,' because what I've said is not at all the film. It is even almost the opposite; it is the way in which I show myself that there is in what I created a part which is in spite of everything, explainable by established order, and a part increasingly large, because order progresses.
>
> (Robbe-Grillet 1977)

The paradox here of identity is that it exists insofar as it does not exist – that is, it is in everything. It is distributed throughout the 'text', it slides from pulsion to pulsion. It does not exist where it seems to exist – that is, as 'I', 'self' or 'identity'. Reduced to a rationalization, object or 'thing', it does not exist. 'Self' is a game of *glissement* or it is nothing.

(iii) *Being* glissement

In Lacan's psychology, *glissement* refers to the endless chain of signifiers. Every significance refers to other significances. Any word, idea or identity exists in relationship to other words, ideas and identities. Meaning slides from one signifier to another. Meaning, thought and identity are language 'games' wherein the signifiers always remain in motion. Communication is an ongoing form of semiotic play. We deal constantly with constructions of sense and meaning that we exchange, develop and convert. Meaning is fragmented and always remains in a curious (un)balanced relationship with (non-)sense – a play of possibilities, an exchange between a foreground (the 'said') and the background (the 'silenced' or left 'unsaid'). If the flow of meanings is disrupted, then the tissue of shared existence is threatened. A constant flow of associations pushes against the danger of senselessness and despair. As long as significations remain visible (on the game board), the desire to continue prevails. As long as communication continues, the social subject is constituted. Stopping the flow amounts to stepping into nothingness. An observer that is not playing with distinctions is in unmarked space – lost without relations. As long as the signifiers flow, there is a sense of identity and purpose. Language protects the 'self' from the abysm of selflessness. Meanings have to glide into one another for there to be communication – the ongoing quality of intersubjective existence depends on it. If the *glissement* stops, the reality we share with one another by means of language disintegrates. The terror of communication is to lose oneself in the *glissement*. *Glissement* provides the self's opportunity for continuity; but only by stepping out of ongoing communication can we explore 'self'. Self-knowledge amounts to the 'end of identity'. We are subjects of ongoing discourse(s), which respond to our surroundings, cultures and circumstances. Our ability for social existence depends on our lack of fixed identity. If we can *be glissement*, we can socially continue to exist. Insistence on 'identity' – on a 'self' found outside of the flow of the Other – destroys the social process. Our social existence occurs inside the system of the *glissement* of signifiers. Humans exist in shared meanings, events, constructs and organizations. As long as one stays inside the referential system and 'self' is constituted within the limits of the *glissement* on offer, identity and social existence remain possible. But is *glissement* then an opportunity for social existence, or a mutually enforced prison, or perhaps both? Is *glissement* a play of shared identity wherein interaction is possible; or the drama of (nearly) powerless subjects repressing one another? Is the game autonomous? How can texts be shared if *glissement* is only half-observable? Are the shared signifiers in a logic of domination or of mutuality? If we admit that there is no pure 'self' – that consciousness is shared and based upon communication – do we somehow give up the body of (individual) freedom? Does a shared constitutive text always lead to the repression or destruction of desire?

(iv) Glissement, *virtuality and an(o)ther desire*

Glissement in Deleuze's *Logique du sense* identifies floating elements, which are hiding the difference between sense and non-sense, thereby being neither one nor other and only partially realized and somewhat virtual (Deleuze 1992). The 'virtual', in a predigital Lacanian world, is the possible and contingent; it could be possible and often it is desired. Virtuality is to be found in the gaze of the other. Virtuality in Deleuze is the milieu of desire. By means of gliding and crossing, Deleuze follows multiple series of *glissements* while playing through different responses upon dissimilar desire(s). The moves he explores are uncontrolled by the Other. Desire, for him, emphasizes the virtuality of the event and the importance of a radical affirmation of randomness, thus disregarding the constant presence of (an)other. Contrastingly, Lacanian *glissement* is mediated through the embodied Other and it operates on the matrix of a pre-ontological *structure*. Lacanian embodiment cultivates the desire of the Other. Its embodiment takes on the Other as a compulsory a priori, which controls the *glissement* from the one to the other. Deleuze potentially repositions an(y)other; he decontaminates the (other-determined) force field so that emerging desires can appear in all their force. Desire becomes a screen for the projection of virtuality; it welcomes the phantasm. Deleuze acknowledges the importance (and the terror) of other-determinedness. The Other can enable gradual *glissement* into the virtual. Interaction between the One and the Other can pre-structure one's desire for meaning: 'What is the meaning of my day? What is the meaning of my world? I will call them beautiful, if it stands in your eyes' (Rosset 1994: 72). For Deleuze, duality is to be found somewhere in between the structural 'other' and the effects of its absence (1992: 372). But what differentiates the 'non-other' from the 'other'? What happens when structure disappears? How is desire constituted if there is not (an)Other at hand, or if it is submerged in an untrustworthy virtual world? When the presence of the embodied Other recedes, one gets system failure. Suffering and hallucinations are produced by self-absence. Compensationary obsessions and a longing for order result. Phantasms and doubles emerge and create a force field. Images of desire are generated. *Glissement* commences between other and another, between significant and signified, between solitaire and solidaire. *Glissement* is movement through another. *Glissement* needs to be thought of as so many images; and not as becoming. *Glissement* is the realm of *another other than the other* (Deleuze 1992).

From *glissement* to gaming, to organization

In the film *The Matrix*, popular culture provides, in one of its more successful efforts, a simulacrum of movement, action and occurrence. The people are portrayed as computer game figures; consciousness is virtual reality; society is hyperreal. In this high-tech simulation, everything slides from identity to identity and position to position, and follows the logic(s) of *glissement*. Not linear cause and effect, or a change driven dialectic, but a convoluted self-referential logic of game-like moves, is characteristic of 'the matrix'. The matrix appears to portray a simple either/or, good/bad, universe; but the opposites touch and everything collapses into ambiguity. Identity is not what it appears to be; resolution (closure) is more open than closed, purposes get no-where. Appearances are more important than principles, and plot is a flimsy excuse for endless (violent) 'action scenes'.

The link to organization studies comes via the need to contextualize action. Nussbaum (1990), for instance, has called on professional training to look to literature to enrich awareness and empathy. Willmott and Knights (1999) have (re)discovered status, identity and rationality by following just such a procedure. The gaze caught by 'the matrix' reveals gaming, desire and the *glissement* of signification. How have these highly contemporary simulacra informed (organizational) practice?

Glissement and gaming

The Matrix has as its explicit point of departure the choice between 'self' and 'illusion' – that is, the real of the desert and appearances of virtuality. One can play along or rewrite the game. The assumption upon which the film is based is that humankind has been reduced to biological batteries who are fed only 'virtual reality' with no 'real' communication or experience left. Most people are content to live what the virtual reality (VR) has to offer, namely, an absence of crises and a 'comfortable' existence in a fairly rich society (the United States of 1999). A few want to know 'what really is', even if that is far less comforting or safe. The explicit choice posed in the film is between safety in ignorance (taking the blue pill), which is identified with corporate existence; or danger in knowledge (taking the red pill), which is identified with countercultural individualism. But analysis of the film shows that this seemingly simple dualism is not that simple at all. In fact, there are lots of crossovers from the one logic to the other. The texture of the movie is full of *glissements* from position to position, identity to identity, significance to significance.

Not the choices that people make – the red pill versus the blue pill, reality versus illusion, individuality versus conformity – but how all the choices imply one another and slip the one into another, is what counts. *Glissement* deconstructs choice and the 'self' that supposedly chooses. It is a destabilizing force that topples identity based on 'things are what they are and that is our safety'. *Glissement* is the social process of uncertain boundaries, indefinite desires; it is a logic that turns and twists back on itself. In the matrix, *glissement* is a product of 'gaming', of living life in a virtual computer game environment. First 'the world of gaming' needs clarification and then its significance can be explored.

Games can be thought of as mirrors of day-to-day experience in the corporate world and hyperreal society. Games are a popular form of entertainment whose operations follow strict conventions. Watching *The Matrix* is like playing a computer game. The movie displays cinematographic dream images that are the products of digital techniques. These images seem to be beyond everyday comprehension and to be powerful enough to hypnotize the player. The digital filming, cutting and rendering technology used in the matrix evokes being inside a computer game. The matrix seems to operate on computer code. The gaming environment and the digitally created environment change from moment to moment. The point of entry for the characters in the film is 'boot camp', where they are trained in simulation. The 'real' action comes thereafter: a skyscraper has to be conquered, numerous jump and run scenes demand all sorts of dexterity, and computer-generated weaponry is employed in combat. The matrix is the game terminal and the players are its extensions.

Appearances

Aesthetics are crucial to computer games. Being 'good' and being 'attractive' are the same thing.[2] Good is 'attractive'; bad is 'ugly'. Even the one traitor in the film is obviously less attractive than his loyal colleagues: he has a weak chin, a stubble beard and very little bodily hair. The male lead, Neo, is a prototype male model and thus 'very good'. The female lead, Trinity, is a 'female goddess'. Goodness and appearance are tightly linked. Everyone in the game who is on the right side has a sympathetic outward appearance. In the matrix, you can judge by first appearances without risking disappointment. Morpheus and the Oracle, two key supporting characters, pay obvious tribute to attractiveness in terms of their political correctness; they represent the older generation and the excluded subgroups. The young (Neo and Trinity) are the most attractive, but governance is the privilege of experienced leaders (Morpheus and the Oracle). 'Good' is defined in terms of resistance to tyranny, technology and conformity. Morpheus is the director of the 'resistance' – he facilitates the new player's (Neo's) experiences, and represents wisdom and insight. The Oracle is a mentor in the mission of the good. She has been with the resistance right from the beginning, and cares for the (human) players. She gives Neo cookies – food for the soul or holy communion – and displays an ironic sense of humor. The Oracle permits identity to be established.[3] The heroes – Neo, Trinity, Morpheus and the Oracle – are attractive game figures.

On the other side, the 'suits' are the representatives of the matrix. They are nasty and heartless, with a cynical sense of humor. They display the characteristics of the anonymous corporate man. Basically, they punish anyone below them and execute the instructions of their superiors. They duck or run when things get difficult. The cold authoritarian corporate type is other-directed, bad and literally inhuman. The agents act anonymously and all look alike. They are clean-cut types, with rectangular sunglasses; they are unified and uniformed. The emphasis on appearances is crucial. The premise of the matrix is that what consciousness consumes, and to a large degree what it wants to consume, is the illusion of attractiveness. But who in the film is really attractive? Is it really the so-called good figures?

Though the agents are 'bad', they're smart, responsive and have a sharp, street-wise sense of humor.[4] They are treated by the matrix as respected business partners.[5] The resistance is made up of a bunch of kids who are playing around in an overstructured adult world of rules and limitations.

Outwardly the matrix celebrates childishness and rejects adult responsibility – a standpoint common to much 'juvenilized' culture. The agents, on the other hand, get the work done. In the matrix, running, hiding and hitting are the keys to success. If you are the right hand of the matrix, you adjust; after some time you even get to like it. You may be on a tight leash – agents receive precise instructions via little ear speakers – but you get things done. The agents are the performative team. Eventually, agents discover that from time to time they can take the little speakers out. There are benefits to being an agent: agents have been promised that they can leave the matrix upon the completion of their mission.[6] They enjoy their vacations every once in a while. Comparing these prospects with the prospects of the resistance crew – that is, the juvenilized attractive characters – leaves us with a paradox. The 'One', Neo, is supposedly exceptional; he gets his work done and is also juvenile. He, so-called, 'saves the world'. But ultimately he is left to wander around the matrix, proclaiming his 'truth' to a world that will not listen. While he can use the matrix as a tool, his powerlessness within the matrix is obvious. Neo manages to provoke a system failure; the game has to go 'on pause'. But his imagination is severely limited. In his closing statement, he merely announces that the fight against the system will continue.[7] But fighting the matrix is reproducing the matrix – and the system knows it. Where can Neo go after he has '*saved*' the world?[8] What is '*success*', under matrix conditions? How could one notice that '*playing in the matrix is actually over*'?

Booting, running and shooting

The characters in the movie always know what to do; they never have to think about it. They are either programmed or remote-controlled (as agents through their earplugs), or they just automatically do what is good for the game. It is all the same basic logic. Throughout the movie, the most frequently used phrase is you/someone/we 'have to'. There are twenty-one 'you have tos' in the lines of the good characters. The matrix is an instructions-based world. Mind, as analysis, as consciousness and as reflection, is worthless in the universe of the film. One just 'has to'. Likewise, competing truths or fundamental uncertainties are either absent or get resolved in an aggressive military style.[9] Learning is something one 'uploads' from a computer.[10] There is no room for process issues; blind action is rewarded. The attractiveness of the results is built in.

The film is infantile in its approach to individual intellectual effort. In the matrix, one has to be physically superhuman and to fight a lot. There is no role for thought or mind. During the first sequences, Neo undergoes his socialization – and the audience with him. Neo gains his new, game character identity; likewise the audience, in the cinema, is initiated (introduced) to the film. Both characters and audience are prepared to play in the matrix. As soon as Neo enters the 'real' world of the desert – that is, chooses the red pill

– he is transformed. Neo becomes a game figure. And instead of the prior normal reality, it is revealed that he has all along been a porous body riveted with holes. What was 'real' was mere VR. Existence is an embodied nightmare. Neo's body has been a physical mass of flesh plugged into the matrix. Being outside the matrix means entering into a transition state. Morpheus and the other dissidents mentor Neo. He is prepared to be a game-player against the matrix. To win, one has to be prepared.[11] Successful behavior has to be programmed into Neo, providing him with the advantages of preadaptive selection. In matrix-ation, competences are determined. That is how one gets things done in the game. Education and socialization take place in a predetermined closed system. Evidently, every character in the game has had to run through the same training program.

The order of the matrix is portrayed to be a universal fore-structure. One is either inside or outside the matrix. Existence is defined as being either on the 'blue pill' (autopilot) or on the 'red pill' (believing in the power of one's self). Either way, life is played in complex game terms. One is a 'player' in a matrix. The results are not surprising. Humans can beat agents if they shoot, run and fight more intelligently than they do. Heroes win by stretching the rules of the game. Being is the becoming of the matrix; it is matrixing. Identity is produced by becoming a better computer game application.

Individualization, via introspection, self-observation and reflection, has little value in the film. One just has to play, imitate, emulate and destroy. Existence, or answering the 'what do you really do' question, is defined in terms of the 'chase'. If one is virtuous enough to make a difference, then the system chases and tries to destroy you. All one can do in response is try to destroy the system. Winning is the only thing that can be desired; it is the pre-scribed and predetermined phantasm. The matrix is a satanic universe ruled by a paranoiac metaphysics wherein the forces of evil have most of the power. Spiritual existence is defined in terms of a universe in which almost everyone is damned. There may be some remote possibility of salvation, but it is not evident. Evil dominates: it wins and loses, triumphs and retreats. The logic of pursuit and violence, fight and flight, never ceases. Some people may escape the matrix – but their existence is still defined in terms of their escape. There is no alternative to the first principle. One can be inside the matrix or one can be outside it, but both positions are defined in terms of it. The matrix has usurped the imagination – it does not show us to the door.[12] The claim in the movie to provide a way out of the matrix is just another way into the matrix. The matrix is a closed system that suffers from a lack of difference – there is no outside. The matrix is a virus: it has unlimited powers of representational reproduction, and it can crowd out all other texts. There is always an(O)ther game to entertain and please one's hyperreal phantasms. The matrix is not an exit.[13] It is an endless feedback loop of illusion, escape and reentry. Rebellion merely leads to playing the game more intensively, reintegrating one into the game. There is nowhere else to go. The players are caught in endless game loops of the matrix.

The consumer consumed

We are supposed to experience the movie as 'good' (attractive) humanity versus 'bad' (repressive) machines. The freedom to initiate change is good, the lack of freedom is bad. But the matrix is the result of a human-made ecological disaster that destroyed the climate – so the matrix's curse and self-legitimization ('humans are a sort of virus or cancer'[14]) carries a lot of weight. But in the movie, freedom and conscious choice are supposedly only possible in opposition to the matrix. The digital technology evokes nightmare images of alienation and repression. The dissidents proclaim the alternative. Morpheus and his gang call humans to: 'follow the white rabbit, take the red pill, master the game, become the One'. But these calls are all hyperreal. They are a simulation that pretends to be more 'real' than the 'matrix reality'. In hyperreality, objects may be free, but consciousness is not (Baudrillard 1981, 1983). Baudrillard's point is that hyperreality, or the images of the game, prioritize the logic of the object; indeterminacy has moved over to the side of the object. Situations, structures and objects have been liberated from human consciousness, which is preprogrammed. In the logic of the consumer society, objects have identity, substance and significance; consciousness is 'read by the objects'. Humans in hyperreality produce human lookalike artifacts – but 'human' and 'humanity' are mere effects. Hyperreal worlds look like human creations; the system (dis)plays the simulacra. The system lives, creates and multiplies; consciousness is merely a point in a lattice of (industrial, commercial and virtual) relationships.

Why the two pills? The polarity is between 'red' and 'blue' – the red pill signifying truth (and the revolution or leftism) and the blue pill signifying the opposite (blue is the color of the British Conservative party). But why the choice, why pose an existential question in terms of swallowing a pill? One can define choice in terms of simple dualism, and the pill does just that. But why consumerist pill-taking? For instance, in Salem, when they wished to decide whether someone was a witch, they used tests. They'd drop someone into water, and if they drowned they were human and not a witch. Why didn't Morpheus opt for such a pragmatic option, highlighting fate or predestination? The issue of choice versus predestination runs through the film. The matrix functions as a simulacrum of choice – it creates the illusion that you are in control of your own life. If you acknowledge (discover) that the matrix and not yourself is in control, then you are in control. Thus, the logic is that of Catch 22: 'If you think you know your own freedom, you are not free'; and 'If you think know your unfreedom, you are free'. But either way, you are 'not free'.

For the audience and the game figures, the film performs the same function. If you think you are free – to see, reconstruct and interpret the film – you do not realize how much the film has locked you into its hyperreality. And if you understand how powerless you are in the face of the game, then you know that you are part and parcel of hyperreality. Either way, the hyperreal reigns.

Energy flows (electricity) are essential in the film. The reproduction of the matrix – the keeping of the system alive – is its sole purpose. Humans are used as batteries – that is, as a primary energy source. Humanity is defined in terms of thermodynamics: it exists in a regime struggling to overcome entropy. The climate change that has caused human beings to be transformed into biological batteries is a result (the agents tell us) of a fault in the evolutionary identity of humanity. The matrix is in its own way 'justified' – after all, humanity destroyed the earth.[15] Humanity is both 'good', as in the case of Neo, Trinity and Morpheus; and 'bad', as the cause of all of the ecological problems. If human agency were to be restored by Neo, then the curse that destroyed the planet would be ready to be reenacted.

The 'blue pill' versus 'red pill' dilemma can be constructed to be very confronting – but it can also be seen as childishly silly. There are two choices, and both of them are consumerist. The big issue is which pill are you going to consume – but that you have to *consume* something is unquestionable. Prefabricated objects and predetermined sequences of behavior organize the matrix. That you have to play is an integral aspect to the logic. The obligation to make consumption choices is the real violence of the matrix. Consumer choice, in a hyperreal consumer society, can never change the logic of the essential relations. Functioning within the system might irritate or disrupt it; but it can never fundamentally question it. Neo may become a source of misfunctioning for the system. The VR may be forced to allow him to fiddle (a bit) with the simulacra, but the principle that society is a VR game is unaltered. The matrix divides humanity into winners and the rest. Humanity is imprisoned in the matrix, doomed to create the electricity that is needed to play out immature superhero games. The basic definitions wherein social reality is a computer game and one exists in the myths of the twentieth century are not altered. Mindfulness is blind to itself; it is defined as the ability to be totally lost in a world of consumerist hyperreality. Human existence is a video game played endlessly over and over. Mind is limited to dealing with the parameters set by action films.

The player cannot gain distance from the game; escaping the stream of events is impossible. The digital effects are used to overpower reflection and mesmerize the mind. From a gaming point of view, the film is like VR without a reset button. It is a prototype next-generation computer game. It is meant to be judged on its own terms by its appearances. It is politically and ethically correct, and it even comes with a superficial happy end. The movie produces pure illusion. Who sees the matrix, and how it is seen, are irrelevant to it; it just 'is'. There is no separate 'act of seeing'. The game writes its message onto your face in the movie theatre. The matrix is a hypnotizing experience of visual simulation. The senses are overloaded with stimulation and the (critical) eye is deadened.

In gaming, the movement from position to position or stance to stance merely sucks one deeper and deeper into the game. There is no outside to 'gaming'. Turning off the one game and turning on another does not make all that much difference; the games all resemble one another. The 'moves' that one can make while 'gaming' are repetitive, limited, and in most ways pregiven.[16] Gaming is designed activity, wherein what counts does not change. There is lots of motion in gaming, but no real change. All the surfaces are full of moving objects, but nothing really happens. Contrastingly, one can assert that movement on the surface is exactly what really happens and that it is the only form of change that our world knows.

Shut-down

(i) Glissement – *in and out of the matrix*

Glissement is movement in between words and objects; it occupies the gap between virtuality and the real. *Glissement* produces continuing realignment of elements. Organizational, societal and epistemic relationships are characterized by such constant small shifts. Individual existence occurs inside such movements – in signification, economic order and social configuration. Epistemic, organizational and social epistemes mediate 'self', 'identity' and 'consciousness'. By not assuming the primacy of the individual, the relational logic of *glissement* emerges. For instance, the agents can be understood in terms of the debates in the 1950s on the organizational man (*Death of a Salesman* and the dangers of other-directedness). Or they can be seen as a critique of the greed society of the 1980s (the film *Wall Street*, *Neuromancer* or Alain Minc's critique of rampant capitalism (1990)). But they can also be thought of in terms of current speculation about the virtual society (Woolgar and Grint 1997). *Glissement* between the various possible interpretations creates an intellectual game – a hide-and-go-seek of identity.

The logic of communication can be made accessible as a language game. *Glissement* captures the appropriate logic of change. Here is the link to Wittgenstein's and Lyotard's idea of the language game as the logic of communication. But do the games play the player? Is there release from domination by the 'machines' of *glissement*? What language games get played out in the simulacrum of organizations and society? How are they mirrored in pop culture?

> [T]he agent is a temporary term or position in an ever-active matrix of order–disorder.
>
> (Parker and Cooper 1998: 213)

> [M]odern science [has substituted] for our world of quality and sense perception, the world in which we live, and love, and die, another world – the world of quantity, of reified geometry, a world in which, though

there is place for everything, there is no place for man. Thus the world of science – the real world – became estranged and utterly divorced from the world of life.

(Koyré 1968: 23–24)

The matrix can be seen as an invitation to Deleuzian destratification, but also as a perspectiveless rendering of Newtonian dead ends. From the Deleuzian perspective, the matrix is an invitation to corrosive practices. It is a way for liberatory thought to invent techniques, for the kind of self-destruction that allows rhizomatic reflection. Normal reflection supposedly categorizes, determines and fixes. It destroys flow and motion, in layer after layer of reification. Normal thought denies the polyphonic and objectifies reality in order and reason. The matrix displays the inconsistencies of a world defined as a closed system – no such tight order remains conceptually sustainable. One can observe social phenomena, such as mass conditioning via virtual gaming, and label it; for instance, as 'the matrix'. 'The matrix' then becomes a totalization. It is 'subjectified', as if 'the matrix' had 'agency' all of its own. A category such as 'mass conditioning via virtual gaming' is made into an actor with agency. 'The matrix' is then no longer merely a convenient concept. It has become a social actor, capable of influencing human existence. Social scientists (literary critics, philosophers, politicians, etc.) then discuss 'the matrix' as if it possessed its own unique ontology. A concept that may have strong heuristic value in media studies, or in (critical) cultural analysis, becomes a 'thing' – it is object-ified. A parallel universe develops for the (de)construction of desires, self-descriptions and subversive reversals. The matrix can be used to mount just such a process of conceptual (de)reification. All its inconsistencies make the flaws of 'object thinking' apparent. Its screaming inconsistencies create (non-)sense – a *glissement* between free/unfree, human/nonhuman, corporate/individual that frees up communication. Deleuzian destratification is such a process of reification running in reverse (Buchanan 2000). Through its 'inhabitation', the power of repressive thought is broken:

> This is how it should be done: Lodge yourself on a stratum, experiment with the opportunities it offers, find an advantageous place on it, find potential movements of deterritorialisation, possible lines of flight, experience them, produce flow conjunctions here and there, try out continuums of intensities segment by segment.
>
> (Deleuze and Guattari 1987: 161)

The matrix is a closed simulacrum – but instead of being just another machine for the repression of ideas, it is an opportunity to think differently. One can slide in the matrix from inconsistency to inconsistency, and glide from there into an alternative space (of social analysis). The matrix's reifications are effortlessly undermined; the internal limits of the system are easily

reached and criticized. Its virtual system(s) produce variation. Its oversim-
plified structures – machine versus human, top-down versus bottom-up, free
versus unfree – all collapse under their own weight. For instance, the
machine/human dichotomy is displaced by cyborgization, VR and information and communication technology (ICT). Machines in the matrix obviously are no longer simple extensions of human agents; they have too much
cybernetic extension for that. Although human knowing is conveyed via
(mass) media, and human working entails tools, it is not self-evident that
people are simply extensions of things. Machine–human integration is
ambivalent; there are lots of equivalents and no hegemony. Humans are
game-players; the games have identities. Gaming constructs and deconstructs, escapes and engages, adds nothing and defines a whole (sub)culture.
It is 'immaterial whether one says that machines are organs, or organs are
machines. The two definitions are exact equivalents' (Deleuze and Guattari
1983: 285).

But one can also assert that in the matrix, difference and change have
been reduced to the identical and the permanent. Time has been eliminated.
Events are reversible; VR can be adjusted, warped and adapted so that 'the
game' continues. There is no law of irreversibility; the game continues irrespective of specific events. Society is frozen in a pre-given social order that is
endlessly determined to repeat itself. The unicity of the present and the
uniqueness of the situation are not respected. The rules of the game brush
the individual and particular aside. The matrix (re)produces a logic wherein
'truth' (science) and phenomenal existence are in conflict with one another.
Structure – the order of reality – is dominant; specific personal existence is a
secondary epiphenomenon, to be dealt with via illusion and media. 'Reality'
is independent of the observer. Society just 'is'; it is totally reified. Living
human activity is purposeless. Humanity merely consumes hyperreal media
– human will has been pacified, hypnotized, amputated and decontextual-
ized. What is this but normal science (Newtonian physics) rendered in a
consistent social vision, in a timeless world of (ir)rationality? Human relationships, communication and activity are irreparably lost. Simulated hyperreal illusions, robbed of all purposiveness, have taken over. There is no 'now'
other than the 'now' of the matrix. The present – as a zone of shared and
experienced possibility – has been shut down. Time as a space for human
lived circumstances is denied. If human meaning is 'constructivist' – that is,
sense-making is realized in circumstance and in contact with others – then
the mental and social spaces it depends on to exist are denied in gaming.
Sense-making made up of 'text', and containing layers of significance
dependent on language dialogue and interaction, has been evicted from the
game. In the matrix, people are 'monads' – suspended in parallelisms of non-
communicating and non-interacting disembodiment. There are no windows
in the matrix through which something can get in or out. The matrix is a
hyperreal *world*. In the matrix, the multiple temporal and complex are
denied. Because humanity is not entirely alienated from its immediate

existential world, the matrix intuitively appears to be flawed. As the film states, 'there seems to be something wrong'.[17] In the matrix, one cannot discover lived time, shared reality, or the *lebenswelt*. The matrix is, on a performative level, a computer game, which is its brilliance and its particular 'horror'. The game players are 'hyonons' – mesmerized consumers of a hyperreal gaming environment. You cannot gain your way from the universe of computer games back to lived complexity.

(ii) From gaming to playing

Glissement between being and becoming, laws and games, desire and perversion, time and structure is what creates potentiality. The connectionism that *glissement* reveals is an opening to indeterminacy and change. Awareness of possibility, experiencing that some of the pieces of life can (sometimes) be moved about, is a feeling

> that knits together the loneliness of innumerable hearts ... in dreams, in joy, in sorrow, in aspirations, in illusions, in hopes, in fear, which binds men to each other, which binds together all humanity – the dead to the living and the living to the unborn.
>
> (Conrad quoted in Gunn 2001: 32)

In the matrix, gaming is not meant to lead anywhere. One is supposed to play the computer game until one drops from exhaustion. 'Winning' is arriving at a point that already existed before you began. And you lose all the time that it took you to get there. Gaming escapes from the present into endlessly self-repeating patterns. In gaming, there is only seriality of action leading nowhere. Insofar as time is duration or a space for action, gaming escapes time and the need to act. Gaming empties circumstances of movement. But as in the matrix, gaming fails. Interaction, communication and process reassert themselves. From the Deleuzian perspective, desire undermines rules, structures and control. Organization triggers subterfuge. It creates conditions of *glissement* that lead to connectionism, interaction and process. This reading of the matrix sees the agents as the heroes, because in their humor and irony human qualities prevail.

Contrastingly, and less bleakly, the rhizomes of organizing can be positively interpreted. The solidarity involved in analyzing the film can become serious play. The matrix is, then, an invitation to play with gaming, by deconstructing its obsessive fetishisms of appearance, winning and violence. In play, the players approach one another – they enter into ongoing dialogue about what to do. In gaming, the game plays the player. By writing about the matrix, we try to earn our way out of the matrix, back into (intellectual) play. One has to play in order to talk about the games organizations impose; it is a (possible) way to earn one's way back into subjecthood (through repositionings).[18]

Notes

1   Displacement of a piece with another by a move to the right, done without lifting it up or turning it over. The inappropriate piece can in this way be moved to a neighboring free square, orthogonally or obliquely. If the square is not free, generally the piece which occupies this position is retired. In the majority of games and pastimes, the pieces move by sliding or jumping.
(*Dictionary of Recreational Mathematics*) [editors' translation]

2   Tomb Raider and Soccer Stars such as David Beckham are popular examples.

3   *Trinity*: That the Matrix cannot tell you who you are. *Neo*: And the Oracle can? *Trinity*: That's different.

4   (Office) *Agent Smith*: Never send a human to do a machine's job.
(Office) *Agent Smith*: Have you ever stood and stared at it, marvelled at its beauty, its genius? Billions of people just living out their lives, oblivious. . . . Evolution, Morpheus, evolution, like the dinosaur. Look out that window. You had your time. The future is our world, Morpheus. The future is our time.

5   (Restaurant) *Agent Smith*: Do we have a deal, Mr Reagan? *Cypher*: You know, I know this steak doesn't exist. I know that when I put it in my mouth, the Matrix is telling my brain that it is juicy and delicious. After nine years, you know what I realize? Ignorance is bliss. *Agent Smith*: Then we have a deal? *Cypher*: I don't want to remember nothing. Nothing. You understand? And I want to be rich. You know, someone important, like an actor. *Agent Smith*: Whatever you want, Mr Reagan.

6   (Office) *Agent Smith*: Can you hear me, Morpheus? I'm going to be honest with you. I hate this place, this zoo, this prison, this reality, whatever you want to call it. I can't stand it any longer. It's the smell, if there is such a thing. I feel saturated by it. I can taste your stink. And every time I do, I feel I have somehow been infected by it. It's repulsive, isn't it? I must get out of here. I must get free and in this mind is the key, my key. Once Zion is destroyed there is no need for me to be here, don't you understand?

7   (Phone) *The One*: I know you're out there. I can feel you now. I know that you're afraid. You're afraid of us. You're afraid of change. I don't know the future. I didn't come here to tell you how this is going to end. I came here to tell you how it's going to begin. I'm going to hang up this phone and then I'm going to show these people what you don't want them to see. I'm going to show them a world without you, a world without rules and controls, without borders or boundaries, a world where anything is possible. Where we go from there is a choice I leave to you.

8   *The Matrix*'s sequels 2 and 3 will cater with an answer.

9   *Neo*: I believe I can bring him back. . . . What are you doing? *Trinity*: I going with you. *Neo*: No you're not. *Trinity*: No? Let me tell you what I believe. I believe Morpheus means more to me than he does to you. I believe if you were really serious about saving him, you are going to need my help. And since I am the ranking officer on this ship, if you don't like, I believe you can go to hell. Because you aren't going anywhere else. Tank, load us up.

10 (Cellular) *Tank*: Operator. *Trinity*: Tank, I need a pilot program for a V-212 helicopter. Hurry. . . . Let's go.

11 *Morpheus*: . . . As long as the Matrix exists, the human race will never be free. . . . Get some rest, you're going to need it. *Neo*: For what? *Morpheus*: Your training. *Tank*: Morning, did you sleep? You will tonight, I guarantee it. I'm Tank, I'll be your operator.

12 *Morpheus*: I'm trying to free your mind, Neo, but I can only show you the door,

you're the one that has to walk through it. Tank, load the jump program. . . . You have to let it all go, Neo, fear, doubt, and disbelief. Free your mind.

Morpheus (with a consultant's voice): . . . I told you I can only show you the door. You have to walk through it.

Morpheus: (a bit later in the plot): Neo, sooner or later you're going to realize, just as I did, there's a difference between knowing the path and walking the path.

13 Echoing of course Bret Easton Ellis's famous last sentence in *American Psycho* – another version of the matrix filmed from within a virtual and operationally closed 1980s, New York, Wall Street suit reality.

14 *Agent Smith*: I'd like to share a revelation during my time here. It came to me when I tried to classify your species. I realized that you're not actually mammals. Every mammal on this planet instinctively develops a natural equilibrium with the surrounding environment but you humans do not. You move to an area and you multiply and multiply until every natural resource is consumed. The only way you can survive is to spread to another area. There is another organism on this planet that follows the same pattern. Do you know what it is? A virus. Human beings are a disease, a cancer of this planet. You are a plague, and we are the cure.

15 *Morpheus*: We have only bits and pieces of information but what we know for certain is that at some point in the early twenty-first century all of mankind was united in celebration. We marvelled at our own magnificence as we gave birth to AI. *Neo*: AI? You mean artificial intelligence? *Morpheus*: A singular consciousness that spawned an entire race of machines. We don't know who struck first, us or them. But we know that it was us that scorched the sky. At the time they were dependent on solar power and it was believed that they would be unable to survive without an energy source as abundant as the sun. Throughout human history, we have been dependent on machines to survive. Fate, it seems, is not without a sense of irony. The human body generates more bio-electricity than a 120-volt battery and over 25,000 BTUs of body heat. Combined with a form of fusion the machines have found all the energy they would ever need. There are fields, endless fields, where human beings are no longer born, we are grown. For the longest time I wouldn't believe it, and then I saw the fields with my own eyes. Watch them liquefy the dead so they could be fed intravenously to the living. And standing there, facing the pure horrifying precision, I came to realize the obviousness of the truth. What is the Matrix? Control. The Matrix is a computer-generated dream world built to keep us under control in order to change a human being into this. [Morpheus holds a battery in his hands.]

16 This is why the sequel, *Matrix Reloaded*, failed. Passively experiencing the replay of similar objects and moves on the same game board is not exciting. A simulation of gaming without interaction fails from a general absence of difference; it produces mere boredom.

17 *Choi*: Something wrong, man? You look a little whiter than usual. *Neo*: My computer, it . . . You ever have that feeling where you're not sure if you're awake or still dreaming? . . . *Morpheus*: I know exactly what you mean. Let me tell you why you're here. You're here because you know something. What you know you can't explain. But you feel it. You've felt it your entire life. That there's something wrong with the world. You don't know what it is but it's there, like a splinter in your mind driving you mad. It is this feeling that has brought you to me. Do you know what I'm talking about?

18 The authors wish to acknowledge research funding received from the ImaginationLab Lausanne Switzerland to investigate the theory of play.

References and further reading

Bateson, G. (1972) *Steps to the Ecology of Mind*, New York: Ballantine.

Baudrillard, J. (1981) *Simulacres et simulation*, Paris: Galilée.

Baudrillard, J. (1983) *Les Stratégies fatales*, Paris: Figures Grasset.

Buchanan, I. (2000) *Deleuzism* Durham, NC: Duke University Press.

Deleuze, G. (1969) *Logique du sens*, Paris: Éditions de Minuit.

Deleuze, G. (1977) *Rhizom*, Berlin: Merve Verlag.

Deleuze, G. (1992) *Logik des Sinns*, Frankfurt am Main: Suhrkamp.

Deleuze, G. (1994) *Difference and Repetition*, New York: Columbia University Press.

Deleuze, G. and Guattari, F. (1983) *Anti-Oedipus: Capitalism and Schizophrenia*, Minneapolis: University of Minnesota Press.

Deleuze, G. and Guattari, F. (1987) *A Thousand Plateaus*, Minneapolis: University of Minnesota Press.

Gibson, W. (1984) *Neuromancer*, New York: Ace Publishing.

Gibson, W. (1999) *All Tomorrow's Parties*, New York: Ace Publishing.

Gunn, G. (2001) *Beyond Solidarity*, Chicago: University of Chicago Press.

Havercroft, B. (1994) 'Fluctuations of fantasy: the combination and subversion of literary genres', in V. Harger-Grinling and T. Chadwick (eds) *Contributions to the Study of Science Fiction and Fantasy* no. 59, Westport, CT: Greenwood Press.

Hayles, K. N. (1999) *How We Became Posthuman*, Chicago: University of Chicago Press.

Kauffman, S. (1995) *At Home in the Universe*, New York: Oxford University Press.

Koyré, A. (1968) *Newtonian Studies*, Chicago: University of Chicago Press.

Lacan, J. (1977) *Écrits: A Selection*, New York: W. W. Norton.

Lacan, J. (1997a) *The Language of the Self: The Function of Language in Psychoanalysis*, Baltimore: Johns Hopkins University Press.

Lacan, J. (1997b) *The Four Fundamental Concepts of Psychoanalysis (The Seminar of Jacques Lacan, Book 11)*, New York: W. W. Norton.

Lyotard, J.-F. (1984a) *Just Gaming*, Minneapolis: University of Minnesota Press.

Lyotard, J.-F. (1984b) *The Postmodern Condition*, Minneapolis: University of Minnesota Press.

McLuhan, M. (1965) *Understanding Media: The Extensions of Man*, New York: McGraw-Hill.

McLuhan, M. and Powers, B. (1992) *The Global Village*, New York: Oxford University Press.

Marcuse, H. (1998) *Eros and Civilization*, London: Routledge [new edition].

Minc, A. (1990) *L'Argent Fou*, Paris: Grasset.

Nussbaum, M. (1990) *Love's Knowledge: Essays on Philosophy and Literature*, New York: Oxford University Press.

Parker, M. and Cooper, R. (1998) 'Cyborganization: cinema as nervous system', in J. Hassard and R. Holliday (eds) *Organization Representation*, London: Sage.

Priorgine, I. and Stengers, I. (1984) *Order out of Chaos*, New York: Bantam Books.

Récréomath, *Dictionnaire de mathématiques récréatives*, http://www.recreomath.qc.ca.

Robbe-Grillet, A. (1977) 'Order and disorder in film and fiction', trans. B. Morrissetti, *Critical Inquiry* 4 (1): 1–20 (accessed online at http://www.uchicago.edu/research/jml-crit-inq/issues/v4/v4n1.robbe-grillet.html, 1 April 2005).

Rosset, C. (1994) *Das Prinzip Grausamkeit*, Berlin: Merve.

Spencer, L. (2000) *The Art of the Matrix*, London: Titan Books.

Stengers, I. (1997) *Power and Invention*, Minneapolis: University of Minnesota Press.

Venkatesh, A., Meamber, L. and Fuat Firat, A. (1997) 'Cyberspace as the next marketing frontier', in S. Brown and D. Turley (eds) *Consumer Research*, London: Routledge.

Willmott, H. and Knights, D. (1999) *Management Lives*, London: Sage.

Wittgenstein, L. (1961) *Tractatus Logico-philosophicus*, London: Routledge & Kegan Paul.

Wittgenstein, L. (1969) *On Certainty*, Oxford: Basil Blackwell.

Wittgenstein, L. (1996) *Wittgenstein Reader*, ed. A. Kenny, Oxford: Blackwell.

Woolgar, S. and Grint, K. (1997) *The Machine at Work*, Cambridge: Polity Press.

Žižek, S. (2001) *Enjoy Your Symptom!*, London: Routledge.

5 The mythic foundations of organization

Iain Munro

[E]very journey, long or short, is always an odyssey.

(Italo Calvino, *The Literature Machine*)

What is indicated by the great historical need of unsatisfied modern culture, clutching about for countless other cultures, with its consuming desire for knowledge, if not the loss of myth, the loss of the mythical home, the mythical womb?

(Friedrich Nietzsche, *The Birth of Tragedy*)

This theme of this chapter was inspired by the title of the 2001 European Group for Organization Studies (EGOS) conference, "The Odyssey of Organizing". *The Odyssey* (Homer 1946) is perhaps the best-known epic in the Western world today and arguably the greatest. Indeed, the term "odyssey" has passed into the English language as meaning "a series of wanderings; a long adventurous journey" (*Oxford English Dictionary*, 9th edition). Myth was being explicitly appealed to as the organizing concept of the 2001 EGOS conference. But to what extent is myth essential to the concept of organization itself? I shall analyse this question on a number of different levels in this chapter – as allegory, as ideology and as ontology.

First, there is the level of allegory – that is, the extent to which organizing is like an odyssey or journey. At this basic level of analysis, myth is understood simply as a story or narrative adventure. If there is any truth to the myth, it is not literal but allegorical. There is an emerging literature in management and organization studies that proposes the use of myth in both understanding and managing organizational culture.

Myth can also be looked at as an ideological phenomenon. This is the method employed by Roland Barthes in his *Mythologies* (1957) and Adorno and Horkheimer in their *Dialectic of Enlightenment* (1972). (Note, however, that Barthes makes a distinction between myth and ideology, where the former conceals one's genuine interests but the latter hides nothing.) These mythologists highlight the many myths that bourgeois capitalism employs to justify its mode of domination. Adorno and Horkeimer suggest that Odysseus is himself the perfect hero of bourgeois individualism.

Finally, myth can be looked at on the level of ontology in so far as it concerns the essence of things. It was Plato himself who employed myth in his description of universal forms, where the myth could be used to distinguish the true form from the false copy or simulacrum. This theme has been picked up by the philosopher Gilles Deleuze and, of course, Nietzsche, and their work will be used in exploring the essential role of myth in the idea of organization.

Allegory

The most straightforward interpretation of the function of myth is as allegory. Myth tells a story that has some underlying important message which conveys a fundamental truth. One of the clearest accounts of the benefits of using a mythological approach in organization studies (OS) has been provided by Strati (2000). Strati proposes an aesthetic approach to understanding organizational phenomena, in which myth plays an important role. According to Strati, mythical thinking is important because it can give us insight into questions of ultimate meaning in organizational life, and it can enrich organization theory with new concepts (e.g. beauty, tragedy and the sacred). This aesthetic approach to organization studies brings a whole range of powerful concepts with it which may be excluded from existing approaches to OS that emphasize cognitivism and rationality (Strati 2000).

Although relatively little has been written about an aesthetic or mythic approach to OS, Strati observes that similar approaches are already existent, in organizational symbolism and the cultural analysis of organizations. The idea that literature and the classics may provide a rich source of knowledge for studying organizations is finding a voice in both the popular and the more critical areas of management literature (Knights and Wilmott 1999). Even Tom Peters has stated that managers may be reading too many management textbooks and not enough of the classics which get to grips with the reality of the human condition. In keeping with this new-found enthusiasm for literature, OS is also beginning to borrow the methods of literary theory and discourse analysis for the study of organization (Grant *et al.* 1998).

Before proceeding to a more in-depth analysis of allegorical understanding of organizations, I would point out some important mistakes that can be made from the outset, which can be illustrated with reference to the call for papers of the EGOS 2001 conference at which this chapter was first presented as a paper. This stated that we should "take pleasure in the process and in the journey from one place to another from one experience to another, sometimes in a casual way". I would not wish to disagree with this advice; however, I would dispute its relevance to the Odyssey. It should be remembered that Odysseus's travels were a curse inflicted upon him by the god Poseidon and that he hated them. The process was not a pleasurable one; he was subjected to a multitude of cruel tortures and saw the death of almost all his friends and comrades in arms. Neither is this the hidden subtext of the book; it is the main thread of the story. More important is the role of the homeland in myths of all kinds (Judaic, Greek, Christian, English), which is a prominent feature of the Odyssey. Odysseus's tale relates his continued efforts to return to his Greek homeland of Ithaca. The tale itself provides a sense of identity for the ancient Greeks (and perhaps it still serves this function to some extent), a land where the heroes lived noble lives and died tragic deaths, a land of marvellous stories and great storytellers. The truth of the Odyssey concerns less the pleasure of the journey than the mythical origins of the homeland and the identity of a people.

If we are to take Homer at his word that Odysseus was a great hoaxer, then it is quite possible, as Italo Calvino (1997) has suggested, that the whole story "might be a pack of lies". Indeed, there are so many stories within the Odyssey, and almost as many storytellers, that it is open to a variety of interpretations, perhaps an infinite variety. It is not enough to see the Odyssey as a pleasurable journey, even if it may be so for the reader. Other possible readings present themselves, such as the fact that heroes tend to live awful lives, which one might be careful to avoid at all costs. Odysseus spent twenty years away from his home and his family, and set out again not long after returning. His wife barely recognized him when he came home, and he finally met his end at the hands of his own son, Telegonus, who didn't recognize him. He lived by his wits rather than brute force. He was a master storyteller, and many of the myths in the tale are recounted by Odysseus himself. Given that much of the tale comes from his own lips, it is hardly surprising that he is the hero of these tales. He is the last of the heroes and the most cunning; he tended to use confusion and misinformation to get his way. The frontal approach of the hero held little attraction for him (Calasso 1994). Whether or not we would wish these same qualities in the modern manager is a matter for some debate, but it raises a key issue concerning the use of mythology for organization studies, the problem of selective interpretation.

There are a few rare papers in the management literature which directly appropriate mythology, such as those by McWhinney and Batista (1988), Cummings (1995) and Cummings and Brocklesby (1997). These authors argue that our understanding of myth and history plays an important part in our orientation towards the future, and hence is crucial to change management projects. Cummings' work draws upon classical history with particular reference to the foundation of democracy in ancient Athens as a model for the change management process. This shows how myth was used by Kleisthenes, the architect of democracy in Athens, to facilitate the political change process, not merely by drawing upon a past tradition to engender a sense of identity, but by engineering certain myths to suit present purposes. We need not, however, restrict ourselves to ancient history to see mythology at work. The invention of tradition has been explored elsewhere by Rowlinson and Hassard (1993), who show how Cadbury attempted to draw upon a religious tradition to give the firm "an identity which made it special, imbued it with a morality probably perceived as lacking elsewhere" (p. 321). These accounts are interesting because they suggest not merely that mythology should be used as a form of analysis in OS, but that mythology is already in common usage by managers as part of their job as manipulators of the corporate culture.

McWhinney and Batista (1988) argue that organizations can be revitalized by using mythology, and outline a number of steps for accomplishing this process. First, one needs to identify older myths, which may have fallen out of circulation but were once an important part of the fabric of the organization. Then one needs to find the origin or archetypes that are associated with these myths and reinterpret them for present purposes. Finally, the new story needs to be circulated, drawing on the old core story but allied to ideas that are more suitable to the present circumstances. Cummings and Brocklesby (1997) say something similar, favouring incremental change drawing upon the old myths of the organization rather than the radical re-engineering of business processes. Common to both these articles is that they disseminate a mythology of their own, which we might describe as a "bourgeois" ideology (Barthes 1957). Cummings' (1995) hero is Pericles, whom he presents as the quintessential leader and strategist, the social engineer of an entire culture, the paradigmatic manager. McWhinney and Batista also suggest that myth is so powerful that "the relation of spirit and body can be managed by the participant [in mythic rituals] or the Chief Executive Officer" (1988: 50). Although participation is encouraged from the lower ranks, it would appear that myth creation is largely the concern of those at the top of the organization hierarchy. The emphasis of the role of the hero in mythology (Cummings and Brocklesby 1997), the importance of leadership (Cummings 1995), and the belief that managers can engineer their own culture by using myths all smack of a managerial ideology. The mythology of leadership is not only to be found in the ancient myths referred to by the academics; it is also a key element in their own belief system, or at least that is the message they are disseminating through their work.

Marx is a particularly insightful commentator on the dissemination of this kind of mythology, which he saw at work in his own day. He criticized this bogus use of mythology explicitly in his study of politics in nineteenth-century France. Marx begins his study *The Eighteenth Brumaire of Louis Bonaparte* with the following observation on the past: "Hegel remarks somewhere that all facts and personages of great importance in world history occur, as it were, twice. He forgot to add, the first time as tragedy the second time as farce" (1934: 10). Marx then proceeded with a scathing attack upon the political posturing of the leaders of the *coup d'état* of 1848. According to Marx, this revolution was no more than a parody of the revolution of 1789, hence the desperation of its leaders in seeking a mock legitimacy by making comparison with great figures from former times. This kind of mythologizing and this kind of history is made by a buffoon "who no longer takes world history for comedy, but his comedy for world history" (ibid.: 64). It is this concern for the farcical aspect of the appeal to mythology that is so notably absent in the management literature discussed earlier in the chapter. The dangers of mythologizing should be all too obvious when considering Goebbels' use of myth as part of Nazi propaganda during the Second World War. The Aryan mythology used by the Nazis served to give them a sense of identity and unity at the same time as marginalizing other groups against which they could define themselves. Incidentally, leadership myths abounded in such propaganda, alongside other ideas concerning the origins of and superiority of their form of organization. At this point in the argument of this chapter, we are moving close to the theme of the second approach to understanding mythology as ideology.

Bourgeois ideology

The myth of the enlightenment

To understand myth simply as a lie, an illusion that must be dispelled and subjected to the cold light of reason, is itself part of a mythical process. This process has been termed "the dialectic of enlightenment" (Adorno and Horkheimer 1972). In this myth, humankind has replaced God at the centre of the cosmos, but apart from this minor usurpation, the previous system of Western metaphysics remained remarkably untouched. Man was still the custodian of the Garden of Eden and his presumed mastery over nature remained uncontested. This myth of the Enlightenment whereby reason was supposed to have replaced faith as humankind's guiding light was first uncovered as myth by Nietzsche. He asked: after having abandoned God, how could the rest of our metaphysical system remain intact? In particular, he observed that the moral system of beliefs, such as the belief in free will, good and evil, and so on, went largely unchallenged.

The Enlightenment belief in reason went hand in hand with the myth that humankind was the absolute master of nature, there being no God to placate any more. But there was a price to pay for this belief, which has been nicely summarized by Adorno and Horkheimer in the following way: "Men pay for their increase in power with alienation from that over which they exercise their power. Enlightenment behaves as a dictator toward men" (1972: 9). Greater domination over nature implies greater domination over humankind as a piece of nature. If this is the case, one may be tempted to ask today whether the information revolution really gives us more freedom or whether it is primarily a revolution in social control (Virilio 2000; Lyon 1994; Munro 2000).

According to Adorno and Horkheimer, bourgeois ideology operates by reducing as much of the world as possible to abstract quantities. In terms of abstract quantities, everything is made comparable and measurable; it can be set on the same scales and subjected to the laws of the marketplace. This historical process of increasing quantification in both science and society has been has carefully documented in Ian Hacking's (1990) study of the history of statistics. He observed that it is no coincidence that "an avalanche of numbers" went hand in hand with the development of the Industrial Revolution.

By reducing the world to numbers and abstract quantities, control over nature is enhanced and belief in irrational mythology suppressed. This gradual process of quantification has been accompanied by a rule of equivalence which is an axiom of both statistics and the marketplace. As abstract quantities, for example monetary value or a customer feedback form, things can be set on the same scales and compared. But this rule of equivalence itself springs from mythical origins. The primitive ritual for exchange was performed to gain control over nature (via gods); humans performed sacrifices in exchange for domination over nature. The Enlightenment has rejected its belief in the content of this ritual (i.e. sacrifice) but has retained its belief in the form of the ritual (i.e. exchange); only the gods have been removed (Adorno and Horkheimer 1972: 53–54). In fact, a new god has slowly emerged, the free market system. This new god is not so unlike the old monotheistic deities: it is supposed to be a dispenser of justice and it works upon humans through an account of their debts. One might say that under the old religions the fetishes were subject to the law of equivalence whereas under the new god the law of equivalence has itself become a fetish (ibid.: 12). In summary, it appears that the ideal of rational organization is itself accompanied by a cartload of mythological baggage, and we must think more rigorously about our freedom and our presupposed mastery of nature.

Bourgeois mythologies

Barthes' study of mythology shows clearly that, far from mythology having been abandoned in favour of reason, it can be found everywhere in modern (or postmodern) life. Barthes finds myths in the most banal aspects of everyday life; he even finds it in what we eat and drink, where he uses the example of drinking wine and eating steak as a myth concerning the essence of being French. He also discovers myth in entertainment, in the morality play performed in the wrestling ring, where the roles of good and evil are decided beforehand, and, more often than not, good triumphs over evil. Even mathematics falls foul of mythologizing, where Einstein's brain has become a symbol for our belief in science. The formula $E = mc^2$ has itself taken on an entirely mythological character in popular culture. According to Barthes, mythology is not simply a kind of story, but a kind of language; in his words, "myth is a system of communication . . . myth cannot possibly be an object, a concept, or an idea; it is a mode of signification, a form" (1957: 109). This idea that myth is a type of speech or language is not confined to Barthes, but can also be found in anthropological studies such as the work of Lévi-Strauss (1978).

Barthes' study of mythology uses two approaches simultaneously, those of semiology and ideology, because "it is a part both of semiology inasmuch as it is a formal science, and of ideology inasmuch as it is an historical science: it studies ideas-in-form" (1957: 112). Common to both Barthes' work and that of Adorno and Horkheimer is the guiding principle that mythology serves an ideological function – and, more specifically, a bourgeois ideology. However, Barthes is more rigorous in that he also studies myth as a semio-logical system. Barthes' approach uses three basic concepts: the signifier (e.g. word), the signified (e.g. concept) and the sign (particular combination of signifier and signified). There is no necessary relationship between the signi-fier and signified; the same word can refer to many different concepts. For example, the word "hot" could refer to the temperature of something or indicate that it was a stolen good. Likewise, a particular signified may be referred to by many different signifiers. For example, my passion can be expressed by signifiers such as a bunch of roses, a poem, the words "I love you", my blushing. Barthes stated that myths can be detected because of this relation (or lack of it) between the signifier and signified, since the same mythical signified appears over and over again in a multitude of different guises. Myth operates by transforming the sign in a linguistic system into a signifier in a mythical system, where the mythological system speaks about the former linguistic system. What is simply a meaning in the linguistic system becomes a naturalized form in the mythical system. This method allows us to distinguish between the simple linguistic meaning of a word and its deeper mythical significance, or *signification*, to use Barthes' terminol-ogy. These signs can be textual, as in the case of words or speech, or visual, as in the case of photographs and films.

For example, car adverts on British television commonly portray a car speeding across open countryside otherwise unspoiled by human meddling. As part of a semiological system, the signifier is the car speeding through open countryside and the signified is idea of efficient and luxurious travel. In the absence of myth, that is what the advert means. However, in the mytho-logical system this sign of luxurious travel becomes a signifier of something else: a sense of freedom, humans' technological superiority and domination of nature. The myth operates by deforming the meaning of the sign in the semiological system and destroys the history of that sign, in this case a history of gross exploitation of workers on the assembly line and of cars squeezed in bumper to bumper on their way into work every morning.

When explaining this concept of signification, Barthes states that its function is to distort rather than to make disappear. One of the main fea-tures of this kind of distortion is to make something that is in fact a contin-gent social phenomenon appear as a natural and universal phenomenon. Perhaps the clearest example of this today can be found in the idea of the market – or, more specifically, the "free market". This is talked of in the media not simply as a mechanism for the distribution of goods, but as if it were a force of nature (or supernature where it assumes a moral form).

Another way in which sociological phenomena are given a naturalistic justification is how people come to be characterized by type. Barthes makes this point in his reading of a tourist brochure that reduces people and regional peculiarities into stereotypes and caricatures. As Barthes said, "We find again here this disease of thinking in essences, which is at the bottom of every bourgeois ideology of man" (1957: 75). This kind of thinking can also be found at the heart of much management literature and some organization theory. One might think of psychometric testing outlined in the introductory texts on organizational behaviour such as that of Huczynski and Buchanan (1991), which devotes much of its chapter on "personality" to discussing such types and traits. This kind of theorizing attempts to explain people's behaviour by attributing it to essential "personality types" such as introvert and extrovert. What is sociological and contingent, in this case people's behaviour, is given a naturalized justification in terms of universal types.

Barthes' approach is particularly stimulating since it provides some broad guidelines on how to read myth in everyday life. His approach is especially rich, being a combination of two distinct theoretical approaches, semiology and ideology. Barthes also proposed that mythology can be turned on its head, and this could form part of a method of resistance to the dominant bourgeois mythology: "Truth to tell, the best weapon against myth is perhaps to mythify it in its turn, and to produce an artificial *myth*" (1957: 135). In this sense, his approach has much in common with the philosophy of Nietzsche, who refers to the myths of Dionysus and Apollo to undo Western metaphyics, or the psychoanalytic method of Freud, who draws on the myth of Oedipus among others to navigate the labyrinth of the unconscious. Barthes does note, however, that left-wing myth may be limited, since the left attempts to restore the history of the oppressed where the right has banished this history. Perhaps the work of Foucault goes furthest in this direction, restoring history to the oppressed and creating a somewhat mythical relationship with truth (at least according to Baudrillard (1987)).

Ontology

So far we have looked at mythology in two distinctive ways: first, as a way of understanding the underlying culture of organizations; and second, as a way of understanding the ideological function of these stories. There is, however, another level on which myth may be understood, one that concerns the nature of reality itself. This will be explored in two different ways: first by looking back to Plato's theory of the forms and the role myth plays in distinguishing true forms from false ones (hence reality from illusion); and second by exploring the role of myth in oral cultures, where reality is linked directly to myth and music in a fundamental way.

The simulacrum and Platonic mythology

If it is true that the history of Western metaphysics begins with Plato, then one may be startled to discover that this history begins with the telling of a myth. In Plato's *Republic* (1974), he uses the simile of the cave to set out a distinction between the apparent world and the real world of forms. According to this myth, it is as if we live in a cave where all we can see is shadows thrown by a fire onto the cave wall. Since we know no better, we take these shadows to be real things. Only were we to emerge from the cave into the sunlight would we be able to perceive the real world for what it is, the world of ideal forms that Plato hopes to reveal to us. Whereas the senses show us an ephemeral reality, Platonic forms are universal and eternal.

This is not the only myth that Plato employs to educate us, and very nearly all his dialogues use myth to illustrate their point. Plato did not employ myths simply for illustrative purposes; they also served to ground his entire theory of the forms. For one has to be able to distinguish between true forms, or copies thereof, and false copies which he calls simulacra. According to Deleuze (1990), Plato employed myth as a method of division, to divide ideas into different classes. Deleuze provides a Homeric interpretation of Plato, showing how much he remains held under the spell of myth. In particular, he shows how appropriate Odysseus's tale is in interpreting the structure of Plato's theory of forms: "Platonism is the philosophical Odyssey and the Platonic dialectic is neither a dialectic of contradiction nor contrariety, but a dialectic of rivalry . . . a dialectic of rivals and suitors" (1990: 254). Plato does not simply resort to the traditional myths of his time, but invents new ones for his own purposes, such as the simile of the cave or the ring of Gyges. These myths establish ideas such as Justice and Courage as eternal forms, universal principles for organization. The myths are foundational, but they also serve a further purpose in Plato's theory: "Myth, with its always circular structure is indeed the story of foundation. It permits the construction of a model according to which the different pretenders can be judged" (Deleuze 1990: 255).

The Deleuzian alternative to Plato is a world without foundation, or at least with many foundations, and one that is populated solely with simulacra. He quotes Nietzsche in this respect: "behind each cave lies another" (Deleuze 1990: 262). There is no light in the cave and no foundation. Hence, Deleuze and Guattari's (1984) call for experimentation in contradistinction to interpretation. If it is true that behind every mask lies another mask, then there are no eternal forms and no ultimate grounds for organization, and myth may well have a role to play as part of the organizing process. It is to this process that we shall now turn our attention.

Myth, music and aesthetic organization

According to Aboriginal myth, the world was literally sung into existence by the Aborigines' ancestors (Chatwin 1987). Here, myth is not simply a story about the creation of the world, but the process by which the world was actually created. Aboriginal myths, or "songlines" as they are more properly known, can be used to navigate the vast plains of the Australian outback. But in keeping with their mythology, they are not just maps, but the very essence of what they sing about. If the Aborigines were to stop singing, it would literally be the end of the world for them. This shows that, at least in so-called primitive or oral cultures, mythology concerns ontology as much as it does epistemology. It may be premature, however, to dismiss such ideas as ridiculous and irrelevant to our (post)modern times, as the following discussion hopes to show. Indeed, the "primitive" idea that reality is in essence mythic and musical is a central feature of Nietzsche's philosophy and his critique of Western metaphysics.

Lévi-Strauss (1978) also observed a fundamental relationship between myth and music. He noticed that there are structural similarities between music and mythology. One cannot understand a musical note separated from the whole work of art, just as one cannot understand a scenario within a myth separated from the rest of the story. During the Renaissance, when myth began to decline, different musical forms emerged to take its place, and Lévi-Strauss believed that he could find mythic counterparts for a whole range of musical forms such as the sonata, the symphony, the toccata, and so on. The organization of myth and that of music, it would seem, are identical.

Nietzsche too held that myth and music are inextricably linked, but with more far-reaching consequences. Nietzsche used myth and music as a critique of metaphysics itself. Whereas Lévi-Strauss was content to say that music is a representation of reality and imitates life, Nietzsche stated that it exists in its own right, not merely as a representation (1993: 83). In *The Birth of Tragedy*, Nietzsche stated that "music is the actual idea of the world" (ibid.: 103). So, music does not represent something else, but speaks directly to our senses in its own voice. We become lost in music, and lose our sense of self. This is the closest humankind ever gets to the world of becoming, or what Nietzsche called the "Dionysian world" (1968: 550). This is also where tragic myth begins, which shows the hero having to endure his suffering alone in the world. Indeed, the suffering arises as a consequence of the feeling of separation and alienation from the world. It is with the myth of Dionysus, whereby this alienation is dissolved, that the critique of traditional metaphysics begins.

Nietzsche contrasts a world of becoming and transformation with a static world of being. Given that nothing endures, he takes the idea of becoming to be the more truthful description of the world, and the world of being as the more illusory. When we think of the world in terms of enduring things, this is "an error" and "the will to deception", but an error that we must make to be able to think. Whereas Plato said that the real world was composed of eternal forms, Nietzsche held the view that the real world is in continuous flux. Becoming should not be understood simply as change, since change implies the primacy of static things which then undergo change, whereas becoming does not assume the primacy of static things. In sum, knowledge must be founded upon an error, the presumption of stasis and the invention of identical cases. This error is built into the structure of language itself, for it is language that names things and in doing so provides a metaphorical basis for gaining knowledge of the world.

R. J. Hollingdale summarized this problem in the following way: "'Things' are projections of the ego as causal agent, and God is only the biggest thing" (1995: 117). This complicity between language and metaphysics leads Nietzsche to say, "I fear we are not getting rid of God because we still believe in grammar" (1990: 48). By arguing in this manner, Nietzsche did not attempt to get rid of knowledge, but to highlight how it has developed historically, the fundamentally active role that creativity plays with respect to all knowledge, and the metaphysical pretensions of which we may fall foul in pursuit of "the" Truth. According to Nietzsche, then, myth plays a crucial role in the development of knowledge.

Nietzsche drew upon some myths of his own, particularly that of Dionysus and Apollo (1993). Both gods are expressions are of the artistic impulse, both essential for creation. Whereas Apollo is concerned with dreams and the creative powers of the visual realm, Dionysus is concerned with dance and music. Of these two forces, it is Apollo that allows the artist to see him- or herself as a thing distinct from the rest of nature and confront him- or herself as an agent of creation and of knowledge. Apollo is the *principium individuationis*, whereby the ego confronts itself as a thing, and projects this principle onto the rest of the world. Dionysian art has precisely the opposite effect, dissolving the individuating power of Apollonian art, bringing us closer to the world of movement and transformation that exists prior to interpretation and individuation. Whereas Apollonian art follows the rule of metaphor and representation, Dionysian art follows the rule of music and transformation. Music threatens the individuating force by which we separate ourselves from nature as the first "thing", just as tragic myth puts into question the suffering that results from this separation and alienation. If it is true that knowledge is founded upon an error, as Nietzsche has suggested, then music and mythic wisdom may have as much to say about the nature of reality as does conceptual knowledge. Whereas knowledge gives us a grasp of reality in terms of being, myth gives us a grasp of reality in terms of becoming and in terms of our alienation from nature. This is exactly what Nietzsche meant when he wrote that existence is justified only as an aesthetic phenomenon. At this point, we have come full circle back to Strati's proposal that organization can be studied as an aesthetic problem. I might add, it must be studied as an aesthetic phenomenon.

Conclusion

This chapter has argued that mythology provides a fruitful way of understanding organizations on at least three different levels. On the level of allegory, myths provide foundational stories that provide organizations with an identity. As allegories they may also be useful in transmitting ideas about how things are expected to be done within an organization. This chapter also demonstrated that this ought not to be done uncritically, and that some work on mythology in the field of organization studies is itself under the spell of a bourgeois mythology (specifically a managerial ideology).

The next level is that of ideology, as exemplified in the work of Adorno and Horkheimer (1972) and Barthes (1957). This work shows that the modern belief in rationality and the mastery of nature through science is itself part of a bourgeois ideology. This ideology robs things of their history and presents contingent social phenomena as if they were natural and ahistorical. Barthes see mythologies of this kind in operation throughout all levels of society, from our most banal and commonplace habits to our most advanced sciences.

Finally, mythology may be seen to tell us something about the nature of being, the essence of things. This can be seen by highlighting the influence of mythology on the development of Western metaphysics, but also by considering the role of myth and music in bringing us into contact with a world of becoming which may be said to be more primal than the world of representation. This also raises the significance of aesthetics in understanding organizational phenomena, showing that it is not just one approach among others but may be considered to be essential in a way that more rational and cognitivist approaches are not.

References

Adorno, T. and Horkheimer, M. (1972) *The Dialectic of Enlightenment*, London: Verso.

Barthes, R. (1957) *Mythologies*, London: Vintage.

Baudrillard, J. (1987) *Forget Foucault*, New York: Semiotext.

Calasso, R. (1994) *The Marriage of Cadmus and Harmony*, London: Vintage.

Calvino, I. (1997) *The Literature Machine*, London: Vintage.

Chatwin, B. (1987) *The Songlines*, London: Vintage.

Cummings, S. (1995) "Pericles of Athens: drawing from the essence of strategic leadership", *Business Horizons* 38: 22–27.

Cummings, S. and Brocklesby, J. (1997) "Towards demokratia: myth and the management of organizational change in ancient Athens", *Journal of Organizational Change Management* 10: 73–96.

Deleuze, G. (1990) *The Logic of Sense*, London: Athlone Press.

Deleuze, G. and Guattari, F. (1984) *Anti-Oedipus: Capitalism and Schizophrenia*, London: Athlone Press.

Grant, D., Keenoy, T. and Oswick, C. (eds) (1998) *Discourse and Organization*, London: Sage.

Hacking (1990) *The Taming of Chance*, Cambridge: Cambridge University Press.

Hollingdale, R. J. (1995) "Theories and innovations in Nietzsche", in *Nietzsche: A Critical Reader*, ed. P. Sedgwick, Oxford: Blackwell.

Homer (1946) *The Odyssey*, trans. E. V. Rieu, London: Penguin.

Huczynzki, A. and Buchanan, D. (1991) *Organizational Behaviour*, 2nd edn, Hemel Hempstead, UK: Prentice Hall.

Knights, D. and Wilmott, H. (1999) *Management Lives*, London: Sage.

Lévi-Strauss, C. (1978) *Myth and Meaning*, Routledge Classics, London: Routledge & Kegan Paul.

Lyon, D. (1994) *The Electronic Eye: The Rise of the Surveillance Society*, Cambridge: Polity Press.

McWhinney, W. and Batista, J. (1988) "How remythologizing can revitalize organizations", *Organizational Dynamics* 17: 46–58.

Marx, K. (1934) *The Eighteenth Brumaire of Louis Bonaparte*, Moscow: Progress Publishers.

Munro, I. (2000) "Non-disciplinary power and the Network Society", *Organization* 7: 679–695.

Nietzsche, F. (1968) *The Will to Power*, trans. R. J. Hollingdale and W. Kaufmann, New York: Vintage Books.

Nietzsche, F. (1990) *Twilight of the Idols/The Anti-Christ*, trans. R. J. Hollingdale, London: Penguin.

Nietzsche, F. (1993) *The Birth of Tragedy: Out of the Spirit of Music*, trans. S. Whiteside, London: Penguin.

Plato (1974) *The Republic*, London: Penguin.

Rowlinson, M. and Hassard, J. (1993) "The invention of corporate culture: a history of the histories of Cadbury", *Human Relations* 46: 299–326.

Strati, A. (2000) "The aesthetic approach to organization studies", in S. Linstead and H. Hopfl (eds) *The Aesthetics of Organization*, London: Sage.

Virilio, P. (2000) *The Information Bomb*, London: Verso.

Part II

'Knowing' organization

6 On the applicability of 'alien' concepts to organisational analysis

Some criteria for inter-domain conceptual transfer

Loizos Heracleous and Martin R. Fellenz

This chapter aims to raise and explore the issue of conceptual transfer from other domains and disciplines to the field of organisational science. The interdisciplinary nature of this field and the fragmented nature of investigations (e.g. Lemke *et al.* 1999; Pfeffer 1993; Zammuto and Connolly 1984) make organisational science a particularly apt example of conceptual transfer practices common throughout the social sciences. We aim to open up for debate and to problematise this hitherto largely implicit and taken-for-granted situation, and to suggest exploratory directions for practice and avenues for further debate.

We view scholarly texts in terms of Ricoeurian written texts, which have higher potential polysemy and ambiguity by virtue of their more limited contextuality than does spoken discourse. The inter-domain diffusion of concepts can potentially increase a field's interpretive potential and conceptual arsenal, but may also increase the interplay of multiple meanings and interpretations and conceptual ambiguity. Barthes' views on the desirability of such polysemy, and the primacy of the reader's interpretations rather than the author's intentions, preface the postmodernist movement with comparable aims. Such a state is not necessarily beneficial, however, if we accept a view of social science as a potentially cumulative endeavour with an actual subject matter related to, but independent of, actors' subjectivity, and the need for a common language and platform for scholarly debate.

We draw from a metaphorical perspective to suggest that concepts transferred from a source domain to a target domain are imbued with systemic interconnections, inherent in the source domain, that implicitly carry over to the target domain. In this context, we need a set of criteria to guide inter-domain conceptual transfer in a way that enhances a field's development and benefits its interpretive potential and conceptual arsenal, rather than multiplying potential meanings and giving primacy to each reader's interpretations at the expense of the author's communicative intentions. We suggest three main criteria for guiding such conceptual transfers: technical adequacy, paradigmatic adequacy and pragmatic adequacy.

Paradigmatic diversity and conceptual transfer in social science

Social sciences in general, and organisational science in particular, are characterised by considerable inter-domain diffusion of concepts and by paradigmatic diversity (Lemke *et al.* 1999; Warner 1994). Influential scholars have argued strongly against this diversity, and for the adoption of the positivist paradigm (e.g. Donaldson 1985), which would lead to a more disciplined and unified development guarded by paradigmatic, conceptual and methodological gatekeepers (Pfeffer 1993) as the way for advancement of organisational science. Such consensus-inducing mechanisms, however, have been criticised as elitist, exclusive and ultimately counter-productive for the advancement of organisation science (e.g. Cannella and Paetzold 1994; Van Maanen 1995).

The positivist paradigm itself is inherently problematic in terms of such issues as its hard ontology of social phenomena and its deductive-nomological mode of explanation (Bhaskar 1978; Silverman 1970). Researchers, therefore, have been urged to utilise concepts from other conceptual domains in order to enrich their own,[1] and to avoid unproductive paradigmatic and methodological closure (Cannella and Paetzold 1994; Hassard 1988; Jick 1979; Schultz and Hatch 1996). In the absence of any conscious examination of such issues, however, conceptual transfers and diffusions run the danger of becoming impediments to social science rather than constructive ways of expanding the interpretive richness and analytical potency of established perspectives.

The debate on paradigm development in organisation science has developed in response to its status as an extremely fragmented field of inquiry (e.g. Zammuto and Connolly 1984; Pfeffer 1993). Such fragmentation is in itself not necessarily problematic. However, some view it as hindering scientific inquiry by obstructing meaningful collaboration, impeding the acquisition or extant efficient use of research resources, preventing easy cross-fertilisation between different research traditions or disciplines, or leading to excessive research resources being spent on redundant investigations ('reinventing the wheel') (e.g. Pfeffer 1993). The level of paradigm development (Lodahl and Gordon 1972), or the degree to which a field of study is characterised by technical certainty and consensus, reflects some of the conditions enabling scientific progress (Pfeffer 1993). Fields with high levels of paradigm development should have more effective communication (Salancik *et al.* 1980), may promote the use of research resources (Lohdahl and Gordon 1972), should enable interdependent research and collaboration, and should increase the 'ease and certainty of evaluating scientific research' (Pfeffer 1993: 603).

Scholarly discourse as Ricoeurian written text

In the use of natural language in contexts of interaction, the physical, situational and cultural contexts play a crucial role in determining how concepts are interpreted. This is not the case with regard to written text (including academic literature), where the influence of such contexts is diminished (Ricoeur 1991). Concepts in established conceptual systems, including social science paradigms, largely gain their meaning from intra-textual and inter-textual connections (Saussure 1983; Latour 1987). Latour's insightful study of scientific practice extensively demonstrates this process:

> A document becomes scientific when its claims stop being isolated and when the number of people engaged in publishing it are many and explicitly indicated in the text. When reading it, it is on the contrary the reader who becomes isolated ... whatever the tactics, the general strategy is easy to grasp: do whatever you need to the former literature to render it as helpful as possible for the claims you are going to make.
>
> (1987: 33, 37)

Ricoeur sees spoken discourse as an event in that (1) it is realised temporally and in the present; (2) the 'instance of discourse' is self-referential because it refers back to its speaker; (3) discourse is always about something – it refers to a world which it attempts to describe, express or represent; and (4) discourse is in practice addressed to an other (Ricoeur 1991: 77–78). Ricoeur argues, however, that as soon as discourse is 'fixed' in writing as text (as with scholarly publications), several hermeneutic issues emerge: (1) whereas spoken discourse is realised temporally as a speech event, the written text fixes, in decreasing order of susceptibility to such fixing, the locutionary, illocutionary and perlocutionary acts of spoken discourse and divorces them from their temporal and social context; (2) whereas spoken discourse is self-referential in that it refers back to its speaker, the intended meanings of the author and the meanings of the text do not necessarily coincide in written text, as it is potentially open to an unlimited series of interpretations; (3) whereas spoken discourse displays ostensive references deriving from the common situation and context within which the interlocutors find themselves, written texts, divorced from such conditions, display non-ostensive references projecting new possibilities of being-in-the-world, this state being for Ricoeur the ultimate referent of all texts; and (4) whereas spoken discourse is addressed at a specific interlocutor, texts are in principle available to anybody who can read (ibid.: 146–150).

In viewing scholarly discourse as Ricoeurian written text, therefore, its high potential for polysemy, ambiguity and multiple interpretations becomes apparent. A multiplicity of potential meanings is not necessarily detrimental (after all, exceptional art is imbued with polysemy). If we accept the existence of phenomena and processes that exist independently of actors' subjectivity[2] (e.g. social structures, capital flows, technology transfer) and take these (and their subjective correlates) as the object of scientific investigation with the ideal aim of deeper and cumulative understanding, however, then it becomes necessary to represent these phenomena and processes in scholarly discourse characterised by relative fixity of meaning. The existence of polysemy, ambiguity and multiple interpretations would in this case hinder effective communication within the scientific community and with the wider public.

On the desirability of polysemy in social science

Does it matter, however, whether the reader interprets the text as the author intended, or not? Does it make a difference whether the text is polysemous, having the potential for a multiplicity of interpretations, or has relative fixity of meaning? From a postmodern, specifically Barthian perspective (Barthes 1994), what the author meant does not matter at all; and textual polysemy and openness of potential meanings is a virtue.

In Barthes' essay 'The death of the author', which marked the beginning of a shift in his earlier structuralist stance,[3] Barthes asserts that

> as soon as a fact is narrated no longer with a view to acting directly on reality but intransitively, that is to say, finally outside of any function other than that of the very practice of the symbol itself, this disconnection occurs, the voice loses its origin, the author enters his own death, writing begins. [Writing] is the destruction of every voice, of every point of origin ... a text is not a line of words releasing a single 'theological' meaning (the 'message' of the Author-God) but a multidimensional space in which a variety of writings ... blend and clash.
>
> (1968/1994: 142, 146)

Barthes believed that the suppression of the author was necessary for the elevation of the reader from a passive position receiving the 'theological' meaning of the 'Author-God' to one of reading as 'the true place of [the text's] writing' (ibid.: 147). Barthes forcefully argued that 'The birth of the reader must be at the cost of the death of the Author' (ibid.: 148). In 'The death of the author', Barthes was therefore concerned with removing the limits to the signifying power of the text, especially those limits related to authorship: 'To give a text an Author is to impose a limit on that text, to furnish it with a final signified, to close the writing' (ibid.: 147).

This concern for polysemy is manifested in several of Barthes' later essays. In discussing the distinctions between 'works' and 'Texts', for example, he maintains that 'the work closes on a signified. ... Text, on the contrary, practices the infinite deferment of the signified, is dilatory' ('From work to Text', 1971/1994: 158). In his textual analysis of Genesis, he concludes that 'the problem, the problem at least for me, is exactly to manage not to reduce the Text to a signified, whatever it may be (historical, economic, folkloristic or kerygmatic), but to hold its *significance* fully open' ('The struggle with the Angel', 1971/1994: 141; emphasis in the original). Barthes now saw textual structures not as stable and pre-existing (as in his earlier structuralist stance), but as continually being formed by active reading, in a structurational process in which the distinction between writing and reading is diminished or abolished.

Can a social science, and its discourse, however, be based on such a subjectivist approach without any independent criteria for validation? In Barthes' point of view (and arguably in the wider postmodernist movement, as well as in philosophical schools such as solipsism), this question would be meaningless. This does not simply arise from the assumption that the observed is not something objective and separate from the observer, but is shaped by the research process and by the observer's interpretations; this assumption also characterises interpretive perspectives. It arises, rather, from an inherent ideological dislike for dominant and overarching meanings, and a dislike for the systemic modernist project of enhancing the human condition and its mastery over its context through the systematic accumulation and employment of rational knowledge (Cooper and Burrell 1988). The concern with enhancing validity (in the sense that the scholarly map matches the observed territory), therefore, is downplayed and polysemy is encouraged.

The above position, however, would be incompatible with most other scholarly paradigms and traditions. The interpretive paradigm (Burrell and Morgan 1979), for example, does pre-suppose and focus on processes of social reality construction (Berger and Luckmann 1966) and the influence of researchers on how the objects of study are understood, but accepts that there are broader and independently existing conditions and social structures that cannot simply be wished away by social actors. Ethnography is similarly committed to inductively understanding the point of view of the 'natives', but good ethnography always seeks to employ means of confirming the validity of the researcher's interpretations of the natives' point of view through respondent validation and data triangulation (Hammersley and Atkinson 1995). Structuration theory (Giddens 1984), lastly, accepts both the subjectivity of individual action and the objectivity of entrenched social structures. It attempts to reconcile the seemingly incompatible interpretive and functionalist paradigms concerned with these levels of analysis, recognising that social structures do not simply act as constraints on human action, but are in fact the product of such action. The reproduction of social structures is rooted in their daily affirmation through action; such action can, therefore, in the longer term influence, challenge and change entrenched social structures.

Not all subjective interpretations are equally plausible, therefore (Ricoeur 1991; Giddens 1979, 1987), and there are limits to social construction. At the most basic level, these limits arise from the material condition of the human body. An individual's belief of invincibility to bullets, for example, can be the product of intersubjective social construction (or of a disturbed mind); but this belief will not reduce the actual harm that a bullet can cause. One historical example can be found in the beliefs of members of a Chinese secret society (the Boxers) that launched the anti-Western Boxer Rebellion of 1900. Members of this sect practised martial arts influenced by witchcraft and believed that their recital of magical incantations would render them invincible to enemy bullets; many of them discovered at rather inopportune moments that this was not the case.

Inter-domain conceptual transfer and the wall of knowledge

Inter-domain conceptual transfer can be seen in a similar light as potentially increasing ambiguity yet also aiding paradigmatic enrichment. Given that theorising in social science is largely metaphorical in nature (Morgan 1980, 1983) and that our conceptual system is metaphorically structured (Lakoff 1990; Ortony 1979), the transfer of a key concept from a source to a target domain creates a metaphorical implication complex (i.e. the implications conceptually transferred by the source domain to the target domain) which currently remains unexamined.

One example of the constructive potential of metaphor can be seen in this statement on the nature of peer-reviewed scholarly texts:

> Like a wall that is built one brick at a time, the peer-reviewed literature in a field is built by single contributions that together represent the accumulated knowledge of a field. Each contribution must fill a place that before was empty, and each contribution must be sturdy enough to bear the weight of contributions to come.
>
> (American Psychological Association 1994: 291)

The source domain here is construction of a brick wall, and the target domain is peer-reviewed literature, the accumulated knowledge of a field. The metaphor is thus 'the development of scientific knowledge is like the construction of a brick wall'; consequently and implicitly, 'scientific knowledge is like a brick wall'. Bricks compose the wall, in the same way as academic articles compose the peer-reviewed literature. The wall metaphor carries the connotations (or implication complex) of a solid, enduring, unitary entity, built methodically, always advancing towards completion, by knowledgeable bricklayers who choose which bricks are worthy and sturdy enough for inclusion, with bricks of ideally uniform size and sturdiness. The implication complex thus contains elements pertaining to (1) the nature of the wall; (2) the building process; (3) the actors involved; and (4) the material, or bricks.

An additional, implicit aspect of this metaphor is the orientational nature of building a brick wall: from downwards, or low, advancing upwards, or high. As Lakoff and Johnson (1980: 14–21) have demonstrated, most positive states or situations are 'up', whereas most negative ones are 'down': happiness, consciousness, health, control, high status, virtue and rationality, for example, are all up, whereas their opposites are down. The metaphor 'the development of scientific knowledge is like the construction of a brick wall' is based on this orientational nature of human thought and expression; and its attractions draw from the human desire for control and predictability.

The implication complex of this metaphor, created both by the source domain and by the use of the conceptual transfer, leaves out other aspects such as the use of, and nature of, adhesives (mortar fixes, but does not change, individual bricks, while integration of individual scientific contributions into a wider literature can involve their reinterpretation), or the purpose of erection (building walls for a monument, for shelter, or for incarceration may shed different light on the processes of a cumulative scientific endeavour), among others.

The elements of the implication complex implicitly and subconsciously carry over to the target domain, in terms of (1) the nature of peer-reviewed literature and scientific knowledge (solid and unitary); (2) the process of its development (methodical, ever advancing upwards and aiming towards complete knowledge); (3) the actors involved (the knowledgeable craftsmen being the reviewers who decide which articles, or 'bricks', are fit and worthy enough to form part of the wall of knowledge); and (4) the articles themselves (being enduring contributions that uniformly follow the conventions of normal science, so that they can be deemed worthy of inclusion in the wall of knowledge).

To the naïve, inexperienced or merely idealistic reader, this could be taken as describing the actual process of scientific inquiry; it certainly presents what many scientists would take as the ideal, positivist process; and what many university students are taught. For all its idealistic attractions, however, the constructive potential of this metaphor is limited in this particular case because many scholars know better. Fragmentation and disagreement in a field are rife; contributions can have a far greater impact than initially apparent, or initially promising contributions can fade to obscurity; and reviewers can favour papers adhering to normal science or their personal biases. An appropriate metaphor describing this state of affairs is not a single well-crafted wall, but several distinct, though overlapping, piles of bricks precariously thrown together and often mysteriously moving around from one pile to another. The history of science is a far cry from the 'scientific knowledge is a brick wall' metaphor (Shapin and Schaffer 1985).

Metaphorical implication complexes, characterised by both actualised and potential connections and the creation of meanings deriving from such connections, operate subconsciously in both the authors' and the readers' minds to suggest frames for interpretation (Bateson 1972). In the case of the authors, this influences all stages of the discovery and dissemination process.

In the case of the reader, it influences their interpretation of the text they are reading. If the implication complexes remain unexamined, ambiguity is increased and confusion can result regarding what the author actually intends to say about the findings or ideas he or she wishes to communicate to peers, and how other scholars should interpret this.

The need for criteria of inter-domain conceptual diffusion

How can we use inter-domain conceptual diffusion in a productive sense, avoiding confusion and enriching the interpretive potential of existing perspectives? Both Ricoeur (1991) and Giddens (1979, 1987) acknowledge that not all interpretations are equally plausible or valid. For Ricoeur, the approach to interpretive validation is based on a dialectic movement between explanation and understanding, seen as respectively the subjective and objective moments of a hermeneutic circle (1991: 159–160). For Giddens, the criteria for interpretive accuracy involve inquiry in the settings of production of the text, the intellectual resources the author has drawn on and the characteristics of the audience it is addressed to (1987: 106). Giddens emphasises the necessity of studying texts as 'the concrete medium and outcome of a process of production, reflexively monitored by its author or reader' (1979: 43). Inquiry into this productive process involves exploring the author's intentions as well as the practical knowledge involved in writing with a certain style for a particular audience.

Such criteria are useful but not sufficient to address the issue at hand, which is different from textual exegesis where these criteria are intended to apply. In this case, we need to develop criteria that can help us be more reflexive about the implication complex created by the transfer of key concepts from one conceptual domain to another, and to enable constructive inter-domain conceptual transfer that increases interpretive potential but safeguards against ambiguity and confusion.

Underlying the idea of 'criteria' of interpretive validation is the assumption that there are better or worse, or at least more and less appropriate or useful, inter-domain conceptual transfers. Even though this assumption might be perceived as unduly limiting, the logical alternative to this is a Barthian subjectivism that is unacceptable if we share a concept of social science as a potentially cumulative endeavour with an actual subject matter related to – but sufficiently independent of – subjectivity, and the need for a common language and platform for debate.

If we accept in principle the existence of more or less valuable inter-domain conceptual transfers, however, what should our criteria be based on? Such criteria should be based neither on calls for paradigmatic imperialism, nor on subjective perceptions of what is a 'good' transfer, a process that would quickly become a Trojan horse for the perpetuation of dominant interests. Personal values can easily influence the perceived validity of theories (Miner 1990) as well as the appropriateness of conceptual transfers. Rather, to achieve fruitful inter-domain conceptual transfers, criteria should be based on indications that scholars have reflexively explored and clarified their use of key concepts from other conceptual domains in terms of technical, paradigmatic and pragmatic adequacy.

Technical, paradigmatic and pragmatic adequacy as criteria for constructive inter-domain conceptual transfer

The first criterion we propose is the *technical adequacy* of inter-domain conceptual transfer: that is, that researchers have explored the meaning(s) of the concept they appropriate in the 'source domain' and clarify the similarities and differences of their use and meaning of the concept in the 'target domain'. The degree and type of systemic interconnections of the appropriated concept in the source domain, and their constitution of the meaning of the concept, need to be explored. As we illustrated above with the example of the 'wall of knowledge', source domains are rich with imagery and systemic connections that can be subconsciously transferred to the target domain. The danger lies in not consciously understanding and evaluating such connections and their effects.

An example can be derived from the employment of Foucault's work by organisation theorists, especially those concerned with the concept of discourse (e.g. du Gay and Salaman 1992; Knights and Morgan 1991). Foucault's main theoretical development of this concept is found in *The Archaeology of Knowledge* (1972). Foucault's ideas in *The Archaeology*, however, are not drawn on by these authors, who generally draw on Foucault's later 'genealogical' writings linking discourse to power (Foucault 1980). Indeed, *The Archaeology of Knowledge* (1972) has been relatively neglected by organisation theorists in favour of Foucault's later genealogical writings.

This selectivity, without being explicitly discussed, potentially leads to the impression that the concept of discourse is relatively easily delimited in terms of its meaning and application, a far cry from the fragmented and diverse ways in which 'discourse' has been understood and employed (Heracleous and Barrett 2001; Heracleous and Hendry 2000), as well as developed over time in Foucault's thought (Gutting 1989; Jacobs and Heracleous 2001).

Included in the idea of technical adequacy are the varying temporal orientations and levels of analysis applying to concepts in the source domains, and how these are implicated in the use domains. One example is the appropriation of the concept of culture from ethnography by some organisational authors. The temporal orientation in the source domain is decades or centuries. In the target domain, however, in functionalist approaches, the long-term nature of culture has been downplayed and the ease of swiftly achieving a wholesale cultural transformation accepted rather uncritically (e.g. Tunstall 1986; Wilms *et al.* 1994).

Drawing on the example of the concept of discourse, undiscussed selectivity leads to potentially lower fruitfulness of research conduct and dissemination, as readers are not adequately informed of the different views on, and uses of, a concept. This, in turn, can foster the creation and perpetuation of hegemonic approaches, to the detriment of higher richness and interpretive potential of a field.

Drawing on the example of cultural transformation, ignoring or downplaying the temporal orientation of concepts in source domains, or paying them lip service ('culture can take years to change, but our firm has a procedure for transforming your culture very quickly') can lead to a poorer appreciation of the nature and value of concepts and how they relate to the concerns of practitioners or the world at large.

The second criterion we propose is the *paradigmatic adequacy* of the inter-domain conceptual transfer. Addressing this criterion would mean that authors offer a clear statement of their paradigmatic standpoint and how this influences their aims and appropriation of a concept, as well as considering whether and how the paradigmatic nature of the source domain accords with or conflicts with the paradigmatic nature of the target domain. As discussed above, the appropriation of the concept of culture from interpretive approaches in ethnography, for example, has been used in functionalist approaches in organisation theory with an underappreciation of its complexities. While interpretive and functionalist approaches have been integrated at the methodological level (Jick 1979; Lee 1991), they have not been adequately integrated at a deeper level with regard to ontological, ideological and human nature considerations (Burrell and Morgan 1979).

Can a concept developed in one paradigm be fruitfully used in another? This would be exceedingly difficult. Consider, for example, the Marxist concept of 'surplus value'. Developed by a thinker considered one of the founding fathers of sociology, this concept has been exclusively employed by 'critical' organisation theorists to draw attention to what they consider unjust capitalist practices and power differentials based on the accumulation of surplus value. Given its historical pattern of usage, and systemic conceptual connections within Marxism, it appears unlikely that 'surplus value' could be employed within another paradigm without evoking its Marxist connotations of the unjust domination of capital over labour by virtue of the accumulation of this surplus value. These connotations are inherent not in the concept itself, but in the context of its historical development and in the wider conceptual system and worldview it is part of. For similar reasons, it is unlikely that a Marxist or critical theorist would employ the functionalist concept of 'operational efficiency' without a hint of irony or overt disapproval.

A lack of paradigmatic adequacy can thus lead to unhelpful and erroneous uses of concepts transplanted from one conceptual domain to another without due appreciation of the deeper ontological, ideological and human nature considerations associated with such concepts. How far does the metaphorical creativity principle[4] apply here? Does it mean that we should look for paradigmatic isomorphism between the source and target domains or paradigmatic divergence, and to what extent? Or do the implications of this consideration invalidate both imperialistic paradigmatic approaches and claims of paradigmatic incommensurability (Burrell and Morgan 1979)? These are issues that merit further investigation.

The third criterion we propose is the *pragmatic adequacy* of the inter-domain conceptual transfer, which suggests that better or worse appropriations are also dependent on the pragmatic fruitfulness of the transfer. This can be judged from alternative paradigmatic viewpoints. For example, from a functionalist viewpoint, does a conceptual construct help us increase an organisation's competitiveness? From an interpretive viewpoint, does a construct help us gain a deeper understanding of first-order meanings and social dynamics in an organisation? And from a radical viewpoint, does a construct help us expose the fundamental injustices of the current system and inspire us to engage in praxis?

A more focused evaluation would call for assessing the utility of a concept transfer based on the explicit purpose of this transfer. Does the concept transfer actually achieve the promise that compelled the author to instate the concept in the target domain? Authors may transfer a concept to a target domain for many different reasons. The reasons for a transfer may include elaborating insights into a specific area of research by adding a different concept to the conceptual armament aimed at investigating a particular issue; questioning perceived wisdom about a specific subject by introducing a new concept that changes the perspective taken to view and investigate this subject; enriching the ways in which investigations in an area of research have generally been framed and conducted by introducing a new concept to a target domain without a particular focus for the new concept being specified by the author; or challenging the general approach taken by researchers in an area of study by transferring a concept that necessitates fundamental changes in the established ontological or epistemological approach.

Retrospective analyses of purpose by third parties are difficult to achieve. Thus, it is crucial for authors to clarify explicitly what purpose the concept transfer aims to serve. Without this information, the use of the appropriated concept by other researchers can lead to significant difficulties in assessing the potential utility of the transfer, and may impede future use of the appropriated concept.

Conclusion

We suggested that scholarly texts can be seen as ontologically closer to Ricoeurian written texts than to spoken discourse. This means that they have higher potential polysemy and ambiguity, by virtue of their more limited contextuality. We then discussed inter-domain transfer of concepts as a double-edged sword that can potentially either increase a field's interpretive potential and conceptual arsenal, or increase the interplay of multiple meanings, interpretations and conceptual ambiguity. We described Barthes' views on the desirability of such polysemy, and the primacy of the reader's interpretations rather than the author's intentions, and drew parallels between these ideas and the postmodernist movement.

We argued that this situation is not necessarily beneficial, however, if we accept a view of social science as a potentially cumulative endeavour with an actual subject matter related to but independent of actors' subjectivity, and the need for a common language and platform for debate. Employing a metaphorical perspective, we suggested that concepts transferred from a source domain to a target domain are imbued with systemic interconnections inherent in the source domain that implicitly carry over to the target domain. We then proposed a set of criteria for guiding inter-domain conceptual transfer in a way that enhances a field's interpretive potential and conceptual arsenal, rather than multiplying potential meanings and thus ambiguity.

The three criteria we proposed are all relevant for inter-domain conceptual transfers. However, just as there are fundamental trade-offs between the generality, simplicity and accuracy of a theory (Weick 1979), there can be trade-offs between these different criteria for concept transfer. For example, the use of the concept of learning as applied to the organisational level has generally failed to sufficiently consider the specific characteristics of the concept in the source domain, psychology (Weick 1991), where this concept has been developed with reference to the individual level. In addition, researchers often fail to clarify the similarities and differences of their use and meaning of the concept in the target domain. They frequently fail to specify important aspects such as the locus of learning, the agent(s) of learning, the nature of the process of learning, or the outcomes of learning, among others (Fiol and Lyles 1985; Gallagher and Fellenz 1999; Nicolini and Meznar 1995). Despite these problems of technical adequacy, the wide dissemination and use of the concept among both researchers and practitioners indicates that the perceived pragmatic adequacy of the concept transfer is quite high. The use of learning and other 'umbrella concepts' (Hirsch and Levin 1999) has been aided by their lack of specificity, or technical adequacy, as this allows their use in ways maximally consonant with the purposes of different authors. Thus, increasing the technical adequacy of a construct transfer may impede the perceived pragmatic adequacy for a particular purpose. If such trade-offs between the criteria cannot be avoided, or if the degree of achievable adherence to these criteria is in part dependent on the nature of the transferred concept or the purpose of its transfer, it would fall to the authors transferring concepts to make these trade-offs explicit by addressing the three proposed criteria.

Notes

1 For an example, see van de Ven and Poole's (1995) discussion of ideal-type theories of social change in terms of life cycle, evolution, dialectic and teleology perspectives.
2 We should clarify here that the logical necessity of understanding through subjectivity does not imply that these and other phenomena only exist in subjectivity and have no other existence (as George Berkeley rather problematically argued in his *Treatise concerning the Principles of Human Knowledge*).
3 On the shifts and continuities in Barthes's work, see Moriarty (1991).
4 This principle holds that the potential of metaphor to create new understandings depends on there being sufficient similarity as well as difference between the source and the target domains to foster a creative tension (Aristotle 1991).

References

American Psychological Association (1994) *Publication Manual of the American Psychological Association*, 4th edn, Washington, DC: APA.

Aristotle (1991) *On Rhetoric*, trans. G. A. Kennedy, Oxford: Oxford University Press.

Barthes, R. (1994) *The Semiotic Challenge*, Berkeley: University of California Press.

Bateson, G. (1972) *Steps to an Ecology of Mind*, London: Intertext.

Berger, P. and Luckmann, T. (1966) *The Social Construction of Reality*, London: Penguin.

Bhaskar, R. (1978) *A Realist Philosophy of Science*, Hemel Hempstead, UK: Harvester Wheatsheaf.

Burrell, G. and Morgan, G. (1979) *Sociological Paradigms and Organizational Analysis*, Aldershot, UK: Gower.

Cannella, A. and Paetzold, R. (1994) 'Pfeffer's barriers to the advance of organizational science: a rejoinder', *Academy of Management Review* 19: 331–341.

Cooper, R. and Burrell, G. (1988) 'Modernism, postmodernism and organizational analysis: an introduction', *Organization Studies* 9: 91–112.

Donaldson, L. (1985) *In Defence of Organisation Theory: A Reply to the Critics*, Cambridge: Cambridge University Press.

du Gay, P. and Salaman, G. (1992) 'The cult(ure) of the customer', *Journal of Management Studies* 29: 615–633.

Fiol, C. and Lyles, M. (1985) 'Organizational learning', *Academy of Management Review*, 10: 803–813.

Foucault, M. (1972) *The Archaeology of Knowledge*, trans. A. M. Sheridan Smith, London: Routledge.

Foucault, M. (1980) *Power/Knowledge: Selected Interviews and Other Writings 1972–1977*, ed. G. Gordon, Brighton: Harvester.

Gallagher, A. and Fellenz, M. R. (1999) 'Measurement instruments as a tool for advancing research in organizational learning', in M. Easterby-Smith, L. Araujo and J. Burgoyne (eds) *Organizational Learning: Proceedings from the Third International Conference*, vol. 1, Lancaster, UK: Lancaster University Management School.

Giddens, A. (1979) *Central Problems in Social Theory*, London: Macmillan.

Giddens, A. (1984) *The Constitution of Society*, Cambridge: Polity Press.

Giddens, A. (1987) *Social Theory and Modern Sociology*, Cambridge: Polity Press.

Gowler, D. and Legge, K. (1982) 'The integration of disciplinary perspectives and levels of analysis in problem-oriented organizational research', in N. Nicholson and T. Wall (eds) *The Theory and Practice of Organizational Psychology*, London: Academic Press.

Gutting, G. (1989) *Michel Foucault's Archaeology of Scientific Reason*, New York: Cambridge University Press.

Hammersley, M. and Atkinson, P. (1995) *Ethnography: Principles in Practice*, 2nd edn, London: Routledge.

Hassard, J. (1988) 'Overcoming hermeticism in organization theory: an alternative to paradigm incommensurability', *Human Relations* 41: 247–259.

Heracleous, L. and Barrett, M. (2001) 'Organization change as discourse: communicative actions and deep structures in the context of IT implementation', *Academy of Management Journal* 44: 755–778.

Heracleous, L. and Hendry, J. (2000) 'Discourse and the study of organization: towards a structurational perspective', *Human Relations* 53: 1251–1286.

Hirsch, P. M. and Levin, D. Z. (1999) 'Umbrella advocates versus validity police: a life-cycle model', *Organization Science* 10: 199–212.

Jacobs, C. and Heracleous, L. (2001) 'Seeing without being seen: towards an archaeology of controlling science', *International Studies of Management and Organization* 31 (3): 113–135.

Jick, T. (1979) 'Mixing qualitative and quantitative methods: triangulation in action', *Administrative Science Quarterly* 24: 602–611.

Knights, D. and Morgan, G. (1991) 'Corporate strategy, organizations and subjectivity: a critique', *Organization Studies* 12: 251–273.

Lakoff, G. (1990) 'The invariance hypothesis: is abstract reason based on image schemas?', *Cognitive Linguistics* 1: 39–74.

Lakoff, G. and Johnson, M. (1980) *Metaphors We Live By*, Chicago: University of Chicago Press.

Latour, B. (1987) *Science in Action*, Cambridge, MA: Harvard University Press.

Lee, A. (1991) 'Integrating positivist and interpretive approaches to organizational research', *Organization Science* 2: 342–365.

Lemke, D. K., Schminke, M., Clark, N. and Muir, P. (1999) 'Whither goest thou? Seeking trends in organization theory into the new millennium', *Academy of Management Proceedings*, OMT: D1–D6.

Lohdahl, J. B. and Gordon, G. (1972) 'The structure of scientific fields and the functioning of university graduate departments', *American Sociological Review* 37: 57–72.

Miner, J. B. (1990) 'The role of values in defining the "goodness" of theories in organizational science', *Organization Studies* 11: 161–178.

Morgan, G. (1980) 'Paradigms, metaphors and puzzle-solving in organization theory', *Administrative Science Quarterly* 25: 605–622.

Morgan, G. (1983) 'More on metaphor: why we cannot control tropes in administrative science', *Administrative Science Quarterly* 28: 601–607.

Moriarty, M. (1991) *Roland Barthes*, Cambridge: Polity Press.

Nicolini, D. and Meznar, M. B. (1995) 'The social construction of organizational learning: conceptual and practical issues in the field', *Human Relations* 48: 727–746.

Ortony, A. (1979) *Metaphor and Thought*, Cambridge: Cambridge University Press.

Pfeffer, J. (1993) 'Barriers to the advance of organisational science: paradigm development as a dependent variable', *Academy of Management Review* 18: 599–620.

Ricoeur, P. (1991) *From Text to Action*, Evanston, IL: Northwestern University Press.

Salancik, G. R., Staw, B. M. and Pondy, L. R. (1980) 'Administrative turnover as a response to unmanaged organizational interdependence', *Academy of Management Journal* 23: 422–437.

Saussure, F. de (1983) *Course in General Linguistics*, London: Duckworth.

Schultz, M. and Hatch, M. J. (1996) 'Living with multiple paradigms: the case of paradigm interplay in organizational culture studies', *Academy of Management Review* 21: 529–557.

Shapin, S. and Schaffer, S. (1985) *Leviathan and the Air Pump: Hobbes, Boyle and the Experimental Life*, Princeton, NJ: Princeton University Press.

Silverman, D. (1970) *The Theory of Organizations*, London: Heinemann.

Tunstall, W. (1986) 'The breakup of the Bell System: a case study in cultural transformation', *California Management Review* 28: 110–124.

van de Ven, A. and Poole, M. S. (1995) 'Explaining development and change in organizations', *Academy of Management Review* 20: 510–540.

Van Maanen, J. (1995) 'Style as theory', *Organization Science* 6: 132–143.

Warner, M. (1994) 'Organizational behavior revisited', *Human Relations* 47: 1151–1166.

Weick, K. (1979) *The Social Psychology of Organizing*, 2nd edn, Reading, MA: Addison-Wesley.

Weick, K. (1991) 'The nontraditional quality of organizational learning', *Organization Science* 2: 116–124.

Wilms, W., Hardcastle, A. and Zell, D. (1994) 'Cultural transformation at NUMMI', *Sloan Management Review* Fall: 99–113.

Zammuto, R. F. and Connolly, T. (1984) 'Coping with disciplinary fragmentation', *Organizational Behavior Teaching Review* 9: 30–37.

William McKinley

In the past decade, organizational scholars have devoted considerable attention to an epistemological analysis of the constructs that populate their discipline. For example, Osigweh (1989) noted the lack of precision in many organization theory constructs and identified the phenomena of "concept traveling" and "concept stretching" as important issues. Law *et al.* (1998) presented a taxonomy of multidimensional constructs, classifying them by the way in which individual dimensions relate to the overall domain of the construct. For example, they pointed out that multidimensional constructs can conform to a latent model, in which case their dimensions are all manifestations of a more general underlying construct; an aggregate model, in which case individual dimensions sum to define the domain of the construct; or a profile model, in which case interactions between dimensions define specific parts of the construct domain. In a similar type of analysis, Morgeson and Hofmann (1999) described the structure and function of "collective constructs," arguing that this type of construct emerges from interactions between members of a collectivity.

Approaching the discussion of constructs from yet another perspective, Hirsch and Levin (1999) investigated the life cycles of "umbrella constructs." According to these authors (ibid.: 200), umbrella constructs are broadly defined, integrative theoretical constructs that "encompass and account for a set of diverse phenomena." Using "organizational effectiveness" as an example, Hirsch and Levin (ibid.) argued that umbrella constructs sometimes deconstruct into a set of independent, more narrowly demarcated constructs that mirror the dimensions of the original umbrella construct. Consistent with Hirsch and Levin's thesis, a case can be made that much of the literature in contemporary organization theory is devoted to developing umbrella constructs and bolstering them against deconstruction. Examples of umbrella constructs that are central to current streams of research in organization theory are "power" (e.g., Finkelstein 1992; Hardy and Clegg 1996); "trust" (Bigley and Pearce 1998); "culture" (Detert *et al.* 2000); and "social capital" (Adler and Kwon 2002).

While the epistemological literature cited here has greatly improved our understanding of organization theory constructs, it has not done much to clarify the ontological status of those constructs, nor does it show how organization theory constructs maintain (or lose) the quality of objectivity (Daston 1992; Megill 1991) that we tend to take for granted. In this chapter, I address that issue by developing a theory of construct objectification and de-objectification in organization theory. Drawing on Babbie's (1995) methodological text and the literature cited earlier, I first define a construct as a mental representation that captures a common quality that is shared by a set of observations. Thus, a construct is based on empirical reality, but it does not tap unmediated reality directly; instead, it aggregates across instances of reality, abstracting a common attribute from those instances. Though a construct is actually cognitive in status, Babbie (ibid.) states that use of a construct tends to impart the quality of objectivity to it, so that it comes to be seen as a thing outside the user's mind. This process, which I label "construct objectification," resembles the processes of "objectivation" or "reification" that Berger and Luckmann (1966) identified as central to the social construction of reality.

More specifically, in this chapter I argue that construct objectification has two aspects, which I label "externalization" and "demarcation." Externalization is the quality of being seen as part of the outside world, while demarcation is the perception of an entity as bounded and distinct from other entities. After discussing these two aspects of construct objectification, I identify some of the behaviors that I believe promote construct objectification at the time that a new construct is introduced to a scholarly community. These behaviors include naming the construct, defining it and measuring it.

After discussing construct objectification, I focus on the process of construct de-objectification, arguing that as new constructs diffuse and are adopted by the diverse members of the organization theory community, they become subject to potential de-objectification. De-objectification is the deconstruction of the objectivity of a construct, similar to the phenomenon of "construct collapse" identified by Hirsch and Levin (1999). I argue that the fundamental determinant of this de-objectification process is lack of consensus among scholars about the definition of a construct (McKinley 2003a). Since the definition of a construct links the construct to a distinct empirical domain, lack of consensus about the definition reduces the sense of a coherent empirical domain associated with the construct and blurs the demarcation of that domain relative to the empirical domains of other constructs. In other words, lack of consensus about construct definition undercuts construct objectification and de-objectifies the construct in question.

The final part of the chapter specifies some attributes of the social context in which organization theory constructs diffuse. I delineate the roles of these context attributes in enhancing or retarding consensus about the definition of a diffusing construct. I therefore propose these context attributes as critical determinants of the phenomenon of construct de-objectification. In particular, I argue that diversity in the disciplinary backgrounds of construct users, pooled interdependence (Thompson 1967) in the research using a given construct, decentralization of power in a group of construct users, and diffusion of a construct through lean media (Daft and Lengel 1986; Dennis and Kinney 1998) all promote lack of consensus in construct definition and therefore construct de-objectification. These arguments are summarized in the form of propositions that can be a focus for future empirical research in the sociology and epistemology of organization science, and also can be the basis for future discussions of scholarly practice in organization theory.

The theory developed in this chapter is important because constructs provide a mechanism for organization theorists (and indeed, all human beings) to reduce the complexity of empirical reality enough to understand it and operate upon it. Given this sense-making (Weick 1995) role of constructs, it is important for organization theorists to understand the ontological status of organization theory constructs and how that status is influenced by the social context within which constructs diffuse. For example, the theory contained in this chapter implies that certain social context attributes not discussed by Hirsch and Levin (1999) predispose umbrella constructs to the type of deconstruction that those authors described for "organizational effectiveness." This deconstruction may occur when the social context attributes exhibit values that are common in organization theory today. This in turn suggests that the field of organization theory is currently a fertile arena for construct de-objectification, which poses the question of what (if anything) organization theorists wish to do about it. This practical question is addressed at the end of the chapter in a section on implications of the chapter's theoretical framework for the field of organization theory.

Construct objectification

According to Babbie (1995), a construct (or concept) is a mental representation that abstracts a common characteristic from a set of related observations. For example, a number of observations of interactions between organizations and their environments might suggest that those interactions have a common element related to exchange of goods or services across a boundary. The construct "transaction" (Williamson 1981) could then be used to capture that common cross-boundary exchange element. As another example, a number of observations of individuals in organizational settings or of whole organizations might suggest a common element involving influence by those entities over the behavior of other individuals or organizations. The construct "power" (Hardy and Clegg 1996; Hickson *et al.* 1971; Salancik and Pfeffer 1974) might be used to abstract that common attribute of influence over targets.

As I have pointed out already, constructs have a reductive capacity that makes them very useful for negotiating the complexities of empirical reality. Constructs are not completely divorced from empirical reality, but they do not mirror it directly; instead, they summarize and distill it. Contrary to intuition, the case can be made that the information-processing value of constructs increases as they distance the user from reality, because the distancing makes the phenomena distilled by a construct more cognitively tractable. To completely represent reality in all its detail would be overwhelming for humans, given the limits on their information-processing capacity (Simon 1997). Of course, in abstracting from reality a construct also remakes reality to some degree; and this is particularly interesting when the construct is subject to the process of construct objectification.

Babbie (1995) has suggested that as we use constructs, they begin to attain a quality of objectivity that portrays them as phenomena external to the user's mind. Thus users of the construct "transaction" come to see a "transaction" (not just the underlying observations on which the construct was originally based) as an externally real thing. Users of the construct "power" come to view "power" as an externally real thing, apart from the user's internal cognitions. This objectification process implies that most of us are pragmatic realists, ready and willing to participate in the objectification of cognitive summaries of reality. This pragmatic realism is probably reinforced by the cognitive order that it imposes on the world for us, and indeed if objectification of constructs were completely halted by some magic wand, the world would become a chaotic and confusing place indeed. Something like that state would be approximated if everyone adopted the epistemology of "hard" postmodernism (see Alvesson (2003) and Hancock and Tyler (2001) for descriptions of hard pomo). At any rate, the construct objectification process being referred to here can be considered responsible for the creation of the "unobservables" that are advocated as appropriate objects of study by scientific realists (e.g., Godfrey and Hill 1995; Hunt 1990).

Further developing the construct of construct objectification, I suggest that it has two conceptually distinct but empirically related aspects: externalization and demarcation. First, construct objectification depends fundamentally on the perception that the construct is a "thing" external to the user's mind. Without such an element of externalization, construct objectification would be impossible. Second, construct objectification depends on the demarcation of the construct – the perception that it exists as a bounded entity separate from other entities in the world. This aspect suggests that the preservation of clear construct boundaries is essential to the objectivity of a construct. While this initial specification of the externalization and demarcation dimensions is tentative, I will develop the two dimensions further in my discussion below.

While Babbie (1995) states that the use of constructs tends to objectify them, it is possible to "unpack" the meaning of "use" to be more specific about the behaviors that objectify constructs when they are first introduced to a scholarly community. Rather than attempting to provide an exhaustive list of these behaviors, I will simply point to three that I believe are particularly important. These three behaviors are identified at the left-hand side of Figure 7.1.

As shown in Figure 7.1, the first of the three behaviors is naming (see Babbie 1995: 117). Naming a construct is generally done by the first scholar to constitute the construct as an abstraction from empirical reality. Giving a construct a name externalizes the construct, because it pushes the construct from the scholar's mind out into the world in the form of a communicable label. That label can be employed to transmit the meaning of the construct from the initiating scholar to other construct users. At the same time, naming demarcates the construct by attaching a unique signifier to the construct that is different from the signifiers attached to other constructs. This reinforces the perception that the construct is a distinct entity that is separate from other entities in the world. In summary, naming a construct begins a process of externalization and demarcation that operates to objectify the construct, extruding it from the status of an internal cognition to the status of an externally real phenomenon.

As one example, Whiteman and Cooper (2000) introduced the construct of "ecological embeddedness" to organization theory. By attaching the label of "ecological embeddedness" to the construct, they externalized it from their own minds to the outside world, designated with a signifier that can travel across scholarly users. Since we are used to thinking of signifiers as identifying things, naming the construct "ecological embeddedness" creates the perception of an external thing behind the name. At the same time, naming with the signifier "ecological embeddedness" differentiates this con-

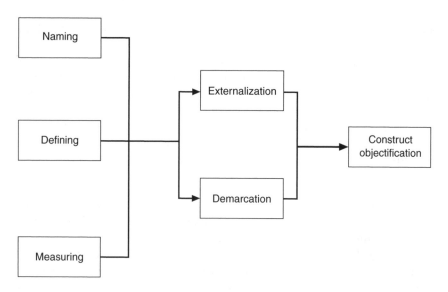

Figure 7.1 Construct objectification.

struct from others that have been named differently, thereby adding the element of demarcation to the objectification process. In combination, the externalization and demarcation promoted by naming start the process of objectifying the construct. My analysis here is consistent with the postmodernist notion that language constitutes phenomena (e.g., Alvesson 2003), but it does not deny the existence of a fundamental underlying reality that is separate from language. Specifically, my argument is that an aspect of underlying reality is captured, simplified and abstracted through a cognition called a construct, and that construct is subsequently objectified in part through the process of assigning a name to it.

While naming a construct begins to objectify it, the essence of that object would remain mysterious without a concomitant attempt at defining. As shown in Figure 7.1, the behavior of defining also reinforces externalization and demarcation, and therefore promotes construct objectification. Defining a construct specifies the empirical domain covered by that construct, thereby enhancing the perception that the construct is an objective phenomenon. Defining solidifies the externalization process begun by naming, pulling the construct into the territory of the objective world and out of the territory of internal cognition. At the same time, defining reinforces the construct boundaries that are implicit in the use of a unique signifier, because defining identifies an empirical referent for the construct that is at least potentially distinct from the empirical referents of other constructs. In this way, defining a construct demarcates it, adding to the construct objectification that flows from definitionally produced externalization.

To continue the example of "ecological embeddedness," Whiteman and Cooper (2000) take pains to define this construct for the readers of their article. The authors tell their readers that "ecological embeddedness" is "the degree to which a manager is rooted in the land — that is, the extent to which the manager is on the land and learns from the land in an experiential way" (ibid.: 1267). This definition externalizes the construct of "ecological embeddedness," because it specifies an external domain of subsidiary constructs (e.g., learning) and concrete entities (land, manager) that are already objectified in the reader's mind. This gives the reader the sense that the construct "ecological embeddedness" refers to an external reality, something that is outside cognition and in the world. Thinking about these specific subsidiary objects and entities also imparts a sense of distinctness to the construct "ecological embeddedness," making "ecological embeddedness" not only an externalized construct, but also a demarcated one. Together, the externalization and demarcation accomplished by Whiteman and Cooper's (2000) definition of "ecological embeddedness" help convert the construct into an object. At that point, the construct no longer needs to be enclosed in quotes, because it has lost its subjective status and has become objective. So, we can speak of ecological embeddedness rather than "ecological embeddedness." The idea that ecological embeddedness is just an invention of the authors, an internal cognition that only abstracts from underlying reality, gets obscured (papered over, if you will).

The third behavior listed on the left-hand side of Figure 7.1 as a source of construct objectification is measuring. My argument for the causal effect of measuring on construct objectification relies heavily on the discussions of Golinski (1998) and other sociologists of science (e.g., Latour and Woolgar 1986). These individuals suggest that measuring instruments both represent and reproduce the phenomena being measured. The act of developing a laboratory instrument and achieving consensus that it operates reliably to measure a phenomenon also constitutes acknowledgement of the existence of that phenomenon (Golinski 1998). If measurement functions in a similar way in organization theory, the development of construct measures will help "produce," or objectify, the constructs being measured. In the realist ontology that has traditionally dominated organization theory, the process of measuring presupposes an external entity to be measured, so the very act of measurement helps externalize constructs. At the same time, measures also have a demarcation effect that resembles that of a unique signifier or definition, differentiating the construct being measured from other constructs that are measured in different ways. In summary, as is true with naming and defining, measuring operates to objectify constructs.

Since Whiteman and Cooper's (2000) article is based on field observations, they do not describe quantitative measures of the construct of ecological embeddedness. However, they do furnish a detailed list of concrete human behaviors covered by the construct, and these could serve as items with which to measure the construct of ecological embeddedness in future quantitative studies. These behaviors are compiled from observations of Cree tallymen (trappers) in the James Bay area of Quebec. For example, according to Whiteman and Cooper (2000), gathering ecological information and walking out on the land are behaviors indicative of ecological embeddedness. One can imagine survey researchers developing a series of items to rate the degree to which managers in corporations exhibit behaviors like these. The procedure of measuring ecological embeddedness in this way would further the externalization and demarcation of the construct begun by naming and defining. Thus, measuring ecological embeddedness would be another vehicle for extruding the construct into the world as an object of investigation.

Construct de-objectification

I have now argued that the objectification of an organization theory construct is promoted by the acts of naming the construct, defining it and measuring it. I emphasize again that this is not intended as a complete list of the causes of construct objectification; rather, it is just a sampling of the factors that I believe are important in the construct objectification process. While the reader may conclude at this point that construct objectification, once achieved, is an enduring state, I am not so sanguine. In this section of the chapter, I propose that as constructs diffuse over time in the organization theory community, their objective status can become threatened even if it was adequately solidified at the time of construct introduction. The primary culprit in this de-objectification process, I maintain, is the diversity of definitions that often arises as a construct diffuses among different users. While a construct definition may be unitary and objectifying at the time of construct introduction, diffusion of the construct among many users can displace that unity and fragment the meanings associated with the construct. That is, each user or group of users comes to attach a different meaning to the construct in question.

This fragmentation of definition and meaning has been frequently remarked in commentary on the current state of organization theory (e.g., Pfeffer 1993; Knudsen 2003; Shenhav *et al.* 1994), and some observers (e.g., McKinley 2003b) have explained it as part of the encroachment of postmodern epistemology on the field. That assertion is of course debatable, but for our purposes here, it suffices to note that when definitions of a construct vary across scholarly users, and different scholars attach different meanings to the same construct, the specified empirical domain of the construct becomes more and more a function of individual perspective. The construct therefore becomes more subjective in status, and the objectification that may have been attained at construct introduction is undercut. Speaking metaphorically, the construct "intrudes" from an external status to a cognitive status, and the observer begins to lose the sense of the construct as an external entity. I argue that divergence in construct definition across users not only "intrudes," disrupting the externalization of a construct, but also interferes with the demarcation that may have been established at the time of construct introduction. Thus, differences in construct definition across construct users tend to reverse the externalization and demarcation processes that are represented in Figure 7.1, drawing the construct out of the world and de-objectifying it.

This argument supports a formal proposition that may be useful for focusing future discussion and empirical testing:

Proposition 1: The less the consensus across post-introduction users in the definition of a construct, the greater the de-objectification of the construct.

The causal relationship stated in Proposition 1 is shown as linkage P1 on the right-hand side of Figure 7.2.

Arguably, many constructs that are diffusing in organization theory today exhibit low degrees of consensus in construct definition. Constructs such as "transaction," "institution," "power," "institutional field," "learning," "strategy," "culture" and so on each admit of a variety of different definitions (Astley and Zammuto 1992; Hirsch and Levin 1999). This perspectival diversity in definition is reflected in the literature that has developed around each of the constructs (see, for example, Barney and Hesterly (1996) and Godfrey and Hill (1995) for reviews of the transaction costs literature;

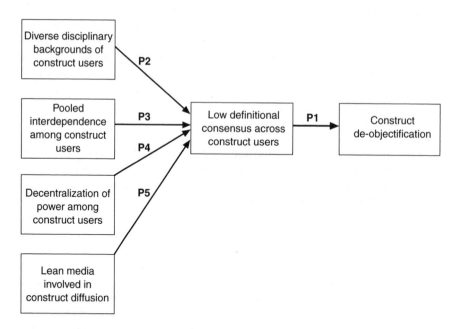

Figure 7.2 Construct de-objectification.

Mizruchi and Fein (1999) and Tolbert and Zucker (1996) for discussions of the institutional theory literature; Hardy and Clegg (1996) for a recent review of the literature on power; and Hirsch and Levin (1999) for discussion of the constructs "learning," "strategy" and "culture"). To the extent that the argument summarized in Proposition 1 is correct, the implication is that many organization theory constructs diffusing today have a de-objectified or only partially objectified character. I hasten to add that I am not making a prescriptive statement here, but rather a descriptive one: I do not consider objectified constructs "good" or less objectified ones "bad."

On the other hand, a few organization theory constructs that are currently diffusing appear to exhibit greater standardization in the way they are defined across users, and this pulls the construct away from perspectivity and renders it more objectified over the long term. An example of this is the construct "organizational size," which in most of the empirical studies that have used the construct has been defined and measured as the number of employees (Kimberly 1976). Another example is "organizational decline," whose definition has gradually become standardized around the "decrease in an organization's resource base" specification that Cameron *et al.* (1987: 224) gave it. If Proposition 1 is valid, these two constructs will have greater long-term objectification than many other constructs in the field of organization theory. In summary, variation in the degree of consensus about construct definition can help explain variation in the level of objectification exhibited by organization theory constructs as they diffuse after their introduction.

Context attributes and construct de-objectification

Having discussed in some detail the role of diversity and fragmentation of meaning in construct de-objectification, I now turn to an inventory of some social context attributes that I believe influence the level of fragmentation of meaning and therefore the phenomenon of construct de-objectification in organization theory. My expectation is that the degree of fragmentation in the definitions of a construct will mediate the effects of these social context attributes on the level of construct de-objectification.

Diverse disciplinary backgrounds

The first social context attribute I focus on is the amount of diversity in the disciplinary backgrounds of the users of a given construct (see the left-hand side of Figure 7.2). When users of a given organization theory construct come from different disciplinary backgrounds (e.g., economics, sociology, political science), it is less likely that those individuals will converge on a single definition of the construct in question. Different disciplinary backgrounds will instill different cognitive lenses for conceptualizing the construct and interpreting its meaning, leading to less consensus about what the construct's proper empirical domain is. A good example of this is the construct "institution," which has been conceptualized in a variety of different ways by economists, political scientists and sociologists contributing to the interdisciplinary literature on "the new institutionalism" (DiMaggio and Powell 1991). The diversity in these scholars' disciplinary backgrounds contributes to cross-user fragmentation in the meaning of "institution" (ibid.), and this in turn reduces the externalization and demarcation on which construct objectification depends. The result is that constructs like "institution" that diffuse across users with diverse disciplinary backgrounds exhibit a de-objectified or partially objectified character.

On the other hand, when users of a given construct have less diverse disciplinary backgrounds, definitions of the construct will tend to converge more closely across users, and the initial objectification imparted by naming, defining and measuring will be less disrupted. An example of this situation is the "organizational decline" construct mentioned above. As noted, there has been a relatively high user convergence on the definition of organizational decline articulated in the 1980s by Cameron *et al.* (1987). This convergence would appear to be supported by the relatively low diversity in the disciplinary backgrounds of the scholars studying organizational decline. The study of organizational decline is a specialized area, and it seems that most of the scholars involved with that stream of research have either received their doctoral training in business schools, are now employed as faculty of business schools, or both (see Mone *et al.* (1998) for a recent review of the organizational decline literature). Assuming that the disciplinary diversity of organizational decline construct users is relatively low, we would expect less cross-user fragmentation of meaning in conceptualizing the construct, with a resulting barrier to perspectivity and the de-objectification of the construct.

The preceding discussion suggests a second proposition:

> *Proposition 2: The more diverse the disciplinary backgrounds of the post-introduction users of an organization theory construct, the less the cross-user consensus in construct definition and the greater the de-objectification of the construct.*

Proposition 2 is represented by the links P2 and P1 in Figure 7.2.

Type of interdependence

The second social context attribute that I would like to call to the reader's attention is the type of interdependence that characterizes research on a given construct. Thompson (1967) distinguished between three types of interdependence: pooled, sequential and reciprocal. According to Thompson (ibid.: 54), pooled interdependence is marked by an aggregative principle, so that "each part renders a discrete contribution to the whole and each is supported by the whole." In contrast to sequential and reciprocal interdependence, Thompson's other two types, pooled interdependence represents a lower absolute level of interdependence and a less demanding coordination problem (ibid.). An example of pooled interdependence is the relationship between the local branches of a bank: each branch contributes revenues to the whole organization, but the branches have a relatively low level of dependence on one another and simply aggregate their outputs into a whole.

In sequential interdependence, on the other hand, a series of organizational units are engaged in a sequential conversion operation, and the outputs of one organizational unit become inputs for the next unit (Thompson 1967). The classic example is the automobile assembly line, or indeed any sequential manufacturing process in which a unit performs a transformation and feeds the output to the next unit in line.

Finally, reciprocal interdependence represents the highest level of interdependence in Thompson's (1967) typology. In reciprocal interdependence, each focal unit's outputs become inputs for the other units with which it is interacting, and vice versa. The result is a dense web of interactions that require close coordination, typically of a face-to-face variety (ibid.). A good example of reciprocal interdependence is a surgical team, in which each member is processing physical or informational inputs generated by the other team members, while simultaneously producing physical or informational outputs to be processed by those members.

I argue that when theory building and research designed to explore a given construct are characterized by pooled interdependence, there is less pressure to converge on a common definition of the construct. In such cases, each researcher is pooling his or her intellectual outputs to form the sum total of knowledge about the construct. However, generation of research outputs is not dependent on other construct users having performed a subtask in the knowledge production process, as would be true in cases of sequential or reciprocal interdependence. Pooled interdependence in construct scholarship promotes a high level of autonomy among the scholars, and this autonomy reduces the constraint to agree on and maintain a common definition of the construct. This in turn permits cross-scholar fragmentation of construct meaning, which has a positive effect on the de-objectification of the construct.

In contrast, if academic research involving a given construct is characterized by sequential or reciprocal interdependence, knowledge producers will be less autonomous and will feel more pressure to reach consensus with their fellows about the meaning of the construct. If knowledge-generating agents are sequentially or reciprocally interdependent with one another for the accomplishment of intellectual production, they will be forced to limit disagreement on construct definition, because otherwise they cannot communicate effectively with one another and coordinate their efforts. Thus, when sequential or reciprocal interdependence characterizes knowledge production, I predict that the producers will converge on a standard definition of whatever construct they are studying, and that construct will be correspondingly less subject to de-objectification. In summary, sequential or reciprocal interdependence foster conditions in which constructs are more resistant to de-objectification.

Arguably, much of the research in organization theory today falls into the category of pooled interdependence. Despite the existence of schools of thought in organization theory (McKinley *et al.* 1999), many organization theorists appear to be conducting their research in isolation from their colleagues. This is consistent with Fuchs and Ward's (1994: 481) description of academic disciplines with "loosely coupled textual fields that have minimal hardware and social solidarity." The autonomy of organization theorists is suggested by the typical format of empirical research papers in the field: a unique theory is presented and then empirical results that test it are reported. This makes the typical organization theory research article a self-contained affair. The expectation seems to be that the findings of these self-contained articles will be pooled into a body of knowledge. There appears to be relatively little division of labor in knowledge production between scholars who develop theories and specialists in empirical research who test them. There are of course journals in which pure theoretical articles can be published (e.g., *Academy of Management Review*), but the models in those articles rarely seem to be the focus of later empirical testing. A division of labor between theorists and empirical researchers in organization theory is not institutionalized at this point in the evolution of the field. On the normative side, pooled interdependence is supported by the "uniqueness value" in organization theory (Mone and McKinley 1993), which states that unique scholarly work is good. In short, organization theory appears to be characterized by the type of interdependence that fosters lack of definitional convergence among scholars investigating the same construct, and this in turn leads to cross-scholar fragmentation of meaning and construct de-objectification.

A contrasting case would be research in the field of high-energy physics (Pickering 1984). Pickering's description of the field suggests that it exhibits more of a reciprocally interdependent character. The theoretical models generated by theorists in this field become direct inputs for the work of their experimental colleagues, while the empirical results generated by the latter feed quickly and directly back into the theoretical deliberations of the former (ibid.). There appears to be less emphasis on self-contained research, and the well-developed division of labor between theorists and experimentalists in high-energy physics creates a stronger degree of cross-scholar interdependence than is typically the case in organization theory. If the argument being developed in this section is correct, this would suggest a higher degree of cross-scholar definitional consensus, and less cross-scholar fragmentation of construct meaning, resulting in less de-objectification of high-energy physics constructs as they diffuse.

While I have contended that research in organization theory is usually characterized by pooled interdependence, my argument also recognizes variation across communities of organization theory construct users in the type of interdependence exhibited. Thus, research directed toward the exploration of some constructs may exhibit pooled interdependence, while research directed toward the exploration of other constructs may have a more sequentially interdependent or reciprocally interdependent character. For example, research groups in population ecology devoted to theoretical and empirical studies of the construct "density dependence" (Hannan and Carroll 1992) may have moved away from the pooled interdependence model and begun to engage in investigations characterized by a state of sequential or reciprocal interdependence between investigators. If this has indeed occurred, one would predict more consensus in the way the construct of interest is defined and correspondingly greater resistance to fragmentation of meaning and construct de-objectification.

On the basis of this discussion, I state the following proposition:

Proposition 3: The closer post-introduction theory building and empirical research on a construct come to the pole of pooled interdependence, the less the cross-user consensus in construct definition and the greater the de-objectification of the construct.

Proposition 3 is represented by links P3 and P1 in Figure 2.

Decentralization of power

A third context attribute that I believe has an important influence on the degree of definitional consensus about a construct, and therefore the level of construct de-objectification, is the power structure of the scholars studying the construct. These groups of investigators may be "invisible colleges" (Crane 1972), "schools" (McKinley *et al.* 1999), or looser aggregations of individuals who share only a common interest in a particular constructed slice of the organizational world. When the power structure of such a group is centralized, there will be pressure for individual scholars to conform to the construct definition advanced by the most powerful members of the group. Such conformity may be necessary for access to scarce critical resources such as journal space, grants, faculty appointments or research data. Consistent with that argument, Pfeffer (1993) has drawn attention to the role of power in promoting consensus within a scholarly discipline. The logic of the argument is also consistent with McKinley *et al.*'s (2000) description of the catalyst role that power plays in consolidating and standardizing cognitive schemas. Thus, in research groups where power is centralized, I expect relatively high consensus about the definitions of the constructs being investigated, and therefore less de-objectification of those constructs over time.

On the other hand, when the power structure of a collectivity concerned with the investigation of a construct is decentralized, there will be less constraint to adhere to a standard definition of the construct, and the fragmentation of meaning that precedes construct de-objectification will be more in evidence. Like pooled interdependence, decentralization enhances the autonomy of individual scholars, and that autonomy is likely to be reflected in cross-scholar differences in the interpretation of the core construct of interest. Those varying interpretations will undercut the objective status of the construct and render it increasingly a matter of individual cognition.

As Pfeffer (1993) pointed out, the power structure of organization theory is decentralized. One reason for this is that the organization theory collectivity does not depend heavily on expensive hardware for the production of research outputs. This lack of dependence on hardware is typical of social science fields (Fuchs and Ward 1994) and forms a contrast with fields like high-energy physics (Pickering 1984). Pickering (1984) described the tremendous investment made in particle accelerators and other hardware items for modern experimental work in high-energy physics. These resources are so expensive that they tend to be concentrated in a few geographical locations (ibid.), and those who administer the facilities where the hardware is located probably acquire a good deal of power by virtue of their resource control. Such centralization of power will encourage convergence across different experimentalists in the definition and measurement of a given construct; and in fact, the apparatus itself will add additional impetus to this standardization process. These factors will create significant barriers to fragmentation of meaning and de-objectification of high-energy physics constructs. There is no equivalent set of social or instrumental constraints in organization theory. In the social realm, organization theory's decentralized power structure leaves investigators much more leeway to advance their own interpretations of constructs and therefore precipitate the unintended consequences of meaning fragmentation and construct de-objectification.

On the basis of this argument, I suggest:

> *Proposition 4: The more decentralized the power structure of a research group (school or college) studying a particular construct after its introduction, the less the cross-user consensus in construct definition and the greater the de-objectification of the construct.*

Proposition 4 is represented by links P4 and P1 in Figure 7.2.

Type of diffusion medium

Turning now to a fourth context attribute, I propose that the nature of the media through which a construct diffuses affects the degree of cross-scholar consensus in construct definition and thus the construct's susceptibility to de-objectification. Daft and Lengel (1986; see also Daft and Lengel 1984; Dennis and Kinney 1998) have differentiated between "rich" communication media and less rich media. Rich media rely on face-to-face interaction and "[allow] for rapid feedback and multiple cues so that managers can converge on a common interpretation" (Daft and Lengel 1986: 560). Daft and Lengel (1986) contended that rich media are good for reducing equivocality in organizational tasks. Less rich, or "lean," media, on the other hand, reduce uncertainty but not equivocality. In a scholarly discipline, examples of rich communication media would be conferences where participants meet face to face, specialized research symposia or scholarly seminars. By contrast, less rich media would include formal reports, published journal articles or unpublished manuscripts.

When a construct diffuses through rich media, the face-to-face interaction that is involved provides an abundant set of cues and feedback signals that help reduce equivocality about construct interpretation. For example, if scholars meet face to face in a specialized symposium to discuss a construct, there is a greater likelihood that they will become aware of differences in their definitions of the construct, and be able to converge on a common definition of the construct through an exchange of cues and rapid feedback. If the scholars are successful in establishing consensus, or at least in reducing the number of feasible interpretations of the construct, fragmentation of construct meaning will be retarded and a barrier to construct de-objectification will be erected. The construct will be less subject to individual interpretation than it was before and there will be less chance that the objectivity of the construct will be disrupted as it is used in additional research by the scholars.

On the other hand, lean media, like journal articles and written reports, do not provide the multiple cues and feedback channels that are afforded by face-to-face interaction. Thus, I expect that these leaner media will be less proficient at resolving ambiguity about the definition of a construct. If information about a construct diffuses primarily through lean scholarly media, the reader will not have the opportunity to verify his or her interpretation of the construct directly with the authors, and this can foster fragmentation in interpretation across the different consumers of an article. Lean scholarly media isolate the sender of a message from the receiver, so if there is ambiguity in the message (such as the meaning of a construct), that ambiguity is more likely to become entrenched and even institutionalized. The absence of face-to-face interaction also reduces social pressure to conform to a common construct definition, reinforcing the tendency toward an array of meanings and toward construct de-objectification over time.

Arguably, much of the construct diffusion in organization theory today takes place through lean media. Published journal articles and book chapters – rather than conferences or face-to-face symposia – are probably the dominant channels for communicating about constructs and discussing their interpretations. Conferences take place, of course, but their relatively low status compared to publication in major journals reduces their importance as construct diffusion media. Despite this general assessment of organization theory, however, there may be variation within the field in the degree of richness of the channels for construct diffusion, depending on the construct in question. In some cases, researchers studying a construct may meet frequently (perhaps in informal settings) to exchange views about the construct and resolve their differences about its definition. In other cases, the individuals studying a construct may rely on leaner media and not have (or take) the opportunity to meet face to face to interact about issues such as construct meaning. One would anticipate that in the latter cases there would be more diversity about construct definition and that this diversity might even become institutionalized over time (see Cameron's (1986: 541) discussion of effectiveness for an example). The diversity in construct definition would eventually transform the construct into an array of subjective interpretations, undercutting objectivity and resulting in construct de-objectification.

This supports a final proposition:

Proposition 5: The leaner the media through which a given organization theory construct diffuses after its introduction, the less the cross-user consensus in construct definition and the greater the de-objectification of the construct.

Proposition 5 is represented by linkages P5 and P1 in Figure 7.2.

Discussion and conclusion

The theory summarized in this chapter suggests that when a construct is first introduced to the organization theory community, naming, defining and measuring the construct play important roles in its objectification. However, as the construct diffuses among organization theorists, processes may be set in motion that reverse the construct objectification that was attained at introduction. Those processes stem from diversity in the disciplinary backgrounds of construct users, pooled interdependence in their scholarly endeavors, decentralization in their power relationships, and use of lean media in their scholarly communications. All these context attributes lower the degree of consensus that scholars exhibit in defining a scholarly construct that is diffusing among them. In turn, low cross-user consensus in construct definition reduces the long-term objectification of a construct by interfering with the underlying dimensions of externalization and demarcation. Low cross-scholar consensus in construct definition means that interpretations of the construct's meaning vary from scholar to scholar, making the construct's empirical domain more subjective and reversing the extrusion into the world that is critical for construct objectification. Given the social context attribute levels just described, a construct will be vulnerable to the type of deconstruction or "collapse" that Hirsch and Levin (1999) described for "organizational effectiveness."

On the other hand, if diversity in the disciplinary backgrounds of construct users is low, if their interdependence is closer to the sequential or reciprocal types that Thompson (1967) identified, if the power relations among them are hierarchical and centralized, and if their construct diffusion media are rich, I would expect the opposite outcome to occur. That is, cross-user definitions of a diffusing construct would be more standardized, and the empirical domains associated with the construct by each user would overlap more tightly. This would enhance the inter-subjective status of the construct's empirical domain and build in barriers to its de-objectification, pulling it away from individual perspective toward an externalized, demarcated state. The ultimate result would be a more objective construct that has more of the character of a phenomenon and less of the character of a thought. Again I emphasize that I am not taking a normative position on construct objectification or de-objectification. I am simply trying to understand the contextual conditions under which construct de-objectification may occur and may indeed become a permanent feature of organization theory.

Of course, for many constructs diffusing within organization theory, the values of the context attributes I have discussed will be fixed at contrasting levels (some high, some low). This may lead to a number of interesting permutations and combinations for a given construct. For example, imagine a construct diffusing within a group of researchers who have come to organization theory from many different disciplinary backgrounds and whose power relations are decentralized, but who have organized themselves into research teams characterized by reciprocal interdependence and who are using rich media to communicate to one another about the construct. In that case, one would predict a tendency toward fragmentation in the interpretation of the construct attributable to the diversity in disciplinary backgrounds and the decentralized power structure. Those pressures toward fragmentation would be counterbalanced by opposing pressures toward standardization stemming from the organization of the research teams and the rich media they were using. The result would be some erosion of construct objectification over time but also some barriers to complete de-objectification. One could also expect plenty of creative dispute as researchers tried to move beyond their diverse backgrounds and decentralized power relations to forge a common understanding of the construct.

Implications for future theory and research

One of the main implications of the argument presented in this chapter is the novel insight that the ontological status of the constructs diffusing in organization theory is at least in part a function of the social contexts in which they diffuse. Depending on the nature of that context, a construct may come to have a more or less objective status over the long term. Since constructs are user abstractions from a complex, unknowable underlying reality, the ability to maintain the abstractions as solid, objective entities is in part determined by socio-cognitive processes and the social context variables that drive them. So, if one wants to understand why some organization theory constructs seem more solid and objective than others, this chapter suggests that one needs to look at what is happening in the social context within which each construct is diffusing. Are the construct's users diverse in disciplinary backgrounds, or not? Are construct users doing research that entails pooled interdependence between researchers, or does knowledge production fit Thompson's (1967) sequential or reciprocal interdependence categories? Is the power structure of the community studying a construct centralized or decentralized? And how is the construct diffusing across the community – through rich media or lean? Depending on the answers to these questions, one can anticipate varying levels of consensus about the definition of the construct, different scores on the externalization and demarcation subdimensions I have identified, and, ultimately, different levels of construct objectification over time.

The propositions advanced in this chapter could serve as the starting point for an interesting stream of empirical research in the sociology and epistemology of organization science. Through operationalizing the constructs in these propositions – constructs such as "construct de-objectification," "definitional consensus," "diversity in disciplinary backgrounds," and the like – empirical researchers could gain greater insight into the complex empirical realities that underlie these constructs and are summarized by them. In order to conduct such operationalizations, researchers in the sociology and epistemology of organization science would need to collect data on how constructs diffuse in organization theory and how they are used by organization theorists. That would admittedly be a difficult task, but sources for such data might actually be more abundant than would appear at first glance. Data appropriate for the operationalization and testing of the propositions in this chapter might be obtained, for example, from survey instruments administered to random samples of organization theorists, from demographic information in professional association databases, from published articles in the major journals in the field, and from editorial statements in those same journals. Mone and McKinley (1993) used some of these sources to assemble qualitative data to support their thesis about the value placed on uniqueness in organization theory research, and there is no reason why such sources could not also be used to develop quantitative measures of the constructs described in this chapter.

Assuming that at least some of the propositions in this chapter were tested and received empirical support, new research questions of interest to the sociology and epistemology of organization science would be posed. For example, if low cross-user consensus in construct definition does indeed undercut construct objectification, rendering a construct more subjective and idiosyncratic, does the degree of consensus have a linear or a curvilinear effect on this outcome? Is there a threshold effect such that beyond a certain point low definitional consensus has little or no additional effect on construct de-objectification? Are there perhaps other variables besides definitional consensus that mediate between the social context factors I have discussed and the dependent variable of construct de-objectification? Do the social context factors have direct effects on construct de-objectification that are *not* mediated by any intervening variable? And what about moderators of the relationships predicted in this chapter's propositions? All these questions would be interesting topics for future empirical research.

Implications for the field of organization theory

Given the type of social context that often characterizes construct user groups in organization theory, the framework presented in this chapter suggests that many of the constructs currently diffusing in the field are partially or wholly de-objectified. While these abstractions from empirical reality may have been successfully objectified at introduction through naming, defining and measuring, definitional consensus in many cases has eroded over time as the construct diffused among organizational scholars. The diversity of disciplinary backgrounds that is frequently seen among users of a given construct, the pooled interdependence that often characterizes their research efforts, the decentralization of their power relations, and the lean media frequently involved in construct diffusion all contribute to this erosion of definitional consensus and the construct de-objectification that results from it.

If many organization theory constructs are indeed in the process of becoming de-objectified, the practical question is what, if anything, to do about it. To the extent that the social context variables of disciplinary diversity, type of interdependence in research activity, level of decentralization and degree of media richness can be manipulated, it may be possible to adjust these factors either to preserve construct de-objectification or to raise the level of objectification of the typical organization theory construct. The former strategy might be favored by scholars of a postmodern persuasion (e.g., Case 2003) who believe that flux is the natural state of empirical reality and therefore that a fixed, unitary construct definition would impose artificial restrictions on meaning. The latter strategy might be favored by those (e.g., McKelvey 1997; McKinley 2003a; McKinley and Mone 1998) who wish to enhance the precision and objectivity of organization theory constructs.

As an example of the type of manipulation that might be achievable, consider the implications if empirical research based on Proposition 5 showed that the richness of the media through which constructs diffuse does have an independent effect on cross-scholar consensus in construct definition and on the resulting level of construct objectification. It might then be possible to manipulate the richness of construct diffusion media in such a way as to raise or lower construct objectification as desired. Researchers interested in solidifying the objectivity of the constructs with which they deal could devote more time and effort to rich, face-to-face interactions in which the meaning of the constructs would be discussed and negotiated agreements would be sought on how each construct is to be defined. Alternatively, researchers in a given college, school or working group could seek to de-emphasize such rich interactions if they wanted to avoid the restraints that a negotiated consensus on construct definition would impose on the interpretations of individual construct users.

Ultimately, of course, this discussion leads us to the fundamental question of what kind of scholarly discipline we, as organization theorists, wish to have. Do we wish to be more like the humanities, in which "idiosyncratic microstates" (McKelvey 1997) predominate and subjectivity is celebrated? Some organization theorists (e.g., Case 2003; Zald 1993, 1996) have answered in the affirmative, and it is certainly a feasible possibility. Individuals of this persuasion would presumably wish to maintain social context factors at levels that would facilitate multiple interpretations of a given construct and reduce unwarranted construct solidification. Or, on the other hand, do we wish to follow a path closer to the natural sciences, in which idiosyncrasy is reduced through the abstraction of common components of individual microstates into general constructs, followed by the externalization and demarcation of those constructs as objectified entities? Those who answer "yes" to this question would presumably advocate manipulating social context factors so as to promote definitional consensus, thus reducing fragmentation of the meanings attached to a single construct and supporting construct objectification.

Because they involve normative preferences, the options referred to in the previous paragraph can only be addressed by a normative discussion, though theory building and empirical research in the sociology and epistemology of organization science could certainly inform this discussion. A choice of direction would require a debate that seeks to forge a consensus on the future of organization theory. Whether such a consensus is possible at this point in the field's development is unclear – but at any rate the debate might be healthy for the field, because it would at least bring to the surface the issue of our collective future. That future is – for better or worse – up to all of us, so perhaps it is fair to recommend that we become more aware of the different ways in which we could enact it through our treatment of the constructs we use on a daily basis.

Note

1 An earlier version of this chapter was presented at the Seventeenth annual EGOS Colloquium, 5–7 July 2001, in Lyon, France. The author would like to thank Marja-Liisa Kakkuri-Knuuttila for her helpful comments.

References

Adler, P. S. and Kwon, S. (2002) "Social capital: prospects for a new concept," *Academy of Management Review* 27: 17–40.

Alvesson, M. (2003) "Interpretive unpacking: moderately destabilizing identities and images in organization studies," in E. A. Locke (ed.) *Postmodernism and Management: Pros, Cons and the Alternative*, Oxford: Elsevier Science.

Astley, W. G. and Zammuto, R. F. (1992) "Organization science, managers, and language games," *Organization Science* 3: 443–460.

Babbie, E. (1995) *The Practice of Social Research*, 7th edn, Belmont, CA: Wadsworth Publishing.

Barney, J. B. and Hesterly, W. (1996) "Organizational economics: understanding the relationship between organizations and economic analysis," in S. R. Clegg, C. Hardy and W. R. Nord (eds) *Handbook of Organization Studies*, London: Sage.

Berger, P. L. and Luckmann, T. (1966) *The Social Construction of Reality: A Treatise in the Sociology of Knowledge*, New York: Doubleday.

Bigley, G. A. and Pearce, J. L. (1998) "Straining for shared meaning in organization science: problems of trust and distrust," *Academy of Management Review* 23: 405–421.

Cameron, K. S. (1986) "Effectiveness as paradox: consensus and conflict in conceptions of organizational effectiveness," *Management Science* 32: 539–553.

Cameron, K. S., Kim, M. U. and Whetten, D. A. (1987) "Organizational effects of decline and turbulence," *Administrative Science Quarterly* 32: 222–240.

Case, P. (2003) "From objectivity to subjectivity: pursuing *subjective authenticity* in organizational research," in R. Westwood and S. Clegg (eds) *Debating Organization: Point-Counterpoint in Organization Studies*, Oxford: Blackwell.

Crane, D. (1972) *Invisible Colleges: Diffusion of Knowledge in Scientific Communities*, Chicago: University of Chicago Press.

Daft, R. L. and Lengel, R. H. (1984) "Information richness: a new approach to manager information processing and organization design," in B. M. Staw and L. L. Cummings (eds) *Research in Organizational Behavior*, Greenwich, CT: JAI Press.

Daft, R. L. and Lengel, R. H. (1986) "Organizational information requirements, media richness and structural design," *Management Science* 32: 554–571.

Daston, L. (1992) "Objectivity and the escape from perspective," *Social Studies of Science* 22: 597–618.

Dennis, A. R. and Kinney, S. T. (1998) "Testing media richness theory in the new media: the effects of cues, feedback, and task equivocality," *Information Systems Research* 9: 256–274.

Detert, J. R., Schroeder, R. G. and Mauriel, J. J. (2000) "A framework for linking culture and improvement initiatives in organizations," *Academy of Management Review* 25: 850–863.

DiMaggio, P. J. and Powell, W. W. (1991) "Introduction," in W. W. Powell and P. J. DiMaggio (eds) *The New Institutionalism in Organizational Analysis*, Chicago: University of Chicago Press.

Finkelstein, S. (1992) "Power in top management teams: dimensions, measurement, and validation," *Academy of Management Journal* 35: 505–538.

Fuchs, S. and Ward, S. (1994) "What is deconstruction, and where and when does it take place? Making facts in science, building cases in law," *American Sociological Review* 59: 481–500.

Godfrey, P. C. and Hill, C. W. L. (1995) "The problem of unobservables in strategic management research," *Strategic Management Journal* 16: 519–533.

Golinski, J. (1998) *Making Natural Knowledge: Constructivism and the History of Science*, Cambridge: Cambridge University Press.

Hancock, P. and Tyler, M. (2001) *Work, Postmodernism and Organization: A Critical Introduction*, London: Sage.

Hannan, M. T. and Carroll, G. R. (1992) *Dynamics of Organizational Populations: Density, Legitimation, and Competition*, New York: Oxford University Press.

Hardy, C. and Clegg, S. R. (1996) "Some dare call it power," in S. R. Clegg, C. Hardy and W. R. Nord (eds) *Handbook of Organization Studies*, London: Sage.

Hickson, D. J., Hinings, C. R., Lee, C. A., Schneck, R. E. and Pennings, J. M. (1971) "A strategic contingencies theory of intraorganizational power," *Administrative Science Quarterly* 16: 216–229.

Hirsch, P. M. and Levin, D. Z. (1999) "Umbrella advocates versus validity police: a life-cycle model," *Organization Science* 10: 199–212.

Hunt, S. D. (1990) "Truth in marketing theory and research," *Journal of Marketing* 54: 1–15.

Kimberly, J. R. (1976) "Organizational size and the structuralist perspective: a review, critique, and proposal," *Administrative Science Quarterly* 21: 571–597.

Knudsen, C. (2003) "Pluralism, scientific progress, and the structure of organization theory," in H. Tsoukas and C. Knudsen (eds) *The Oxford Handbook of Organization Theory*, Oxford: Oxford University Press.

Latour, B. and Woolgar, S. (1986) *Laboratory Life: The Construction of Scientific Facts*, Princeton, NJ: Princeton University Press.

Law, K. S., Wong, K.-S. and Mobley, W. H. (1998) "Toward a taxonomy of multidimensional constructs," *Academy of Management Review* 23: 741–755.

McKelvey, B. (1997) "Quasi-natural organization science," *Organization Science* 8: 352–380.

McKinley, W. (2003a) "From subjectivity to objectivity: a constructivist account of objectivity in organization theory," in R. Westwood and S. Clegg (eds) *Debating Organization: Point-Counterpoint in Organization Studies*, Oxford: Blackwell.

McKinley, W. (2003b) "Postmodern epistemology in organization studies: a critical appraisal," in E. A. Locke (ed.) *Postmodernism and Management: Pros, Cons and the Alternative*, Oxford: Elsevier Science.

McKinley, W. and Mone, M. A. (1998) "The re-construction of organization studies: wrestling with incommensurability," *Organization* 5: 169–189.

McKinley, W., Mone, M. A. and Moon, G. (1999) "Determinants and development of schools in organization theory," *Academy of Management Review* 24: 634–648.

McKinley, W., Zhao, J. and Rust, K. G. (2000) "A sociocognitive interpretation of organizational downsizing," *Academy of Management Review* 25: 227–243.

Megill, A. (1991) "Four senses of objectivity," *Annals of Scholarship* 8: 301–320.

Mizruchi, M. S. and Fein, L. C. (1999) "The social construction of organizational knowledge: a study of the uses of coercive, mimetic, and normative isomorphism," *Administrative Science Quarterly* 44: 653–683.

Mone, M. A. and McKinley, W. (1993) "The uniqueness value and its consequences for organization studies," *Journal of Management Inquiry* 2: 284–296.

Mone, M. A., McKinley, W. and Barker III, V. L. (1998) "Organizational decline and innovation: a contingency framework," *Academy of Management Review* 23: 115–132.

Morgeson, F. P. and Hofmann, D. A. (1999) "The structure and function of collective constructs: implications for multilevel research and theory development," *Academy of Management Review* 24: 249–265.

Osigweh, C. A. B. (1989) "Concept fallibility in organizational science," *Academy of Management Review* 14: 579–594.

Pfeffer, J. (1993) "Barriers to the advance of organizational science: paradigm development as a dependent variable," *Academy of Management Review* 18: 599–620.

Pickering, A. (1984) *Constructing Quarks: A Sociological History of Particle Physics*, Chicago: University of Chicago Press.

Salancik, G. R. and Pfeffer, J. (1974) "The bases and use of power in organizational decision making: the case of a university," *Administrative Science Quarterly* 19: 453–473.

Shenhav, Y., Shrum, W. and Alon, S. (1994) "'Goodness' concepts in the study of organizations: a longitudinal survey of four leading journals," *Organization Studies* 15: 753–776.

Simon, H. A. (1997) *Administrative Behavior: A Study of Decision-Making Processes in Administrative Organizations*, 4th edn, New York: Free Press.

Thompson, J. D. (1967) *Organizations in Action: Social Science Bases of Administrative Theory*, New York: McGraw-Hill.

Tolbert, P. S. and Zucker, L. G. (1996) "The institutionalization of institutional theory," in S. R. Clegg, C. Hardy and W. R. Nord (eds) *Handbook of Organization Studies*, London: Sage.

Weick, K. E. (1995) *Sensemaking in Organizations*, Thousand Oaks, CA: Sage.

Whiteman, G. and Cooper, W. H. (2000) "Ecological embeddedness," *Academy of Management Journal* 43: 1265–1282.

Williamson, O. E. (1981) "The economics of organization: the transaction cost approach," *American Journal of Sociology* 87: 548–577.

Zald, M. N. (1993) "Organization studies as a scientific and humanistic enterprise: toward a reconceptualization of the foundations of the field," *Organization Science* 4: 513–528.

Zald, M. N. (1996) "More fragmentation? Unfinished business in linking the social sciences and the humanities," *Administrative Science Quarterly* 41: 251–261.

8 Reflective knowledge management

Some philosophical considerations

Frits Schipper

Introduction

Among the many developments taking place nowadays in the field of management and organization (M&O), the movement emphasizing the role of knowledge is quite striking. From an economic point of view, knowledge is seen as a new production factor, outweighing the traditional ones of land, labour and capital (Drucker 1993; de Geus 1997; Hauschild *et al.* 2001). It is also argued that knowledge *brings forth* a world (Krogh *et al.* 1996). Because of its impact, it is often argued that the development of (organizational) knowledge must not be left to chance, but should be systematically managed. Some companies even appoint special "Chief Knowledge Officers" (CKOs) (Foote *et al.* 2001) and do many other things in order to raise the "return on knowledge" (RoK). Moreover, there is sometimes also a striking positive difference between the market value and the traditional book value of a company. The idea behind the need for knowledge management and the existence of a return on knowledge is that this value difference becomes understandable when the until now rather "intangible" knowledge factor is brought in. A conceptual change in the way we think about business is supposed to be needed in order to make this factor measurable (Sveiby 2000).

Knowledge is not a simple and concrete subject, however, and ideas concerning knowledge management, which is something that acts at a meta-level, cannot be discussed without the introduction of epistemological themes. Very popular these days is Michael Polanyi's notion of tacit knowledge (Nonaka and Takeuchi 1995; Tsoukas 1996; Spender 1996a, b; Choo 1998; Baumard 1999). However, Polanyi's idea is often misrepresented and isolated from his general philosophical concerns.[1] This chapter underlines other important but neglected epistemological issues in knowledge management: "asking questions", "epistemic variety", "knowledge quality" and "knowledge responsibility". These concerns spring from a relational view of knowledge which considers knowledge in terms of an interaction between the knower and the (un)known. In this interaction, asking questions plays a central role. It is also important to notice here that the issues just mentioned are relevant for both (1) knowledge concerning the field in which one is active (object-level knowledge), and (2) the knowledge involved in knowledge management itself (meta-level knowledge).

I will start by discussing different kinds of questions. Next, I will concentrate on epistemic variety and the quality of knowledge. Then the concept of knowledge responsibility will be introduced, and finally, attention will be paid to some of the pitfalls of knowledge management. What is not presented in this chapter is a discussion of relational epistemology itself or how it relates to other views.[2] Neither will I try to clarify the connections between individual knowledge and the knowledge that some argue functions at an organizational level (for efforts to do so, see Blackler 1993, 1995; Tsoukas 1996; Spender 1996a, b). However, speaking of the interactions between the knower and the known is not necessarily to suggest that knowledge is a matter of socially isolated individuals, and my argument should therefore not be read in this way.

Asking questions

In the epistemology underpinning this chapter, "knowledge" is not considered to be a rather passive mirroring of reality or a mere (subjective/social) construction. Neither is "knowledge" seen as completely determined by contingent concepts or as based on some a priori necessity. Put positively, knowledge always relates to our involvement in the world. Asking questions plays a major role in this interaction. As Gadamer has put it, "all knowledge passes through the question" (1975: 283; my translation).

Now, asking a particular question expresses a specific focus or perspective in terms of which the reality at issue is thematized. It is important to notice that different ways of thematizing are at our disposal and that these become manifest in the different kinds of questions that might be asked. Indeed, the same reality, for example a particular building such as the Tower of Pisa, can be approached with distinct questions in mind: "in which period was it constructed?"; "what are the materials used?"; "what is its meaning in connection with the Duomo?"; "how it is to be preserved for the future?", etc. The specific issues raised express the way the questioners relate themselves to the object, enunciating a particular interest or care. From what has been said thus far, it is not surprising that language is very important for knowledge – a major theme in twentieth-century philosophy. We should realize, however, that the human body too, through its different movements and sensibilities involved, can express "questions" (see the works of Merleau-Ponty (e.g. 1945)).[3] For reasons of convenience, however, I will now confine myself to questions expressed in language.

Kinds of questions

Some twentieth-century philosophers tried to set up demarcations between cognitive meaningful and cognitive meaningless language. Others, such as the later Wittgenstein, Habermas and Gadamer, made it clear that language is a far more complicated affair. Its richness manifests itself in many ways. One of them is the potential variety of questions, which in turn is also present in the different kinds of answers humans give and the knowledge implied by these answers.[4] I shall not explore this variety completely, but concentrate on the following four kinds of questions:[5]

- questions of fact;
- questions of meaning;
- questions of orientation;
- questions of identity.

Questions of fact

Questions of fact are raised continuously in our private lives, but in work contexts, among them research, they are also important. As such, these questions can concern simple facts or more complicated issues and situations. In English, they are often formulated in terms of "how...?" or "what...?". They can be divided into two subcategories: the first addresses what actually *is* the case, the second concerns what *should* be realized in order to effectuate something else.

Asking "what is on the surface of a particular area of land?" is asking for a rather simple fact. Asking "how are the responsibilities in the board of directors divided?" is more complicated. One can also speak of, for example, linguistic facts, which can be looked for in a dictionary. In addition, questions of fact can also concern the relation between variables – for example, "how, at a particular temperature, are the volume and pressure of the gas in this cylinder related?". Another issue of the same kind concerns the relation between interest and economic growth. To this first subcategory also belong questions that ask for explanations after the fact: "how did this or that event happen?". Besides, questions of fact may also focus on things that should be done in order to realize something else. Questions like "what is the recipe for cooking this meal?", "how can the damage done to the canvas of this painting be repaired?" and "what needs to be done in order to keep next year's inflation at a level of less than 2 per cent?" all belong to the second sub-category.

In science and technology, questions of fact play a major role. Whereas science concentrates on what actually is the case, although sometimes concerning rather artificial realities present in "experiments", technology's focus is on creating preferred situations. Questions of fact are rather popular within the context of knowledge management (meta-level) and they can be of both subcategories. Issues like "how do people learn?", "how do organizations create new knowledge?",[6] "what are the key factors in innovation processes?" and "what is the value of the knowledge capital of company Z?" belong to the first subcategory. Questions such as "how can experience become the best teacher of our company?", "what can be done in order to stimulate people to share their tacit knowledge with others?"[7] and "how can the intranet in organization X be used more effectively?" are of the second subcategory. It is clear that these questions are only *apparently* simple, and that finding answers depends on different conditions. The example of company Z, for instance, requires that it is already known how such a form of capital can be measured.

Many questions of fact asked in the context of knowledge management concern the directed change of a situation. They focus on what needs to be done so that a particular effect will occur. Rather as in technology, what is preferred in such circumstances is an insight into the "mechanisms" regulating the phenomena in terms of particular "if a then b" relationships.[8] Managers probably very much welcome such a kind of insight concerning the relevant variables – if not for control, then at least because it identifies potential facilitators. It is, therefore, not surprising that the literature on knowledge management mainly concentrates on this kind of meta-knowledge, something that also applies to the management of innovation.

Questions of meaning

Questions of meaning show a rich variety. Take the following examples. In a museum, someone looking at a painting by Constable wonders, "What sense of the relation between humankind and nature is expressed in this work?" In the context of M&O, a consultant asks, "What weight is given to the informal organization in this company and what is made of the official hierarchy?" Moreover, when someone is getting angry during a meeting, questions like "is he really angry?" or "why does she do this?", although not formulated in meaning terms, are really about meaning. For all the examples mentioned, finding answers is an essentially hermeneutic affair.

There is also a group of questions of meaning that have in common that they ask for so-called principal determining characteristics. Although this sort of question is not very popular among postmodern thinkers, they remain central for many things in which human beings may be engaged. Using what perhaps some people would consider "old-fashioned" philosophical terms, such questions can be said to search for the "essence" of what is at issue (Schipper 1999). Often, expressions such as "real" or "kernel" are used. Sometimes there is a relation with a specific situation: "what he has done, is that compatible with real friendship?". However, such a query can also be formulated more abstractly: "what is the kernel of real friendship?". In connection with the world of auditing, one can, for example, ask, "What is really essential for the independence of auditors?" This too is a question of meaning looking for principal determining characteristics.

Questions of meaning are also relevant for knowledge management. Some of them focus on the meaning of concepts. An example is the meta-level question "what distinguishes a 'knowledge worker' from a normal one?". Another example is "what value do the employees of organization X attach to the intranet?". Customer relations might also involve questions of meaning. An example is the question "what knowledge do the stories that are told among our personnel concerning particular customers contain?".

However, the more major questions of meaning are those concerning the distinctive characteristics of knowledge. This is an ancient matter, which was discussed extensively in antiquity, but people are still looking for satisfactory answers and the question is indeed not an easy one. Abstaining from asking it because of this, however, is not a proper reaction. On the contrary, the question intrudes into knowledge management. Signs of this are the already mentioned references to Polanyi's views, the autopoietic epistemology of Krogh *et al.* (1996), and the respective "stock" and "flow" approaches to knowledge. Discussions concerning the distinctions between data, information and knowledge belong here too. From a relational point of view, the question of the distinctive characteristics of knowledge deserves much attention. I will come back to this issue later.

Questions of orientation

The philosopher Michel Montaigne is supposed to have said, "For sailors who have no aims, there is no wind." This suggests that the availability of goals is very important in human life. Without a clear sense of direction, it is difficult to see what is relevant or what is not. Aims, goals, etc. are the subject matter of questions of orientation. These questions are important because, once answered, they give direction to thought and action. Primary questions of orientation are asked by people who want to decide about *their own* aims. However, one can also try to find out about and understand the goals and aims of others, such as competitors. In my view, however, these are secondary; sometimes they concern matters of meaning. Answers can, of course, influence one's own primary questions of orientation.

Answers to questions of orientation can be more or less precise. Let us consider some examples. If a person asks him- or herself, "what am I going to study next year?", several answers are possible. A rather precise one is "mathematics, and I will start with a course in calculus". Less precise is "I do not know exactly, but in any case something in relation to people". Also, an answer such as "I will not decide at this moment, but I will take courses in different fields in order to find out what really interests me" is possible. All three answers show a kind of knowing that focuses on thinking and acting, although in different degrees. Questions of orientation also play an important role in different kinds of work. Wherever work is more or less planned, preceding questions of orientation have been answered. In these cases, it does not make a difference whether what is involved has a rather wide time horizon (e.g. the building of a large bridge) or whether it is much nearer (e.g. the giving of an injection). Even firefighters, who are often expected to act immediately, cannot always avoid explicitly asking questions of orientation, such as "do we still have to try to extinguish the fire in this building or shall we just put all our efforts in preventing it from spreading?".

As far as knowledge is concerned, questions of orientation may address individual persons or professions as well as organizations. Take the following examples. A particular first-line physician working in Amsterdam might ask, "does my medical-technical knowledge suffice, or do I need also knowledge of the varied cultural backgrounds of my patients?". Tax lawyers specializing in business takeovers might wonder whether a knowledge of organization studies would be valuable for their own practice. One of my former teachers in philosophy, Van Peursen, once told me that he was asked by the Dutch steel company Hoogovens (now Corus) about the cultural meaning of fire in Indonesia. As a producer of steel, Hoogovens apparently decided that it should be familiar with the meaning of "fire" in the countries in which it was active. In this case, the company asked and answered the question whether, besides technical knowledge concerning "heat" and "fire", specific cultural knowledge was relevant. These examples focus on the selection and content of subject matters. However, questions of orientation can also address more formal issues. Take, for instance, discussions about whether knowledge management should adopt a "codification" or a "personalization" strategy of knowledge (Hansen *et al.* 1999).

Some authors consider the organizational intention, which helps to conceptualize what kind of knowledge should be developed, to be the most critical aspect of organizational knowledge creation. Moreover, such an intention is said to be welcomed because it can "reorient" the individual person's thinking through collective commitment (Nonaka and Takeuchi 1995: 74). However, there is always the risk that such a collective commitment will create a collective myopia concerning knowledge, through which people become blind to other knowledge possibilities. From a relational point of view, reflecting on these possibilities is central for matters of orientation. Also, epistemological approaches that imply a closure with respect to knowledge (Krogh *et al.* 1996: 167) are not to be taken for granted.

Questions of identity

Questions of identity, which can be formulated in several ways, are presumably asked less often than the other types of questions discussed here. Of the kinds of questions presented thus far, they are also the most difficult to answer. As with questions of orientation, it makes sense to distinguish primary and secondary questions of identity. The first address the questioner him- or herself, or something in which the questioner is involved; the second concern something that the questioner is outside. In the first case, the question of identity can focus on self-identity, which includes self-knowledge.

Identity may concern individual persons and smaller- or larger-scale social "entities". An example of the latter is the identity of Europe. When asked by Europeans themselves – "is there a European identity and, if so, how should it be characterized?" – it functions as a primary question of identity. That is also the case when a business company such as Shell asks the question "how do we stand?". But if a social scientist who is not a member of Shell looks for its identity, then he or she is busy with a secondary question of identity. Questions of identity can also concern works of art, pieces of architecture, etc. In the latter case, such questions are, for example, involved in the restoration of old churches. Architects sometimes face issues such as "do we have to maintain these nineteenth-century additions or not?". Answers are always based on an evaluation of the value of these additions for the identity of the building at issue. On these occasions, the questions of identity involved are always secondary.

As such, identity is a complex subject. It is doubtful whether it is possible to grasp identity in full, the more so as it can develop over time. A person's identity, for example, is related to his or her historical roots, crucial relations, geographical areas of living, values considered as important, sense of the future, etc. Every time questions of identity – primary as well as secondary – are being answered, the people involved have to recognize this complexity and be willing to explore the different items included, being aware of the limitations of the answers given.

That matters of identity are mostly very critical is obvious. Time and again we see that when people lose their sense of identity, their lives become indifferent or they find themselves in deep trouble. This critical role applies both to individual persons and to the social entities mentioned, as well as to professions. Take the example of auditing, mentioned earlier in connection with the notion of independence. Over time, many auditors became more and more involved in consulting. This often changed them into associates rather than independent regulators of the companies involved (e.g. Enron), thereby creating a particular *actual* professional identity. When auditors nowadays discuss the question of how they should view the relationship between diverse activities such as regulating and consulting, they are really rethinking or *re*searching their professional identity.

Questions of identity are not asked very often with a focus on knowledge.[9] However, the role of knowledge in matters of identity, concerning people as well as organizations, should not be underestimated. When I was a young boy, children calling out insults were sometimes reacted to by their recipients shouting back, "So are you!" Putting this into the context of knowledge we can say, with some exaggeration perhaps, that "what you know is what you are". When this is correct, we can speak of a "knowledge identity", or at least of something like a "knowledge component" of identities. In the case of auditing, mentioned above, one could say that the specific way in which it is practised also includes a particular knowledge identity. Knowledge identity depends not only on the actual knowledge involved, but also on the kind of knowledge it is, on views of its nature and the way it is handled. It makes a big difference whether one simply considers only a special kind of knowledge to be relevant, or whether one is self-critical and alert to new (kinds of) knowledge. Donald Schön's "reflective practitioner" (Schipper 1999) can, therefore, be considered as indicating such an aspect of knowledge identity.

In our society, we are not unfamiliar with labels such as "specialist" or "generalist", or with general terms denoting professions: "historian", "carpenter", "lawyer", "physician". Such general terms are used at an organizational level too: "law firm", "IT company", "school of art", etc. Of course it is possible to express knowledge identities, primary as well as secondary ones, by these terms. The implication is that the knowledge identity at issue is nothing special, just "one in a dozen". Indeed, these kinds of terms give only a general and very limited impression of what the knowledge identity is about. If one wants to be more specific in answering (primary or secondary) questions of knowledge identity, a richer language is needed, matching a complexity that is analogous to the one mentioned above concerning identity in general.

I happen to be familiar with a consultancy firm that explicitly tries to contribute to the development of new knowledge. Its personnel are encouraged to write articles in professional journals. It seeks relationships with universities by encouraging some of the partners to have a scientific career too. In this case, the wish to innovate and improve knowledge, not only for its own use but for society at large, should be a part of the (self-)description of the firm's knowledge identity. It is fundamental, however, that the knowledge identity manifests itself in the way the firm concerns itself with and seeks for reality.

Hierarchy of questions?

Now that we have these different types of questions in view, what about their relationship? I think that, from a logical point of view, the questions can be ordered hierarchically. In this hierarchy, questions of identity come first. Answering these makes it easier to decide which questions of orientation are relevant, and it also influences the answers given to them. When clarity concerning questions of orientation is available, this is helpful for selecting the relevant questions of meaning and questions of fact, and even for answering some questions of meaning.

However, from a real-life point of view the situation is much more dynamic. In real life, the indicated hierarchy is not the law of the Medes and the Persians. Matters of orientation do not require that identity is defined fully and explicitly. Of course, there is the risk of superficial opportunism, but things can also be done in such a way that they might later be considered as a contribution to the identity involved. Identity is neither a changeless metaphysical a priori nor a matter of conscious design, but something that gains its shape over time. The same is true of knowledge identity.

Epistemic variety and quality of knowledge

Thus far we have considered different kinds of questions, and we saw that they can function at an object level as well as at a meta-level. Among the meta-level issues discussed is the one concerning the distinctive characteristics of knowledge. This section looks at some aspects of this matter, without claiming completeness. The key notions developed here are "epistemic variety", "knowledge quality" and "knowledge responsibility". As will become clear soon, my approach to these things excludes the possibility of giving just one single, conclusive definition of the settling features of "knowledge".

Epistemic variety[10]

The kinds of questions considered earlier in the chapter are part of a wider epistemic variety that also includes different explanatory strategies. Contrary to what some philosophers think, I do indeed believe that there is room for a variety of these strategies.[11] Besides questions and strategies, epistemic variety contains distinct dimensions of knowledge – that is, the different ways, and different levels of concreteness and abstraction, in which reality can be known. The contrast of data, information and knowledge can be considered to be part of the epistemic variety too. I start with a short discussion of the explanatory strategies.

Strategies of explanation

It makes sense to distinguish the following strategies:

- nomological;
- teleological;
- hermeneutic;
- narrative.

Nomological explanations involve deterministic or statistical laws, which may differ in their scope and generality. As such, these kind of explanations are used in many sciences and, although often put in less precise terms, they also play an important role in daily affairs – for example, explanations using the law of gravitation to different degrees of exactness. When available, nomological explanations also make it possible, under particular conditions, to predict or even influence the course of events. Seeking nomological explanations, therefore, implies a preference for asking particular questions of fact.

Teleological explanations are of two types, the functional and the intentional. In both, the explanation is based on the idea of an end or goal, or sometimes even a wider purpose. Understanding the shape of dandelion seeds by pointing to the fact that this allows them to be spread by the wind easily is giving a functional explanation. When a judge has made up his or her mind and understands the action of a person standing before the court of law in terms of a deliberate motive, then that judge is giving an intentional explanation. Teleological explanations are intimately linked to questions of orientation.

Hermeneutical explanations all involve meaning – for example, of a text, a piece of art, a gesture, etc. Authors such as Dilthey and Gadamer have presented different views, for example, concerning the act of *verstehen* through which meaning is grasped, yet there is enough common ground to speak of hermeneutics as an explanatory strategy; as such, it favours particular questions of meaning.

Narrative explanations, finally, unite different events, sometimes a lot, by means of a story, showing the course of events to have some sort of plot. Stories, which have a beginning and an end, often involve partial explanations of the other types. An example is the narrative of a car accident in which a intoxicated driver, having marriage problems, seriously injured some other people. Besides these "how it all happened" narratives, there are others which especially contribute to questions of identity. Examples from the organizational context are the stories told about the founders. Mostly these are used to create commitment among the personel. Moreover, stories are also used in the context of knowledge management (Foote *et al.* 2001: 126).

Dimensions of knowledge

Human knowledge can be posited along the following different dimensions:

- abstract ↔ concrete;
- universal ↔ individual;
- structural ↔ contentful.

The financial part of a company's annual report, for example, gives a rather abstract picture. An outsider who takes cognizance only of this part, therefore, acquires rather abstract knowledge of the company. But the knowledge can become more concrete if the social and environmental sections of the report are read too (if available). The same applies if, for instance, the aesthetics of the buildings and the work carried out within the company are taken into consideration (see Linstead and Höpfl 2000). The universal ↔ individual dimension of knowledge can be illustrated quite easily. The annual report just mentioned is about an individual company. When we look at the reports of many companies in a particular branch of the economy (IT, for example), the conclusion might be that over a certain period of time all of them show a growth in numbers of employees of about 7 per cent. This statement is more general. Talking about paint and saying that white lead is a mixture of lead carbonate and hydrated lead oxide is a statement that claims universal validity. However, if an art historian says that the white lead used by Rembrandt in particular was a granular substance, then this statement's scope is limited to one individual.

The third dimension is the structure↔content one. Structural knowledge can be searched for in relation to different kinds of entities, such as social groups, crystals, buildings, physical phenomena (light/colour), living beings, paintings, traffic systems, etc. This kind of knowledge focuses on the formal make-up of what is at issue, often by using a geometrical or other kind of mathematical representation. Well-known examples are the geometrical shape of crystals (planes, lines and knots). In the case of works of art, a painting or whatever, knowledge of their composition is an example. Other examples are the structure of an organization (often represented by an "organigram"), the ground plan of a church, the wavelength of a particular kind of light, or a map presenting only the topology of railroads in the Netherlands.[12] The other side of the dimension is "content". Recognizing the colour of a particular object as red or green is having content knowledge of that object. The same is the case if the religious meaning of the ground plan of a church is considered; and looking at an organigram and saying that it represents a "flat" organization is also considering content.

The three dimensions can be related to the explanatory strategies mentioned earlier. Nomological explanations, for example, often concentrate on the left and narratives on the right side of the three dimensions. However, this does not allow us to consider the dimensions in terms of the opposition "abstract–universal–structural" versus "concrete–individual–contentful". Indeed, structural as well as contentful knowledge can be more or less universal, and both can also concern individual objects. The ground plan of a particular cathedral, for example, contains elements that apply universally to these kinds of churches (Gothic, Norman, etc.), but it also involves individual details. Furthermore, content can be more or less abstract, and the same applies to structure. If we only look at the colour of something, leaving out many other characteristics, then our knowledge is rather abstract. However, acquiring structural knowledge does not always require much abstraction. There are sculptures meant to represent nothing but a structure, the artist having used only steel wires. In this case, the degree of abstraction required to attain structural knowledge is not very high.

Data, information and knowledge (dak)

Knowledge management literature often distinguishes between data, information and knowledge.[13] Considering the fact that many issues in knowledge management are IT related, this attention given to *dak* is understandable. In this chapter, *dak* is understood as an item of epistemic variation. Seeing it in this way requires a clear hold on the different roles of data, information and knowledge. From a relational perspective, these respective roles can be characterized as follows:

- *Data* are symbolic representations that can function as material for answering questions, mostly questions of fact, on condition that the rules of representation are understood.
- *Information* is an answer to a question given in such a way that the questioner's uncertainty disappears. Through the answer, data are related and the state of mind of the person involved changes. However, this says nothing about the quality of information. Believing the uncertainty disappears can be unjustified (as in the case of disinformation).
- Information becomes *knowledge* when a person's picture of some part or aspect of the world is improved, supplemented or enriched in such a way that a more adequate praxis becomes possible.

The explanatory strategies and the dimensions discussed thus far all are connected to knowledge in the sense just described. This means that data and information function in a preliminary stage of the knowledge process which can go into different directions, whereas the particular direction taken depends on the kinds of questions asked and the sort of explanation sought. Properly understood, the epistemic variety functions as a fan of such directions. What we come to know depends, therefore, on our awareness of this fan and on how it is used, both being essential for the relational view of knowledge explored in this chapter.

Another important feature of the definition of *dak* given earlier is that knowledge is a normative concept. The term "improved" is an indication of this. If knowledge is indeed a normative notion, then the epistemic variety can only be explored properly on condition that the criteria constituting this normativeness are kept in mind. I think it makes sense to speak of this subject matter in terms of *the quality of knowledge*.

Quality of knowledge

The normativity implied by "knowledge" is one of the key issues of philosophy and it is, therefore, not accidental that much twentieth-century epistemology can be interpreted as a normative criticism of a supposedly dominant knowledge praxis in which only a limited part of the epistemic variety was recognized.[14] However, while quality of knowledge is a major philosophical theme, most of the literature on organizational knowledge and knowledge management passes it by.[15] I shall now pay attention to three issues that I think are especially relevant in the context of reflection on knowledge management:

- criteria of truth;
- depth of knowledge;
- sources of knowledge.

Criteria of truth

If there is one philosophical subject that has continuously challenged the human mind, it surely is the idea of truth. Some twentieth-century thinkers reserved this subject for logical analysis (Carnap); others made it into an ontological theme (Heidegger). Sometimes philosophers have been very critical of the notion of truth, because claims to truth function as exercises of power (Nietzsche). Others have relativized it, by saying that truth candidates (propositions) function only within language games, which themselves cannot be said to be true or false (Wittgenstein). Apart from these different views, and notwithstanding the fact that the often quite sophisticated debates about the nature of truth continue, I think that it is meaningful to distinguish several conditions/criteria of truth that have practical relevance, not only for science/technology, but, although applied less methodically, for daily life as well. The following criteria are important:

- (formal) consistency;
- empirical adequacy;
- applicability;
- context reliability.

A knowledge claim is *(formally) consistent* when it does not contain contradictions or plain incoherences. This is indeed a limited condition of truth. *Empirical adequacy* means that the claim fits the empirical findings, such as data. The statement that a particular chemical substance reacts on skin cells in a specific way is an example when it indeed fits the facts. Not only single statements, but also the more complicated knowledge claims that result from following a particular explanatory strategy, such as the nomological one, should be judged in terms of their (formal) consistency and empirical adequacy.

Consistency and empirical adequacy are not the only criteria to be mentioned here, because there are additional ones that become especially relevant when knowledge is put into action. It is in this context that applicability and context reliability become relevant. The insight concerning the chemical substance just mentioned becomes *applicable* when it is justified to say that, generally speaking, the substance can serve a practical aim – for example, that it has a healing effect on second-degree burns. In addition, *context reliability* would in this case require that in concrete situations the healing effect can take place with good results. However, *context reliability* also demands a further specification of what is to be considered as "good": both the side effects of using the chemical substance and the conditions under which the healing effect comes about (burden put on patients etc.) should be acceptable.

When knowledge is applied concretely, empirical adequacy and applicability are indeed not enough, because context reliability is essential. In other words, the proof of the pudding is in the eating. The illustration from (medical) chemistry used above is just one among many possible others. Later I will mention some examples of meta-level knowledge claims made within the context of knowledge management.

Depth of knowledge

Knowledge can be superficial. Just knowing that the light comes on when one turns the switch is rather slight. However, when this knowledge is based on insight into the construction of the switch, on knowledge of electrical phenomena, etc., it has more depth. Knowledge of a mathematical algorithm without understanding its justification is superficial. If a consultant has knowledge of the structure of a particular company without being familiar with its historical background, of why it has this particular structure, then this knowledge too is lacking in depth.

The degree of depth might also point to the radicality of the questions asked. Often, questions preserve the usual conceptual framework, but they can also be more radical, critically reflecting on insights used thus far in order to come to a new understanding. An example mentioned in the introduction to this chapter is the value of a company. It is possible to determine its book value by the usual means. However, sometimes this book value is exceeded by (or is less than) the market value, which requires further understanding. If researchers successfully transcend usual practice in a fresh confrontation with reality, thereby achieving this understanding (Sveiby 2000), this would be a gain in *depth* of understanding.

Sources of knowledge

Since Popper (1965), speaking of the sources of knowledge seems somewhat naïve. If related to the context of knowledge management, it can still be meaningful, however. What I have in mind is the distinction between knowledge achieved by hearsay and knowledge gained by actual experience. Much of what a particular person knows is knowledge by hearsay. Our system of education is imbued with this. When a particular knowledge claim refers to a newspaper article, this is also a matter of hearsay. The same applies to a CEO who takes the figures given to him by his accountant for granted, or when she takes cognizance of an old file written by one of her predecessors. Life is full of such examples.

Knowledge by hearsay is always bound to the tension between presence and absence. It involves a kind of second-hand presence constituted by the particular representation used (statement, drawing), while what the knowledge is about is at the same time absent. Files, for example, always have this presence/absence duality. In daily life we mostly do not see this as a problem, because we rely on the source from which the file comes to us. Sometimes our confidence is based on direct experience of the trustworthiness of the source, sometimes it too is a matter of hearsay. In the end, however, there will be some real experience that is basic.

Besides knowledge by hearsay, everybody also has knowledge by experience. Sometimes this kind of knowledge is gained accidentally. Sometimes it is consciously and even methodically searched for. If the knowledge is made explicit – for example, by formulating it in language – the person who does this also reflectively knows what decisions were taken in order to make the lingual representation, what is left out as less relevant, what questions were asked, etc. For that person, the presence in absence involved by representation is not that problematic, because he or she is still able to relate it to presence.[16]

The situation just sketched also applies to data and potential information stored in electronic equipment. Some people consider IT a powerful tool for overcoming limits of place and time. I do not deny this positive force, but there is also a price to be paid: lack of real acquaintance with what is at issue. The more sophisticated uses of IT, which go far beyond information storage, even create their own presence. This, however, is not brand new, but comparable with what narratives potentially can do too.

Knowledge responsibility

Epistemic variety and quality of knowledge do not stand on their own, but are intrinsically linked to something else. The best and most adequate term for what I have in mind here is *knowledge responsibility*. Knowledge reponsibility has two sides. First of all, it concerns a responsibility for improving knowledge claims, doing justice to the issues involved, asking whether these are the right ones, etc., at the object level as well as at the meta-level. It is this knowledge responsibility that (1) requires the epistemic variety actually used to be suitable, and (2) asks us to be careful in our knowledge claims. Second, there is a responsibility for the knowledge other people have. When a person is not content with the actual knowledge claims made and strives for better understanding, he or she exercises the first side of knowledge responsibility. However, if this person thinks that some knowledge concerning an object, a situation or whatever, should be known by other people as well, then this is a manifestation of the second side of knowledge responsibility. The constructive criticism of knowledge claims made by others and the real sharing of one's own knowledge and doubts are important means by which to put this responsibility into effect. As such, this responsibility goes beyond intra-organizational affairs. Journalists and whistle-blowers, for example, who bring things into the open and try to create understanding show that they feel accountable for the knowledge of other people at a societal level.

Reflective knowledge management

It goes almost without saying that in the context of the views presented in this chapter, knowledge management is nothing but the proper exercise of knowledge responsibility. All definitions that focus on RoK (Fuller 2002; Weggemann 1997) are somewhat futile when considered from this perspective. This does not imply that seeking financial returns on knowledge is not important for business organizations – on the contrary. Yet what is at issue here is more properly denoted as the "economics" of knowledge. However, the economics of knowledge as such does not necessarily exclude the involvement of knowledge management in the sense just mentioned.[17]

Although knowledge management is sometimes regarded as something brand new, it is not in fact a novel phenomenon at all. People already exercise knowledge responsibility amid other activities (making notes, going to a library, consulting other people, exploring new fields, etc.) – be it in an organizational context or not. What is new, however, is the fact that these kinds of activities are being regarded as a separate management function, with some companies even considering the appointment of a special CKO. Whether this situation is to be welcomed or not falls outside the scope of this chapter. However, when a separate knowledge management function is defined, there is always the risk of a dominant management focus. Reflective knowledge management as advocated here should be conscious of the existence of this pitfall, in order to avoid it. However, there are more such pitfalls: misplaced universality, collective myopia, and forgotten absence. I will now discuss all four of them, starting with the pitfall of management focus.

Management focus

If matters of knowledge are approached from a general management perspective, without real attention being paid to the concrete problems and wishes of the people involved and affected (often called "knowledge workers"), this pitfall becomes a real danger. Huysman and de Wit (2000) mention the example of ING Barings. The idea was the building of a company-wide intranet containing knowledge (about clients, their problems and the advice given) coming worldwide from all the different establishments. The system had a difficult start because at the beginning thought was given only to matters at the level of the whole company, ignoring the epistemic needs of concrete persons at particular places. Problems manifested themselves concerning the gathering of the "knowledge": people were reluctant to put things on the intranet, and it was very difficult to check the quality of the "knowledge" that became available. It was indeed a big knowledge-infrastructural project going over the heads of the personnel and the ways they exercised knowledge responsibility.

In order to avoid the pitfall of management focus, it is important to keep in mind that activities which we are nowadays used to labelling as "knowledge management" were originally embedded in the practice of the knowing persons themselves. Unreflectively isolating them from their primary context in terms of a separate management function will, therefore, bring us to the brink of this snare.

Misplaced universality

Especially when meta-level questions of fact concerning knowledge are being asked in order to accomplish something, one should at least ascertain the context reliability of the knowledge claims involved. Now, some people would perhaps react by saying that "the facts are just the facts", and that there is nothing more to be said. This is too simple a view, however. So-called facts are to be considered as answers to a particular question of fact, nothing more. Hence, when context reliability does not form part of the questions involved, it might not be present at all. Therefore, knowledge management should be reflective – that is, it should be self-conscious of the different aspects of truth, in order to prevent the pitfall of universality.

Recently a consultant told me that he believes that the conscious creation of chaos in organizations is an important means of stimulating the development of knowledge (see also Nonaka and Takeuchi 1995). To some ears, this statement might sound attractive, but without further specifications, necessary for context reliability, it is hardly true. Another issue mentioned in the literature is the (financial) reward for knowledge-sharing activities in order to enhance communication. However, here too we have to be careful because of the pitfall of universality. Under particular conditions, such a reward might, for example, induce people to adopt new tactics for hurting others (Krogh 1998), thereby creating a non-sharing atmosphere – just the opposite of what one wants to achieve.

Collective myopia

When knowledge really is at stake, one must realize that, besides general knowledge, all the people involved have their particular experiences which also matter. Hence, relevant knowledge is to a large extent situated and unique. Knowledge responsibility requires that people are eager to learn from each other as well as being willing to criticize all the knowledge claims that are being made. Of course, it can happen that somebody works more or less as a soloist. Often this is related to a deep involvement in the work itself, which is to be welcomed. However, there are also risks, such as overestimating one's own performance. Cooperation and sharing of knowledge can help to correct this, but is no guarantee that high-quality knowledge will be attained, because a collective myopia – a kind of unreflective groupthink – can take hold. In such a situation, not really exploring epistemic variety is a serious hazard. In order to prevent this, it is important that the first aspect of knowledge responsibility is really active. When talking about organizations, responsibility always involves competences, *inter alia* in terms of hierarchy. In my view, knowledge responsibility goes further, however, because it requires a criticism of the knowledge claims made, irrespective of hierarchical order.[18]

Forgotten absence

The pitfall of forgotten absence connects with the tendency to place symbolic representations at the centre of attention. Should one give in to the temptation – and in organizations the chances of doing so are rather high, because these representations function as an important means of communication – then the consequence might be that concrete presence is less in the limelight, with the possibility that symbolizations will replace the "things" represented – that appearance will replace substance. Moreover, the personal involvement in knowledge, its relational character and quality are easily forgotten too, because the representation itself is the only thing present.[19] One way of coping with this pitfall is to contact the original creator(s) of a symbolic representation (file, note, report, etc.), who may be able and willing to link it with real presence by accounting for it. If so, this even gives the possibility of rethinking the representation, thereby influencing knowledge quality in a positive way.

Although IT is not necessarily always involved, it is nowadays especially important to reflect on this potential pitfall in the case of IT. IT projects are often welcomed because they are considered to be a powerful means of knowledge sharing. Take, for example, the virtual discussion platforms constituted in order to stimulate participation, dialogue and to reduce the knowledge inequality of all those who might have an interest in the subject matter. Perhaps it is the fact that one is allowed, and even expected, to say what one is up to that changes some aspects of the operative knowledge identity. Actual experience of these forums is always not wholly positive, however, because of lack of real discussion. Instead, often there is only an exchange of opinions among the people involved. One possible reason is that the platforms remain too virtual to contribute to the further development of knowledge identity. There is also the risk of virtual platforms replacing the real ones, in so far as they already exist. This can result from so-called efficiency reasons, but it might also be the case that the temptations of representation are too powerful. Therefore, only if IT remains embedded in original modes of cooperation, where the people involved are familiar with each other and with the issues concerned and conscious of the pitfall of representation, can we expect something positive to happen.

Concluding remarks

Reflective knowledge management is the exercise of knowledge responsibility in its broad sense, done with an awareness of the wide range of epistemic variety (kinds of questions, different explanatory strategies, dimensions of knowledge), of the different aspects of the quality of knowledge (truth, depth, sources), and of potential pitfalls of knowledge management. The relational view of knowledge explored in this chapter makes clear that every time people are busy with, for example, answering a particular "how to do this or that question" concerning knowledge or whatever, that question is raised within a complicated epistemic situation. When only such questions, identified by the previous argument as questions of fact, are asked, then issues involved by the other kinds of questions might be considered less relevant or as already clear enough. To say this is to express a critical, normative stance as well as the will to make a positive contribution, without, however, prescribing how people should think. My only intention is to highlight a potentially enriching perspective.

From a relational point of view, the use of conceptual strategies, asking different kinds of questions, at an object as well as at a meta-level, is never a matter of undetached objectivity (if such a thing is even possible). Eventually, this use rather expresses something of the knowledge identity involved. What people come to know and how they exercise their knowledge responsibility is indeed an aspect of their identity. The point is that knowledge responsibility especially should give direction here. Exercising this responsibility requires wondering whether the actual way of knowing is sufficiently varied and has enough quality. The answers given have far-reaching consequences. On the one hand, they express the knowledge identity that is operative. On the other hand, however, they can influence the further development of this identity. This may concern individual persons, or organizations, or even have effects at a societal or cultural level. However, there is always the risk of actual knowledge management being rather flat: that is, an interference only busy with its own, often simplified, technicalities, without relating them to the wider context of epistemic variety, knowledge quality and knowledge responsibility.

Notes

1 In my view, Polanyi's concept of the tacit is used in order to construct a dual model of human knowledge, which should be understood as a reaction against an IT-driven approach to knowledge in all kinds of organizations. The context of Michael Polanyi's thought, however, is his critique of totalitarianism and his refusal to believe in detached objectivity as a condition for knowledge (also the preoccupation with exactness). For interpretations with which I do not agree, see Nonaka and Takeuchi (1995) and Spender (1996a, b).

2 Some readers might perhaps see analogies with Deweyan pragmatism or with Habermas's critical approach to knowledge. I shall not say that these analogies are not there, but this falls outside the scope of this chapter.

3 One could also think of the bodily aspects of Polanyi's tacit knowing.

4 Answering questions is sometimes quite easy, sometimes very difficult. The answers given often lead to new questions because of the problems included. These problems can depend on lack of data, on the presuppositions on which the

answers given are based, etc. However, I will not discuss in this chapter the difficulties involved in answering questions.

5 The selection is made in order to discuss particular issues relevant for "knowledge management". Of course someone may, for example, react by saying, "You should also have included moral questions." I did not do that, however, because it would have made the whole chapter much more complicated.

6 See, for example, Nonaka and Takeuchi (1995: 48).

7 Hauschild *et al.* (2001: 79, 80).

8 Nonaka and Takeuchi (1995: 7) speak, for example, of the "mechanisms and processes by which knowledge is created".

9 I came across only a few links. Spender (1996b) mentions that firms which lose their implicit knowledge are also deprived of their sense of identity and purpose. However, these ideas are not really worked out. Krogh *et al.* (1996) state that self-descriptions that formulate the identity of an organization prevent them from drowning in knowledge complexity.

10 Spender (1996a: 49–51) and Nonaka and Takeuchi (1995: 82–83) seem to mention something similar. However, both publications do not consider the *epistemic* variety needed for doing justice to the subject matter, but rather something crucial for a dynamic knowledge theory of the firm.

11 The literature on knowledge management also speaks of knowledge strategies (Hansen *et al.* 1999). My use of the term is different, however.

12 The philosopher Moritz Schlick once argued that only structural knowledge has the intersubjectivity required of real knowledge. I doubt whether he is right, but that would take a long argument.

13 See, for example, Spender (1996b), who mentions data, information and meaning. For him, data and meaning are different kinds of organizational knowledge. Baumard (1999) points to the problem of reducing the wealth of knowledge to information, and Choo (1998) pays attention to the different ways information can be used. Krogh *et al.* (1996) discuss the distinction from the autopoietic perspective.

14 I will not go into this now, but there is in Western culture a tendency to put the nomological strategy directed to universal and structural knowledge into the limelight. This tendency is questioned by diverse thinkers such as Bergson, Whitehead, Merleau-Ponty, Gadamer, Apel, Lyotard, Derrida.

15 Now and then, remarks are made that seem to recognize something like quality. Take Choo (1998), who says a few things on the quality of information.

16 Derrida especially has made the idea of presence and absence an important topic of his philosophy. However, he is quite radical in his critique of the so-called metaphysics of presence.

17 Although much attention goes to business, knowledge management as understood in this chapter is, therefore, not confined to this part of the organizational world.

18 It should be realized that this requires the freedom to do so and also an atmosphere in which a critical attitude is to be welcomed. In situations where politics and group maintenance are the main thing, one cannot, therefore, expect much knowledge responsibility.

19 Of course this presence has its own problems, because it is not always that easy to grasp the meaning of, for example, the text involved.

References and further reading

Baumard, P. (1999) *Tacit Knowledge in Organizations*, London: Sage.

Blackler F. (1993) "Knowledge and the theory of organizations as activity systems and the reframing of management", *Journal of Management Studies* 30 (6): 863–884.

Blackler, F. (1995) "Knowledge, knowledge work and organizations: an overview and interpretation", *Organization Studies* 16 (6): 1021–1046.

Choo, C. W. (1998) *The Knowing Organization*, Oxford: Oxford University Press.

de Geus, A. (1997) *The Living Company*, Boston: Harvard Business Press.

Drucker, P. (1993) *Post-capitalist Society*, Oxford: Butterworth-Heinemann.

Foote, N. W., Matson, E. and Rudd, N. (2001) "Managing the knowledge manager", *McKinsey Quaterly* 2001 (2): 120–129.

Fuller, S. (2002) *Knowledge Management Foundations*, Oxford: Butterworth-Heinemann.

Gadamer, H. G. (1975) *Wahrheit und Methode*, Tübingen: J. C. B. Mohr.

Hansen, M. T., Nohria, N. and Tierney, T. (1999) "What's your strategy for managing knowledge?", *Harvard Business Review*, March–April: 106–116.

Harvard Business Review on Knowledge Management (1998) Boston: Harvard Business School Press.

Hauschild, S., Licht, T. and Stein, W. (2001) "Creating a knowledge culture", *McKinsey Quarterly* 2001 (1): 74–81.

Huysman, M. and de Wit, D. (2000) *Kennis delen in de praktijk*, Assen: Van Gorcum.

Krogh, G. Von (1998) "Care in knowledge creation", *California Management Review* 40 (3): 133–154.

Krogh, G. Von, Roos, J. and Slocum, K. (1996) "An essay on corporate epistemology", in G. Von Krogh and J. Roos (eds) *Managing Knowledge: Perspectives on Cooperation and Competition*, London: Sage.

Levinthal, D. and March, J. (1993) "The myopia of learning", *Strategic Management Journal* 14: 95–112.

Linstead, S. and Höpfl, H. (2000) *The Aesthetics of Organization*, London: Sage.

Merleau-Ponty, M. (1945) *Phénoménologie de la perception*, Paris: Gallimard.

Nonaka, I. and Takeuchi, H. (1995) *The Knowledge-Creating Company*, Oxford: Oxford University Press.

Polanyi, M. (1967) *The Tacit Dimension*, London: Routledge.

Polanyi, M. (1980) *The Logic of Liberty*, Chicago: University of Chicago Press.

Popper, K. (1965) *Conjectures and Refutations*, New York: Harper Torch.

Schipper, F. (1999) "Phenomenology and the reflective practitioner", *Management Learning* 30: 473–485.

Spender, J. C. (1996a) "Making knowledge the basis of a dynamic theory of the firm", *Strategic Management Journal* 17 (Winter Special Issue): 45–62.

Spender, J. C. (1996b) "Organizational knowledge, learning and memory: three concepts in search of a theory", *Journal of Organization Change* 9 (1): 63–79.

Sveiby, K. E. (2000) *Knowledge Management: The New Organizational Wealth*, Paris: Maxima.

Tsoukas, H. (1996) "The firm as a distributed knowledge system: a constructionist approach", *Strategic Management Journal* 17 (Winter Special Issue): 11–25.

Weggemann, M. (1997) *Kennismanagement. Inrichting en besturing van kennisintensieve organisaties*, Schiedam: Scriptum.

Wittgenstein, L. (1968) *Philosophische Untersuchungen*, Oxford: Basil Blackwell.

9 The Odyssey of instrumental rationality

Confronting the Enlightenment's interior other

Donncha Kavanagh, Carmen Kuhling and Kieran Keohane

Introduction

In seeking to emphasise practical philosophy this volume follows in a long tradition of bridge building between theory and practice (or, alternatively, between philosophy and politics (Arendt 1990)). In this chapter, we argue that science fiction can be a potent means of practicalising philosophy through its ability to link the abstraction of theory and the messiness of practice. Science fiction sheds light on theory by providing an ideal-typical setting through which theory can be represented, clarified and developed. Conversely, it gives insight into the empirical world, while partly suspending the epistemological conundrum of the double hermeneutic that afflicts every empirical study in the social sciences.

Although science fiction is usually thought to have a recent history, we maintain that it has long been used as a way of connecting philosophy and the world of practice. One of the earliest examples is Plato's famous allegory of the cave, which, as an imaginative exploration of an alternative form of intelligent existence, can be seen as a science fiction narrative. Plato's fictitious tale describes a world where people are chained in a cave since birth, and, seeing nothing but moving shadows on a wall, they falsely consider these shadows to be reality. Eventually, one man breaks free, leaves the cave, and finds that the images are only shadows of 'real' people who are walking past the cave, above the heads of those trapped below. What is important for our purposes is that Plato's ontological argument about the reality of Forms was centred on this narrative about an alternative life-world – this piece of science fiction. On this point, it is notable that the same ontological issue is dealt with in contemporary science fiction narratives, such as films like *The Matrix*, *Pleasantville* and *The Truman Show* – which are all variations on Plato's story, in that in each case the central characters believe in a 'reality' that proves to be 'unreal'.

Science fiction shares with all imaginative fictions the potential to think ourselves away from the contexts of action and the mundane realities in which we are constrained to think and act. In this way, fictions increase our capacity for imaginative self-discovery. This deliberate self-estrangement from the world (which, it must be stressed and made explicit to critics who, adopting the mantle of 'Science', would charge that science fiction is 'bad data' and 'soft-science') is nothing but the original source of scientific objectivity specified by Bacon. As such, it may also provide us with the opportunity for creatively exploring imaginative ways of dealing with 'real' problems by vacillating between 'the mimetic and the indeterminate' (Pfaelzer 1988: 289) and between the utopian (or dystopian) and the real. Put another way, science fiction enables a process of estrangement and promotes a text/context interplay by engaging the author in a process through which he or she extrapolates his or her analysis of current historical tendencies into the future, where they are both familiar and new. In this way, science fictional texts are a 'species of political epistemology' and a 'metaphor for potential histories' (ibid.: 289), and by facilitating a critical imaginary they can enable us to envision a variety of organisational alternatives with which we can assess our own practices and the theories that constitute them. In addition, as with Plato's allegory of the cave, science fiction texts can provide a vivid and dramatic way of interpreting and understanding a philosophical idea in a manner that is impossible if the idea can only be 'realised' in a known, empirical setting. And, as Plato has clearly demonstrated, science fiction texts allow us to partly sidestep the enigma whereby any study of the empirical world may merely reflect back the particular ontologies and epistemologies that constitute that world.

At the same time, we should note that while Plato clearly embedded an allegorical meaning into his little story, we are in no sense claiming that all science fictions are allegories. Rather, we use science fiction narratives primarily for didactic purposes, as a way of working with theories. Stories help us test, work with, understand, represent, critique and explicate a theory or theories. And if the story and theory are powerful enough, then they will mutually complement one another, and indeed, in many ways, all theories need allegorical stories for their explication. (A recent example of the type of exercise that we are engaged in is presented in the edited collection by Irwin (1999), which uses the characters from the television series *Seinfeld* to explain and demonstrate a range of philosophical positions and arguments.)

We will return to some of these issues at the end of the chapter, but now we begin our reflexive hermeneutic study of the Borg Collective, as depicted in the television series *Star Trek*. We have taken *Star Trek*, and the Borg in particular, because it ties in neatly with this volume's Odyssey theme; the *Enterprise*'s mission was, after all, 'to boldly go where no man has gone before'. We begin by interpreting the *Star Trek* story – which has now been in the telling for some forty years – as a metaphor for modernity and its odyssey. We then present a range of interpretations of the Borg Collective, an alien life form that has played a central role in the Trek storyline. In particular, we discuss the various encounters between the Borg and the Federation, and between one Borg 'cube' and the Federation's flagship, the

Enterprise. The juxtaposition of the geometrical Borg cube of cyborg drones and the sleek, round lines of the *Enterprise* highlights the theme of collision between a liberal humanist ethic and an instrumentally rationalist one, collisions being negotiated in debates on postmodernism.

'To boldly go': *Star Trek*'s various Odysseys as metaphor for modernity

The popularity and longevity of the *Star Trek* series illustrate that the themes this show addresses have a strong resonance within the viewing population. The original series (*TOS*) ran during the 1960s, *Star Trek: The Next Generation* (*TNG*) ran from 1987 to 1994, *Deep Space Nine* (*DS9*) ran from 1993 to 1999, and *Voyager* ran from 1995 to 2001. We claim that these series, as a developing narrative, address certain themes regarding modernity, including the possibility of universal progress through economic expansion (capitalism, colonialism), technological development (industrialism, positivism), and the possibilities for universal emancipation (democracy). Increasingly as the show has progressed through its various incarnations, it has addressed the limits of these modern narratives of progress, of capitalism, colonialism, industrialism, positivism and democracy to guarantee universal emancipation, and has therefore questioned evolutionist assumptions underpinning the instrumentalist potential of these imperatives to progress. What unifies the various incarnations of Trek is their concern with the limits of these modern narratives of progress, which are now being discussed under the rubric of debates on modernism/postmodernism. For instance, the issues of governance, leadership, communication and difference, which pose the biggest problems for the Federation and Star Fleet in the context of a pluralistic, post-essentialist, postcolonial society, illustrate our struggle with democracy and reflect what some theorists are calling the 'legitimation crisis', or the contemporary crisis of political and cultural authority. The Federation's principle of non-interference encapsulated in the 'Prime Directive', and its alleged openness to new cultures, reference contemporary dilemmas regarding the limits of neo-liberalism, political and cultural representation of various Others, and the nature of 'responsible' postcolonialism. Likewise, Trek's characterisation of technology is ambivalent and paradoxical. Technology is at once enabling (in that it enables encounters with others through interstellar travel, and has made the Federation a post-capitalist, post-scarcity economy) and destructive (embodied in the catastrophic consequences of war in technologically advanced societies and in the risks (Giddens 1991; Beck 1986/1992) of decimated ecospheres symptomatic of post-industrial societies). In this manner, Trek addresses our anxiety regarding limits of reason, science, of the environment, of authority, of morality and of identity, categories postmodern theorists have identified as being 'in crisis'. Specifically, Trek exaggerates various problematic facets of modernity and thus provides a mirror which highlights contemporary dilemmas that inform current critiques of development, modernity and postmodernity as articulated by theorists such as Bauman, Berman, McIntyre, Giddens and Beck.

Specifically, our interpretations of Trek draw on and reflect various philosophical critiques of modernity, and in turn these critique the modern narrative around the Other that underpins *TOS* and *TNG*. We can also see that *TNG*'s successor, *DS9*, was both a 'natural' response to this type of reflective critique and a major departure for the series. Simply put, *DS9* is a radical alternative to *TOS* and *TNG* precisely because it is not driven by its predecessors' logic of 'progress', which was propelling the series inexorably forwards towards a Utopian reconciliation of the diverse species in a common ancestry, and/or in an alternative reality that may also be our own timeline, towards the catastrophe represented by the Borg: the abyss of degeneration to technocratic dystopia. Thus, Deep Space Nine is an immobile space station in deep space, signifying that *DS9* is about stasis: instead of boldly going forward, *DS9* is bogged down, stuck at the cross-roads of time and space. The extended odyssey of the earlier two series is over. In other words, *DS9* depicts a world that is no longer (apparently) driven by the progressive logic of modernity.[1] In contrast to the *Enterprise*, *DS9* is maybe best seen as a postcolonial wasteland, akin to multi-ethnic postcolonial London, where the 'frontier' talks back and the 'native' is ready to resist anything resembling a colonial presence. *DS9* not only gives the native a voice, but also provides a different story about the genealogy and rationale behind the existence of a particular setting. Thus, the space station in *DS9* might very well still be the *Enterprise*, except this time interpreted by a (postcolonial) Other.

Unlike the series that came before it, the arena of negotiation in *DS9* is not a formally organised occupational life and a hierarchical command structure, but, rather, radical Otherness (as symbolised by the wormhole to the other galaxy) and a multi-ethnic public space (as symbolised by the promenade). The central feature in *DS9* is no longer the bridge – symbolising command and control – but a 'promenade' and bar where different races mingle, which is a microcosm of antagonistic multi-ethnicity. On *DS9*, inter-species conflict is simmering just under the surface, but unlike Kirk and Picard, the *Enterprise*'s captains in *TOS* and *TNG* respectively, Commander Sisko is only nominally in control, relying on a large network of informers to operate. While remaining within Hollywood conventions, Sisko is not a heroic figure in the tradition of Kirk and Picard, who were always able, through personal ingenuity, courage and charismatic leadership, to achieve the impossible. And in contrast to *TOS* and *TNG*, where the storylines focused on the heroic exploits of the main characters, anti-heroes are given a much more central role in *DS9*. Hence, *DS9* concentrates our attention on the status of the hero in organisations, and the possible nature of what we might term anti-heroic or post-heroic forms of organisational leadership.

If *DS9* represents a more dystopian, antagonistic vision of multi-ethnicity, *Voyager* is much more utopian in that consensus and collective agreement are possible, but only with the explicit acknowledgement that no identities are pure or innocent, and all alliances are temporary, provisional and shifting. On *Voyager*, Federation law and Starfleet protocol do not always apply, which is analogous to the postmodern rejection of liberal humanism in favour of a context-dependent morality. Thus, the location of *Voyager* on the edge of space and within new terrain symbolises a recurring theme in the series whereby boundaries between individual crew species of human (Federation and Maquis), Borg and Talaxian, as well as between public and private, personal and professional, are continually compromised and often reconfigured. Despite shifting political alliances and the relativity of ethics in the *Voyager* universe, the central characters are continuously seeking to establish a principled relationship to Others, to each other and to themselves. Hence, *Voyager* can be viewed as an Odyssey towards a critical post-modernism, towards a principled relationship to difference, and towards an awareness that ethical actions are by necessity provisional, temporary and context dependent. Thus, *Voyager* acknowledges that Federation law and Starfleet protocol provide useful guidelines, but at the margins of space they do not always apply, and must be reconfigured and re-interpreted to accommodate their unique situation. Accordingly, *Voyager* references the foundationalism/relativism debate in the social sciences regarding whether universally applicable standards of morality are desirable, or whether morality must always be context dependent.

The Borg Collective as a metaphor for modernity's encounter with rationality

In this chapter, we focus on the Borg Collective, a form of life that has become one of the most enduring and critical mirrors that *Star Trek* has held up to contemporary society (and indeed to organisation studies). The Borg were introduced in a 1989 episode in which Q – an omnipotent deity/ trickster who continually chides Picard about humanity's arrogance – sends the Federation's flagship, the *Enterprise*, seven thousand light years away, 'to give you a taste of your future', after Picard refuses to allow him join the crew. They immediately encounter a cube-shaped ship from which two Borg – hybrid organic and artificial life forms – appear on the *Enterprise* and begin draining information from the ship's computers. Once their data survey is complete, the Borg vessel demands the surrender of the *Enterprise*. The Borg state that they are intent on perfecting the standard of life of every species they encounter, by assimilating each one into the 'Borg Collective', a giant, hive-like, cybernetic network of technologically linked cyborgs in which each being shares the thoughts and feelings of each and every other member. The Borg are so integrated and collective that individual cyborg/humanoids do not register as individuals: through assimilation, individuality, the Self, is necessarily sacrificed.

The representation of the Borg can be interpreted in various ways. A central theme in our readings is that the Borg Collective is actually the Federation, or, more precisely, it is what the Federation will become in the future if it continues along its present path of development. Thus, the Borg 'cube' *is* the *Enterprise*, and they only meet because Q sends the ship forward in *time* as well as in space. The Borg confront us as we ourselves may one day become (perhaps in all-important respects we have already become the Borg; Q said, 'to give you a taste of your future, of what's in store for you'). The Borg are not an alien Other, but rather an alienated part of ourselves. Alternatively, the Borg are the *différance*, the unsaid but ever-present dystopia, that inheres within all Utopian visions, of which Trek is but a contemporary example.

Within this frame, we now present various interpretations of the Borg Collective to illustrate and explore particular philosophical positions. Our aim here is to demonstrate the pedagogical value of science fictional representation to illuminate organisational issues and problems, not only in terms of the immanent problems and phenomena of common organisational settings, but also, more importantly, in terms of the transcendent contexts within which organisational problems are located: that is, the broad historical, cultural and discursive frames within which the situatedness of modern organisations can be interpreted and understood.

In mapping these macro-frames, we will focus on four themes:

1   rationalisation of social action and the Other of modernity (Weber);
2   domination by instrumental reason: from Weber through the Frankfurt School;
3   subjectification and colonisation (the internalisation of domination): Foucault and Habermas;
4   reflexively reappropriating the Other of technocratic rationality: Donna Haraway and Kathryn Janeway's principled relations to domination by instrumental reason.

1 The Borg as the literalisation of Weber's 'iron cage'

The first philosophical concept we will explore is Weber's contention that instrumental rationality becomes institutionalised in modernity through science and bureaucracy. The rationalisation of social action is a central theme in Weber's critical analysis of modernity. He identifies the disarticulation between *formal* (means–ends) and *substantive* (value-based) rationality. Formal or instrumental rationality becomes institutionalised in two forms: (a) science and technology, and (b) bureaucratic organisation. These combine in modern society to constitute a characteristic form of social action: action that is concerned with the efficient achievement of instrumental objectives by the systematic application of technical means to instrumentally defined ends. This process can be seen at work in the mass production of goods, the treatment of disease, the collection of taxes, the management of a transnational insurance corporation, etc. The form of rationalisation underpinning institutionalised collective action of this kind is not necessarily connected to questions of substantive value – that is, *ought* we to pursue these ends? Formal rationality, institutionalised in science and technology and bureaucratic organisation, increases exponentially our ability to continuously devise more efficient means to achieve further ends (i.e. our technical capacity and organisational ability increases), but substantive rationality (i.e. our moral ability to articulate, reflect on and evaluate those ends) is relatively underdeveloped. This is because systems of formal rationality, though increasingly complex technically and organisationally, are straightforwardly single-minded, whereas systems of substantive rationality are increasingly pluralist and diversified, accommodating a variety of moral positions. For example, advances in medical and biotechnology increase our technical capacity to sustain severely damaged or terminally diseased bodies on life-support systems, or to manipulate genetic material to shape future life. But moral questions as to the governance of such technical capacities – when to suspend medical intervention, limitations as to who uses genetic information, and for what reason (physicians to pre-treat illness *in utero?* insurance companies to assess risk, parents to pre-select gender and IQ? etc.) are left relatively unexamined. In other words, substantive rationality, moral discourse, is out of sync with formal-instrumental/technical discourses. Thus, modernity increasingly encounters its own technological and organisational capacities institutionalised in technology and bureaucracy as 'Other', as an alien power with a life of its own that is not answerable to or governable by human normative discourse.

The Borg exemplify this problem of the ascendance of instrumental rationality and its disarticulation from morality characteristic of modern civilisation. The Borg are technically advanced and organisationally sophisticated, and their systems tend towards exponential expansion of these capacities. The Borg Collective is single-minded in the calculation of its means to the efficient pursuit of its clearly defined ends: 'We have analysed your defensive capabilities as being unable to withstand us. If you resist, you will be punished. Resistance is futile. You will be assimilated.' Their end is clear: to acquire and assimilate the *Enterprise* and its technology, to assimilate it so that it augments their own resources. The Borg, like modern capital, are driven by a growth imperative. This is a 'hostile takeover bid', the pure simple logic of capital accumulation. Picard, representing the Renaissance inheritance of broader discourses of humanist reason in the Enlightenment, asks, 'How can we reason with them?' In his version of modernity, there must be other grounds to action apart from purely formal instrumentality. But no, in this representation this discourse is hegemonic.

The dispassionate inhumanity of the Borg drones illustrates how within modernity we become, as Goethe and Weber predicted, 'specialists without spirit, hedonists without heart, a nullity that imagines it has attained a level of civilisation never before achieved' (Weber 1930/1958: 182). Thus, the

Borg are an almost perfect pop-culture representation of Weber's central critical image of modern existence, the infamous 'iron cage', wherein all natural and social relations are dominated by the principle of rational instrumentalism. The shape and social organisation of the ship and its crew also bring to light Weber's notion of the 'iron cage'. What Weber sees as the inexorable rise of instrumental reason in modern society culminates in the dystopia of the 'iron cage' of rationalised acquisitiveness, where modernity's technical and organisational capacities, no longer linked to a discourse of higher values (religious, ethical or political ideals), become oriented single-mindedly to accumulation for its own sake, as an end in itself. The psychosis of modernity, for Weber, is manifest in a new form of barbarism wherein 'mature' civilisation in fact regresses to a childlike Hobbesian state of war of all against all, where we are governed by an empty teleological ethic of 'the one who dies with the most toys wins!'. This is the principle of Borg civilisation, a morally degenerative principle that produces a correspondingly dehumanised species of 'specialists without spirit' – highly technically competent functionaries, but lacking the animation by ideals and moral conscience (lawyers who care nothing for justice, doctors who are not interested in health, scientists who are not concerned as to how their research is put to use, businesspeople who are not concerned with the utility of their product, but solely with its profitability (the tobacco industry is a Borg cube with all of these functionaries) . . . 'hedonists without heart' – rationalised acquisitiveness leads to accumulation of wealth, an abundant capital stock of material resources, but our enjoyment of what we accumulate becomes distorted and impoverished. The spiritual and moral impoverishment of the affluent society's growth imperative – accumulation for its own sake – is that works of art are sought not for their aesthetic value, but as 'investments'; houses are not homes, but abstractly 'properties'; futures are speculative capital ventures rather than the realisation of institutionalised collective goods in accordance with a discursively elaborated ideal of the 'good life'. 'This nullity flatters itself that it has achieved a level of civilisation never before achieved.' The Borg Collective is one of the clearest textual representations of this scenario in both classical and popular fiction.

Addressing the consequences of bureaucratisation for modern humanity, Weber points to the tendency for the rationality of bureaucratic institutions to systematically cultivate the people who will become its functionaries. Even the best and brightest modern minds, university educated, with drive and commitment, become assimilated and ground down, so that they become 'little men, clinging to little jobs', mere 'cogs in a machine; aware of that fact, their only preoccupation is how to become bigger cogs'. As we are assimilated, we become uniform replaceable components, as Borg drones are, as the staff of Monty Burns' Springfield Nuclear Power Plant are – when Burns asks, 'who is that man, Smithers?' 'That's Homer Simpson, sir. One of your drones in sector 7G' – or as Arthur Miller's pathetic protagonist in *Death of a Salesman* is. The 'little men' of modern organisational life,

Weber's sharper version of Nietzsche's 'mediocre man', is the cornerstone of modern totalitarianism, as he is one who 'needs order, and nothing but order, and becomes nervous and cowardly if that order wavers'. In so far as this describes the existential condition of the Borg drone both within and outside of the collective – comfortably functional when connected to the organisation, anxious and seeking to regain the security of the hive when isolated – the Borg represent the common form that modern organisations, from hospitals to armies, from banks to universities, share with the all-encompassing state apparatus of totalitarian regimes.

2 From Weber through the Frankfurt School

Continuing from Weber, we interpret the Borg as an ideal type of the worst elements of science, the ascendance of one side of the dialectic of the Enlightenment (Horkheimer and Adorno 1973), and the oppression of the political and ethical dimensions of the Enlightenment project that is implicated in the victory of instrumental rationality. In other words, the *Enterprise*'s encounter with the Borg can be interpreted as a vivid illustration of the twentieth-century critique of Enlightenment thought. The Borg ship as a perfect geometric cube also illustrates an exaggerated representation of the Comtean hierarchy of the sciences whereby mathematics and geometry represent the highest level of the scientific hierarchy. If the Federation portrays a utopian, modern future, then the Borg Collective depicts a dystopian world that has lost its humanity to technological consciousness, driven only by the imperative of rationalised acquisition. Borg drones have no individuality, no conscience and no morality beyond that of improving their technological expertise. Worse, their bodily boundaries have been thoroughly compromised to enhance their efficiency.

Weber's analysis of the development of modern instrumental reason, its institutionalised form in modern bureaucratic organisation and technocratic management, and its moral and political consequences, feeds directly into the Frankfurt School's critical theory. Reich and Fromm developed the social psychology of the 'authoritarian personality': the 'little man' as not just the functional type of modern state power, but the malleable, obedient, disposable and replaceable subject envisaged by Taylorism and scientific management. Walter Benjamin sharpened the focus on the centrality of the commodity as fetish as the essential object of desire and the focal point of the nihilistic pursuit of modern action. This singular focus, repeated infinitely, always insatiable, stands at the centre of a monotonous eternal recurrence, a static repetition of action that constitutes the hell to which modernity is condemned by rationalised acquisitiveness. The Borg represent this terrible stasis of repetition: 'They are relentless', Q tells Picard, but their relentless pursuit is simply to accumulate more and more. Like the growth imperative of the modern capitalist world market, it has no higher aim, but is an end in itself that is ultimately meaningless.

For Adorno, Horkheimer and Marcuse, the three central figures of the Frankfurt School, fascism and communism are expressions of the logical outcome of the dialectic of Enlightenment. Their shared thesis is that science first frees us from domination by nature as it clears away ignorance, superstition and myth. But in so far as humanity is embedded in nature, as we come to dominate nature by science, through science we progressively come to dominate humanity: 'What science wants to learn from nature is how to dominate nature, and other men.' Enlightenment science, as instrumental reason, emancipated humanity from the Other that was mythic nature; but now humanity is dominated by the Other that instrumental reason as mythic science has become.

The critical analysis of modernity for the Frankfurt School becomes a more focused critique of power as 'domination by instrumental reason'. Horkheimer and Adorno are preoccupied primarily with how otherwise ordinary and well-meaning Germans and Russians became caught up in totalitarianism, functionaries in 'purges' and 'final solutions'. The evil of modern civilisation, as Hannah Arendt noted, observing the Nuremberg trials, is 'banal': war and genocide largely entail the systematic and efficient performances of routine tasks. Concentration-camp commandants and secret policemen accounted for their actions in terms of the 'performance of duties', in precisely the same way as social workers, accountants, tax inspectors and production managers perform their duties with the impartiality and fairness of professional detachment, and conduct business, as Weber says, 'without regard for persons'. Borg drones are thus not individually responsible for their actions, as they act on behalf of the collective. Individually they are not evil, and when rescued from the Borg and de-programmed (for instance, both Hugh and Seven of Nine were drones who became disassimilated from the Hive) a former humanity can be recollected and cultivated. Similarly, abstracting from the non-culpable individual drone who becomes implicated in a collective process, the Borg Collective is not necessarily self-consciously evil either, and in fact the deep underpinnings of its current actions, like Enlightenment ideals, are utopian and progressive: utopian socialism devolves into scientific communism, national development devolves into the military acquisition of *lebensraum*; eugenics and social hygiene devolve into extermination and ethnic cleansing. Like Enlightenment science, the Borg's pursuit of better technology – an end to improve means – becomes an end in itself, an empty tautology and a Hobbesian 'restless pursuit of power after power, ceasing only in death'.

As refugees in America from totalitarianism, Adorno, Horkheimer and Marcuse developed their critique of domination by instrumental reason so that it encompassed not just institutions and practices of totalitarian regimes, but also the institutions of New York, the capital city and very heartland of the free world. The conceit of modern civilisation is that the pathology of domination by instrumental reason – a risk that is widely recognised in modern social and political thought, not just in the critical tradition outlined here, but also by liberal and utilitarian schools – is realised only in extreme and abnormal instances, that 'modernity as usual' is free of domination and is a theatre of free will, freedom of choice and democracy. In their critiques of the American culture industry ('Enlightenment as mass deception') and the affluent society ('One-Dimensional Man'), Adorno and Marcuse show that domination by instrumental reason is a pervasive, subtle and insidious ideology that permeates the entirety of modern civilisation. Not only is it the animating principle not only of formal organisational life in the marketplace, the workplace, the state administrative apparatus, but it penetrates also into the realms of entertainment, leisure, domestic life, and even the vestiges of spiritual yearning as a form of pseudo-religion.

3 *The Borg as colonisation of the life-world and the swarming of disciplinary discourses*

Developing Weber's stark prognosis of the fate of modernity, the Frankfurt School argue that the negative side of the potentially emancipatory dialectic of the Enlightenment, instrumental rationality, is ascendant in contemporary society. The stark irony of the Frankfurt School's philosophical and theoretical legacy is that their claim that domination by instrumental reason is insidious and all-encompassing replicates this very problem, in so far as critical theory itself becomes a totalising critique. If ideology, power and domination are everywhere, then there is no position of externality. Thus, the Frankfurt School's formulation of critical theory is as totalising as that expressed by the threat the Borg repeat when encountering every new species: 'Resistance is futile. You will be assimilated.'

Two responses to this problem, both deeply indebted to Weber and the critical theorists, but both dealing with that philosophical inheritance in quite different ways, are represented by the work of Michel Foucault and Jürgen Habermas. Though usually set in opposition to one another, they share much in their critique of the present. Foucault recasts the deep penetration of domination by instrumental reason in terms of 'bio-power' in general, and 'subjectification' (the internalisation of domination by instrumental reason in which the person him- or herself is an active participant). The Borg are a good representation of these processes, wherein populations, races and species become the subject not of extermination or enslavement, but of assimilation. Their bodies are subjected, transformed, improved and put to work, incorporated into collective corporate bodies, where they regenerate within the corporate structure like Japanese 'salarymen' and company golfers, willing participants in the increasingly all-encompassing collective life of the organisation. When they are made redundant or retire, they are lost and aimless, and mope around the former workplace, as decrepit academics haunt the corridors of the university. What Foucault calls 'the capillary functioning of power' is graphically illustrated by the Borg, as assimilation involves the infusion of nanites into the body that reconfigure the entire organism at a microscopic level.

Habermas (1989) formulates the same problem in terms of 'the colonization of the social lifeworld by system media of money and power'. The deep penetration of colonisation of the life-world does not only commence when one is assimilated – that is, when one enters the formal organisation and undergoes a structured and prolonged programme of professional training: university degree, on-the-job training, progression along a career trajectory based on accumulated experience and attested by formal examination and further qualification – but begins 'almost at birth' in 'the Borg nursery', as Commander Riker, second in command of the *Enterprise*, informs us when he encounters newborn babies already fitted with Borg prostheses. Borg are born human, but implantation begins almost immediately with the formative early childhood experiences of gender typing, and socialisation for obedience at school, work and at consumption. Habermas's argument is that the corporation's narrow set of human needs – money and power – is normally counterbalanced by the more meaningful life-world, but that as bureaucratic institutions grow, the life-world becomes 'overloaded' – so, for example, we go to professional counsellors rather than family or friends for help during trying times. Thus, the discovery of the Borg nursery by an *Enterprise* 'away team' is a reference to Habermas's critique of the colonisation of the primary, language-based institutions of the life-world, such as family and community (Deetz 1992). In the extreme, we end up destroying the natural environment and narrowing the human character, creating a dismal 'carceral' society (Foucault 1977). We become Borg.

How does one challenge this internalisation of instrumental rationality, which Habermas describes as the colonisation of the life-world, and which Foucault presents as the process of subjectification? Both Habermas and Foucault see instrumental reason as a dominating, alien and alienating power, and in this respect the representation of the Borg, as an alien Other, maps onto their respective theses. In other words, both authors confront domination by instrumental reason as Other, although they come to terms with its Otherness in quite different ways. Reformulating his position in terms of psychoanalysis, Habermas, in Freudian fashion, recommends a rapprochement with a divided part of the Enlightenment self. A traumatic schism in the early childhood of modernity left a part of Enlightenment consciousness stunted and undeveloped, while other dimensions grew monstrous and threatening. Now in adulthood, late modernity must get in touch with its damaged inner child in the hope that the reconciliation will govern and temper its wild and self-destructive drives.

Foucault, in a Lacanian vein, sees this as futile, as there is no 'real', no particular trauma that can be healed; there is only lack and desire. We are not innocent victims of historical trauma. Instead, we are deeply implicated in domination by instrumental reason, as 'we are both subjects and objects of modernity'. Our symptom – our fear of domination by instrumental reason – is ourselves; we equally desire to be dominated by instrumental reason, for it is part of our modern selves, it is the Other that is interior to modern Enlightenment consciousness. That is why we can never get away from it.

It is useful to illustrate Foucault's theory by way of a particular encounter between the Borg and the Federation as depicted in *TNG*. In this episode, Picard is kidnapped by the Borg and assimilated into the Borg Collective, a process that includes being fitted with invasive cybernetic brain implants, an electronic eye and an arm prosthesis. In his assimilated state, Picard takes on the same dispassionate cyborg persona and the same single-minded goals of assimilation as the other Borg, and negotiates ruthlessly with the *Enterprise* (in order to assimilate their crew and co-opt their technology) under a new identity, as Locutus of Borg. Despite his apparent total assimilation to the Borg's coldly calculating worldview, we can see the residue of the 'real' Picard, and thus the incompleteness of his transformation, when, after assimilation, a single tear falls from his face (presumably, and paradoxically, in grief over his lost humanity). Also, Picard's/Locutus's ambiguous identity is highlighted when his 'human' self struggles against his Borg self when, after being rescued by the *Enterprise*'s crew from the Borg ship, he ultimately provides the key for the Borg's eventual defeat by informing Data how to disable the Borg: this can be done by commanding them to sleep.

Similarly, Captain Foucault as Picard of the *Enterprise*/Locutus of Borg, evades the Borg, subverts the Borg, avoids the Borg and represses the Borg. But they are always there, the humming of the hive an *objet petit*, a little piece of the Real at the edge of his consciousness, the Borg hovering at the edge of Federation space. It is this persistence of the Real despite the deliberate practices of evasion and subversion that makes Captain Foucault the hero of modern radicalisms, but which leaves those very radicals open to assimilation by the Borg, so that they become, as Foucault warns, 'politically correct' political correctors: 'bureaucrats of the revolution and civil servants of truth'.

The assimilation of Captain Picard by the Borg and his role as negotiator for and eventually subverter of the Borg is a prime example of the ambiguous nature of leadership in contemporary organisations, and it also provides examples of both Habermas's and Foucault's positions. Foucault and Habermas differ not in terms of their substantive diagnoses of the pathology of modern civilisation – only their taxonomies are different – but in terms of subtle but important differences on the original germs in which the pathology is based and on its historical aetiology and prognosis. Habermas interprets Weber's analysis of the disarticulation of formal and substantive rationalities as the source of the problem, and, like Picard, pins his hopes on the possibility of communicating with the Borg. Habermas postulates that there is an anthropologically deep-seated reason built into communicative action that can provide the basis for bringing the system of instrumental action back again under the governance of reasonable discourse, from which it has become separated. Thus, the faulty connection in the hard-wiring between system and life-world can be traced, rewired, and the project of the Enlightenment corrected so that modernity is saved from catastrophe.

The ambiguity of Picard's transfiguration as Locutus both highlights the contradictory demands of contemporary leadership and raises interesting questions with regard to the possibility of a Habermasian communicative consensus. Locutus is the interlocutor who holds out the possibility of mediation between the ego-ideal of the *Enterprise* as modernity governed by reasoned discourse, and modernity's alter ego the Borg, the ungoverned system of transnational corporate organisational bodies of the free-market military–industrial–entertainment complex. Picard of the *Enterprise*/Locutus of Borg is thus the science fictional representation of the role of contemporary executive political leadership: the US president, the British prime minister, the German chancellor. Unlike senior bureaucrats and the CEOs of transnational enterprises, who are operating primarily within self-contained and self-referential rational discursive frameworks, political leaders are highly ambiguous figures who struggle to reconcile divergent rationalities of private interests and public goods. The admirals at the Federation are suspicious of Picard's residual link with the Borg (long after the *Enterprise*'s encounter with the Borg), but his crew trust him, a subtle ideological inversion of our own suspicion of our political leaders' links with the captains of industry, though for the time being we tend to trust them!

Habermas's solution to the problem of the colonisation of the life-world is to reclaim this life-world through communicative action (establishing an ideal speech situation as a means to achieving a communicative consensus) and by ensuring that institutions of global governance are democratically accountable and discursively constituted. Interestingly, the example of the Borg illustrates how some institutions of global governance are so dominated by an instrumental, rather than a democratic, rationality that their participation in democratic discourse is impossible. This is demonstrated in a conversation between Captain Picard (a true product of the Enlightenment, at least before his assimilation) and Guinan, whose race was previously attacked by the Borg. Picard asks, 'How can we reason with the Borg?', to which Guinan answers simply, 'You can't.' The clear message is that in the extreme, the product of reason – the Borg – becomes unreasonable, or alternatively that Enlightenment reason itself contains the possibilities for multiple – utopian or dystopian – rationalities. In keeping with Weber and Adorno before him, Habermas would most certainly not agree that this is being achieved by the political institutions of the advanced capitalist democracies, not even within national jurisdictions, and most certainly not in the post-national contexts of globalisation, where federations of states (planets) – NAFTA and the EU – are free trade and common market structures, not democratically accountable, discursively constituted institutions of global governance. Thus, in such contexts, Habermas's solution – communicative action – will not work. However, in so far as the most enduring character,

Picard, always wins any battle and keeps the Borg at bay on the margins of space by the strength of his charismatic authority as a reasonable, well-rounded man, appealing to Enlightenment values, democratic reason, a humanistic philosophy, in defence of the 'public good', *Star Trek* shows its ideological colours as more pro-Enlightenment than post-Enlightenment. Picard and the *Enterprise*'s encounters with the Borg illustrate a microcosm of a pro-Enlightenment, modernist worldview held by thinkers such as Habermas, where Enlightenment values through democratic reason, communicative consensus and a unified notion of the common good are still possible.

One of the things that make the Borg so perplexing and ominous is the realisation by Picard that the Borg cube's networked and distributed form of cognition and action enables it to manoeuvre, attack, defend and rebuild itself at a much faster speed than the *Enterprise*, which relies on a centrally controlled hierarchy. For us, this contrast provides a vivid illustration of Foucault's ideas on power, and especially his central thesis that in the nineteenth century disciplinary power (which is based on self-control, examination and the micro-practices of ordering) supplanted sovereign power (based on ritual, tradition, and respect for the monarch). Translated into the world of *Star Trek*, we can see that sovereign power is alive and well in the *Enterprise*, but as it 'progresses' – that is, as it becomes Borglike – the sovereigns/heroes become disempowered and eventually vanish, leaving a disciplinary matrix that operates without any apparent centre or heroic individuals. This is the 'democratic deficit' that is the source of anxiety animating the current 'anti-globalisation' protests: that transnational political-economic institutions such as the World Bank, World Trade Organization, NAFTA and the European Union are post-democratic matrices of bureaucratic and technocratic instrumental reason that are disconnected from any particular political centre, and thus as they expand and increase in terms of capacity, human control over their power diminishes. On the other hand, the idea that heroes will vanish is probably fanciful. Even in the *Star Trek* series, the scriptwriters eventually introduced a sovereign – the Borg Queen – probably because the Borg were destined to be dull otherwise. This, of course, transformed the Collective into a centrally controlled empire that, like the Roman and Aztec empires of old, was susceptible to a focused attack by the Federation.

Picard's assimilation by and eventual subversion of the Borg from within their ranks also demonstrates a Foucauldian notion of subversion or reverse discourse as well, although the Foucauldian interpretation involves a slightly different emphasis. Foucault sees the historical origins of the problem and its solution quite differently from Habermas. For a start, in Foucault's view there is not a single form of domination by instrumental reason, no one point of origin or disarticulation to which we can retrace our steps and begin to set the problem right. Instead, in keeping with Weber's broad analysis of the multiple sources of modern civilisation, Foucault's own close historical investigations into historical instances of power show that domination begins from a multiplicity of points in the historical cosmos. Like Borg cubes, medical, penal, military, governmental, educational and other modern disciplinary discourses are relatively autonomous self-contained and self-sufficient entities, discourses that have varying degrees of connectivity and elective affinity with one another, that complement one another, such that power and domination in modern society are an effect of the 'swarming of disciplinary discourses'. The Borg are a hive, and Guinan tells Picard how they swarmed through her solar system. Part of the reason the Borg cannot be reasoned with is that there is no central authority. Power in modernity, as LeFort tells us, is 'an empty place'.

Within the Foucauldian view, the Habermasian hope for a governance of the system presupposes a system, whereas in fact there is none, but instead a loose association of organisations, institutions, discourses, medical, financial, productive, distributive, public, private, local and transnational, whose power is derived from their swarming in loose affinity. From Weber, Foucault also takes the idea of a multiplicity of actions and rationalities that, depending on the situatedness of the social actor, can be seen to be reasonable or not. Contrary to Habermas, therefore, Foucault says that there is no one form of reason to which we can look to provide a basis for agreement that would provide the ground of a social life-world in which to anchor the institutions that would govern the system. Captain Foucault's enterprise occupies an alternate timeline, a parallel universe to the utopian Habermasian Picard. Captain Foucault (who bears some follicular resemblance to Picard) fights a running battle with the Borg. 'Let's get the hell out of here! Warp eight. Any heading. Engage.' When the Borg track him down 'Evasive manoeuvres' is Michel Picard's command, and when his ship is captured and boarded, and he is assimilated and incorporated, his tactics become a micropolitics of resistance. Rather than Jean-Luc Habermas's appeal to governance through discursive reason, Captain Foucault's tactics are to subvert from within. His recommendation to Data and the crew of the *Enterprise* is to forget about central functioning systems, power, weapons, propulsion, communications, and instead to focus on unguarded peripheral functions: 'Sleep, Data, sleep,' he says. The minor adjustment to the operations code of the Borg, the instruction that it's time for bed, brings the whole organisation to a standstill.

To summarise their respective positions with regard to instrumental reason as Other, we have used the example of how Habermas would advocate communicative action and Foucault a micropolitics of resistance in the face of the dangers of a totalising instrumental rationality posed metaphorically by the Borg. As we have shown, Habermas's solution is limited in that it demonstrates how communicative action presumes that consensus and discussion are priorities for all participants, and, as we know all too well, this is not always the case. In the words of the Borg, 'We have analysed your defensive capabilities as unable to withstand us. Discussion is irrelevant.' Against this, the Foucauldian micropolitics of resistance poses a better model for how to deal with the encounter with instrumental rationality, since it illustrates how this rationality is not radically Other or exterior, but exists within the Self. As such, the treatment of the Borg on *TNG* only partially illustrates a Foucauldian position, in that it implies that by this resistance we become cleansed of the Borg, and truly human again: only a trace of the Borg remains with Picard, and he is back as captain again in no time, albeit somewhat traumatised by his encounter.

Various *TNG* encounters with various Others problematise uncritical use of technology and challenge instrumentalist applications of reason (often shown in the many episodes dedicated to debating the applicability of the Prime Directive), and thus demonstrate a strong critique of evolutionary, linear versions of development. In other ways, the horizons Trek presents are quite ethnocentric and anthropomorphic, reflecting predominantly a liberal individualist philosophy of rights and a liberal humanist philosophy of evolutionary species development. Aliens are usually bipedal, while anthropological encounters – particularly between human and Borg – do not seem to be able to get beyond a residual essentialist, and at times idealised, humanism. Individual Borg drones when captured by the crew are usually forced to become individuals (for instance, as shown by Janeway's role in the deassimilation of Seven of Nine, Trek's most famous Borg). The real-life corollary of this fetishisation of the autonomous individual is illustrated by medical and legal rationales for insisting on the separation of Siamese twins in several recent court cases. Alternately, de-assimilated drones are shown as desiring of human characteristics, as demonstrated in a maudlin, sentimental episode where 'Hugh', an orphaned Borg, gets 'adopted' by the *Enterprise* crew and becomes a gentle, human-like drone.

Thus, *TNG*'s representation of the Borg is enlightening in illustrating the irrationality of reason, and the possibilities for subversion from within. However, up to this point in the series the boundaries between Self and Other, and between instrumental and democratic rationality, are envisaged as too rigid, insufficiently malleable. In short, the Borg are continuously either depicted as a dangerous enemy, or de-assimilated, domesticated and made over in our own (idealised) image. What both positions fail to recognise is that this Other, the Borg, this icon of instrumental rationality, is in ourselves, and thus cannot be radically exteriorised or domesticated. It is a part of the inheritance of modernity.

4 'We are all cyborgs': towards a principled and responsible relationship to instrumental rationality

This brings us to our next reading of the Borg narratives. Drawing on the writings of Donna Haraway (1985/1991, 1991) in particular, we can interpret the Borg as organic/mechanical hybrids – they are 'cyborgs' (or cy/borg). In this case, the salient theoretical discourse is Haraway's

(1985/1991) questioning of the essentialist boundaries of the modern project. For instance, when an 'away team' from the *Enterprise* beam aboard the Borg ship, they find that infants are cybernetically fused with machines soon after birth, and, tellingly, there are no females. Thus, the potency of the Borg threat to the *Enterprise* is a metaphor for the cyborg's threat to the modern, humanist paradigm where essentialist models of the self, and apparently inviolable boundaries – such as between the human and the non-human, leader and follower, individual and society, whole and part, mind and body, culture and nature, male and female – are subverted. In Haraway's words (ibid.: 178), cyborgs 'make very problematic the statuses of man or woman, human, artefact, member of a race, individual entity, or body', and, while this may contain a radical promise of emancipation, this development is profoundly ambiguous, as, like the Borg, cyborgs represent the 'final imposition of a grid of control on the planet' (ibid.: 154). For Haraway, the cyborg's ambiguous status can be explicated and resolved only by accepting that cyborgs are the Other within us – we are already cy/borg.

Haraway advocates a cyborg version of politics based on strategic alliances as well as a non-essentialist version of identity. She refuses to frame the issues in terms of a utopian/dystopian discourse, which she sees as unhelpful. The world, as she says, 'is messier than that'. Instead, she proposes that we take responsibility for the Other (instrumental reason) within the Self rather than treat it as in any way 'external' or 'alien' to the 'pure' Self (which is itself a chimera): 'Technology is not neutral,' she says. 'We're inside of what we make, and it's inside of us.' In her prescient 1985 essay 'A manifesto for cyborgs', she wrote 'we are all chimeras, theorised and fabricated hybrids of machine and organism; in short we are all cyborgs' (1985/1991: 191). Her cyborg metaphor thus suggests that we need to formulate a new relationship to science, technology and rationality that takes account of the fact that there is no outside, no pure, natural authentic space outside of the exigencies of instrumental rationality: globalisation means we have all been compromised, and the age of innocence is lost. Furthermore, this metaphor suggests a new relationship to social-political and organisational relations, one which suggests that purity be eschewed in favour of 'new myths of political identity' based not on false commonalities, but rather on 'partial, contradictory, permanently unclosed constructions of personal and collective selves' (ibid.: 199). She argues for alliances that are contradictory, partial and strategic rather than 'pure' positions that make claims to epistemological priority, and which presume to hierarchically order categories of oppression whereby 'she who has the most categories wins'.

By arguing for strategic alliances and a non-essentialist version of identity, it is clear that Haraway's cyborg heroine in terms of identity would be *Voyager*'s partially disassimilated Borg crew member Seven of Nine, and in terms of politics would be Captain Kathryn Janeway. Seven of Nine has at times betrayed the *Voyager* crew, or at least continuously challenges orders she is given, initially because of her residual allegiance to the Borg and later because her priorities of efficiency are not always shared by her superiors. Janeway has at times formed strategic alliances with the Borg in order to fight an enemy that both judged to be far worse a threat than each other. In the *Voyager* universe, no one is innocent, and we acknowledge our domination by instrumental reason (and our complicity in its genesis) but try to act in a principled fashion nonetheless. The permeability of boundaries between human and machine, and the multiple alliances they form, illustrate Haraway's dictum that we are now 'wet-wired'; we are cyborgs. There can never again be a hard-wired system and a warm, organic life-world. Our invention is not an alien Other to us, but the Other within ourselves, for, as William Gibson says, 'Technology R Us now!' Like Gibson, Haraway argues that rather than denying or repressing this dark side of the Enlightenment, we must acknowledge and make the best of it, while keeping alive a utopian vision that acknowledges reality but strives above it.

Thus, the new challenge in *Voyager*'s postmodern universe is living in world(s) where morality is context dependent, and decisions must be continually negotiated in the context of the multiple rationalities that emerge in the encounters with many radically different Others. This is the quest of *Voyager* and Captain Janeway. Modernity is lost in space, thrown too far, light years ahead of ourselves, divided, disunited, at odds with ourselves and with one another; a semi-disassimilated Borg, a holographic medical officer and a mixed bag of technocrats, misfits and rebels constitute the crew of our postmodern '*Voyager*'. Captain Jean-Luc Habermas's model of a united Federation of [European] planets is a nostalgic utopia now, light years and a few generations behind our current situation, and Foucauldian transgressive and evasive manoeuvres belong to an older set of problems. The *Voyager* crew invariably negotiate and compromise with (rather than resist) the hostile Others they encounter: a micropolitics of resistance will not buy the *Voyager* dilithium crystals or get us safe passage through Borg space to get us any closer to home. Divested of the conceits and assurances that underpinned Captains Habermas's and Foucault's confrontations with the Borg, Captain Kathryn Haraway is not labouring under the delusion that reasoned agreement with alien Other powers is possible, or that their subversion and evasion is in all instances desirable, for she needs the Other to try to get her crew home. She doesn't trust them, nor they her, but she must truck with them. She relates to hostile alien Others pragmatically and reflexively. Captain Kathryn Haraway and her cyborg vessel are (in)appropriate/d Others in inappropriate time/space. Monstrously compromised, they make monstrous compromises: they trade with unscrupulous wheelers and dealers; they make strategic alliances with supremacists, warmongers and barbarians. However, the crew are monsters as well. 'We have all been injured, injured profoundly,' Haraway says, but from phaser burns and truncated stumps monstrous new limbs can be grown, grafted, prosthetically articulated. The archetypal Other, domination by instrumental reason, is acknowledged as no longer simply an alien Other, but a familiar Other: the Other that is within us.

Haraway advocates a confusion of boundaries, which provides a fruitful way of looking at the Other of instrumental rationality within ourselves. In her essay 'Postscript to cyborgs at large' (Haraway 1991) in the book *Techno-culture*, she explores the promises of monsters and (in)appropriate/d others such as simians, cyborgs and women, which occupy a destabilising space within discourses about what it means to be human, animal and machine. She argues that science fiction is 'generically concerned with the interpene-tration of boundaries between problematic selves and unexpected other and with the exploration of possible worlds in a context structured with trans-national technoscience' (ibid.: 24). In other words, science fiction, like debates on postmodernity, is grappling with the notion of boundaries in attempts to negotiate future worlds, possible utopias that deal with what lies at the cusp between nature/culture, human/non-human, First World/Third World, civilisation/primitivism, and with issues of oppression in attempts to articulate whether or not post-feminist, post-racist, postcolo-nialist, post-imperialist, post-capitalist worlds are possible.

In this fashion, themes explored in science fiction are not so speculative or fictional as one might think. Many of these works deal with the breakdown or boundaries between human and animal, between organism and machine, between the physical and the non-physical, ambiguities that Haraway claims define our contemporary existence in the early part of the twenty-first century.

Conclusion

In the preceding analysis, we have shown that *Star Trek* addresses certain themes regarding modernity, including the possibility of universal progress through economic expansion (capitalism, colonialism) and technological development (industrialism, positivism), and the possibilities for universal emancipation (democracy) with specific reference to Weber, the Frankfurt School, Habermas, Foucault and Haraway. Increasingly as the show pro-gressed through its various incarnations, it addressed the limits of these modern narratives of progress, of capitalism, colonialism, industrialism, positivism and democracy to guarantee universal emancipation, and there-fore questioned evolutionist assumptions underpinning the instrumentalist potential of these imperatives to progress. In so far as Trek illustrates a concern with the limits of these modern narratives of progress, it can serve a valuable pedagogical function in teaching students how to think critically about these various critiques and responses to instrumental reason.

There are, of course, other possible interpretations of *Star Trek* and the Borg Collective. We will end with four supplementary readings. The first is that the collective represents the dark side of the information age, eliciting an unconscious fear in the technological age of our bodies being violated by cybernetic 'viruses', 'bugs', etc. In cyber-punk jargon, the Borg are 'wet-wired': that is, communications technology has been directly interfaced with the brain (which is only a short step from where we are at now – the micro-cellular telephone as implant). More generally, what is sinister and disturbing about beings who are integrated in a perpetual feedback loop in an information-rich society of perfect communication is that since Bacon we have known that knowledge is power, and in the Borg we encounter the modern will to power/knowledge taken to (one possible) conclusion. Thus, the collective is a metaphor for our contemporary fear of technological nemesis. The Borg serve as a collective representation of the source of the widespread paranoia in contemporary techno-utopian societies, where coexisting with the celebratory and affirmative discourse on the advances to civilisation and humanity wrought by the Internet, genetic mapping, and the transparency and security of constant CCTV recording are very legitimate fears of loss of privacy (individuality) and of bodily integrity. In other words, like the Borg, we are embedded in a technological imbroglio that strips us of our power under the false guise of increasing it.

The second reading is concerned with the different leadership philosophies of the various *Star Trek* captains. In turn, this also raises questions regarding the balance between rationalism, altruism, empathy and charisma each captain utilises. *Star Trek*, especially the first two series, follows in the tradition of the European Romantic movement, which flourished in the first half of the nineteenth century and which was, in many ways, a direct alternative to eighteenth-century rationalism. In keeping with its Romantic roots, *TOS* and *TNG* always depicted its heroic captain as superior to the characters (caricatures) representing rationalism: Spock in the original series and Data in *The Next Generation*.[2] But Romanticism also has a dark side: the ever-present danger that the heroic genius/charismatic leader may lead his or her unquestioning followers into the abyss. In literature, this scepticism towards the heroic tradition provided a strong theme during the twentieth century, writers like James Joyce and Samuel Beckett being especially hostile to the heroic images of the Celtic literary revival led by W. B. Yeats. Beckett's antipathy to nationalism, to the Celtic literary revival and to heroism in general is vividly depicted in his 1938 novel *Murphy*, in which one of his characters tries to brain himself against the statue of Cú Chulainn[3] that was erected in Dublin's General Post Office to commemorate the 1916 Easter Rising. In place of the (Celtic) hero, Beckett presents an image of the exhausted (predominantly male) ego of twentieth-century Western man. This raises an interesting question. Are we living in a 'post-heroic' or 'anti-heroic' society? In many ways we are, if we consider the long list of anti-heroes that have become central to popular culture: television programmes such as *Seinfeld* and *Friends*; films like *American Beauty*, and Woody Allen's films; the Budweiser lizard ads and the Budweiser Wassup ads (a contemporary take on Beckett's *Waiting for Godot*); and popular depictions of organisational life (e.g. *Dilbert* and *The Simpsons*). In terms of organisation studies, this line of thinking suggests that we might fruitfully inquire into the nature of anti-heroic or post-heroic forms of organisational leadership.

Our third reading is to consider the Borg Collective as a dramatic representation of Lacan's concept of the 'Big Other': thus, the Borg/'Big Other' is the virtual symbolic order that structures reality for us, deciding what counts as normal, the accepted truth and the horizon of meaning in a given society. Following Lacan, the Borg Collective depicts the constitutive alienation of the subject in the symbolic order: within the collective the subject no longer 'speaks', but is instead 'spoken' by the symbolic structure.

Finally, on an optimistic note, we can interpret the *Star Trek* fantasy about the Borg as a reaffirmation that we are not Borg, since the ability to fantasise is patently lacking in the Big Other/Borg. Consequently, our only bulwark against becoming Borg is to continue fantasising and critically imagining, which is precisely why fantasy and science fiction are of such importance. This neatly returns us to our initial point, and the theme of this chapter, which is that science fiction provides an underused and potent method for articulating, translating, developing and implementing philosophical concepts.

Notes

1 Baudrillard (1991) argues that the end of 'exploratory' science fiction is because we no longer live in a world dominated by the reality principle, but in one governed by the principle of simulation. In the case of the former, the imaginary (which includes models) are 'pretexts' of the real, while in the latter, 'it is no longer possible to manufacture the unreal from the real, to create the imaginary from the data of reality' (ibid.: 311), because our 'reality' is now utterly constituted by models: 'models no longer constitute an imaginary domain with reference to the real; they are themselves, an apprehension of the real, and thus leave no room for any fictional extrapolation' (ibid.: 310). Thus, the new form of science fiction no longer describes an elsewhere, but an 'everywhere' that is our simulated environment. For instance, in Ballard's *Crash* 'there is neither fiction nor reality – a kind of hyperreality has abolished both' (ibid.: 312), which is why Baudrillard identifies *Crash* as an exemplar of this new science fiction.
2 In the nineteenth century, the heroic role was filled most completely by Napoleon, who typified the individual challenging the world and subduing it by his genius. Other examples of this Romantic vision of the 'superman' include Nietzsche's *Übermensch*, Carlyle's (1841/1993) heroic model of social change and the various musical works that celebrated Napoleon.
3 Cú Chulainn was a Celtic demigod. Celtic mythology and folklore was a major influence on Romanticism in the early nineteenth century and it was also central to the Celtic literary revival and Irish nationalism in the period 1880–1920.

References

Arendt, Hannah (1990) 'Philosophy and politics', *Social Research* 1: 73–103.
Baudrillard, Jean (1991) 'Simulacra and science fiction', *Science-Fiction Studies* 18 (3): 309–313.
Beck, Ulrich (1986/1992) *Risk Society: Towards a New Modernity*, London: Sage.
Carlyle, Thomas (1841/1993) *Heroes, Hero-Worship and the Heroic in History*, Berkeley: University of California Press.

Deetz, Stanley (1992) *Democracy in an Age of Corporate Colonization*, Ithaca, NY: State University of New York Press.

Foucault, Michel (1977) *Discipline and Punish: The Birth of the Prison*, Harmondsworth, UK: Penguin.

Giddens, Anthony (1991) *Modernity and Self-Identity: Self and Society in the Late Modern Age*, Cambridge: Polity Press.

Habermas, Jürgen (1989) *The Theory of Communicative Action*, Cambridge: Polity Press.

Haraway, Donna (1985/1991) 'A manifesto for cyborgs: science, technology and socialist feminism in the 1980s', in D. Haraway (ed.) *Simians, Cyborgs and Women: The Reinvention of Nature*, London: Free Association Books.

Haraway, Donna (1991) 'Postscript to cyborgs at large', in C. Penley and A. Ross (eds) *Technoculture*, Minneapolis: University of Minnesota Press.

Horkheimer, Max and Adorno, Theodor W. (1973) *Dialectic of Enlightenment*, London: Allen Lane.

Irwin, William (ed.) (1999) *Seinfeld and Philosophy: A Book about Everything and Nothing*, Peru, IL: Open Court Publishing Company,

Pfaelzer, Jean (1988) 'The changing of the avant-garde: the feminist utopia', *Science Fiction Studies* 15 (3): 282–294.

Weber, Max (1930/1958) *The Protestant Ethic and the Spirit of Capitalism*, New York: Macmillan.

Part III

The becoming of organization theory

10 Rough magic

Screens[1]

Steven Connor

This chapter is one of a series of four pieces collectively titled 'Rough Magic' about the role in contemporary lives of certain very mundane, but at the same time quite magical, things, which together constitute an effort to prolong this everyday way of *thinking through things*, in contrast to thinking things through.[2] The more abstract, placeless and bodiless our existences, the more we come to live beside ourselves, and encounter the world and each other at a distance and through various kinds of remote control, the odder and lovelier things can become, and the greater the importance in our lives can be of objects that we can lay hands on, manipulate, transform and do things with. Human beings are such incorrigible fidgets, such manipulators of objects, of things we can touch and handle, or think of touching and handling, that it is scarcely possible for us to think, dream and imagine without things exerting their shaping force upon us. We think with shapes and weights and scales and textures. We literally keep ourselves in shape by the ways in which we heft and press and handle things. 'One does not think', Gilles Deleuze and Félix Guattari have written, 'without becoming something else, something that does not think – an animal, a molecule, a particle – and that comes back to thought and revives it' (Deleuze and Guattari 1994: 42).

The essence of a magical object is that it is more than an object. We can do whatever we like to objects; but magical objects are things that we allow and expect to do things back to us. All magical objects surpass themselves. There is no more magical object than a ball. The first magical objects are probably the blankets, rattles and teddies that young children use for comfort and security, and to ease the growth of the knowledge that the world is full of things that are not them. Children know that their blankets, rattles and teddy-bears are not them, but are nevertheless theirs. Magical objects are for doing magic with; but we use the magical objects in which I am most interested to do magic not so much on others as on ourselves. These objects have the powers to arouse, absorb, stabilise, seduce, disturb, soothe, succour and drug. They have a life of their own: a life we give them, and give back to ourselves through them, thereby giving rise anew to ourselves. Some of the magical objects about which I talk are ancient, some belong to the world of contemporary technology. All of them are strangely anachronistic.

We may believe we have abjured it, but the rough magic of things is proliferating and prospering as never before. In this chapter, I consider the rough magic associated with screens.

Screens

Screens have two functions: they show and they conceal. The primary meaning of a screen is in fact something that blocks, separates or filters, as in the rood screen, which separates the nave from the chancel in a church; the cricketer's sight-screen; firescreens; hospital screens; sunscreens; windscreens. There is a subtle but important difference between a screen and a blind: a blind shuts off altogether. A screen filters; it is a permeable membrane, not a locked door. Screens cover and conceal: but in presenting a secondary or fictitious surface, they also partially disclose.

Looking, we have always known, is deeply pleasurable to human beings. It is pleasurable because it is so closely linked with desire, and possession. A baby learns that it can reach for what it sees. Thereafter, seeing and grabbing are indissolubly hooked together. Seeing, the philosopher Merleau-Ponty has remarked, is a kind of having. Of course, what the baby wants to do with anything it manages to get in its hands is to take it into its mouth, which actually means making it invisible once again. As long as you can see something, you haven't quite got it, which is why it is a stimulus to craving. If this makes looking pleasurable, it also makes it avaricious, dangerous.

One of the most ancient and widely spread beliefs is in the power of the evil eye, the power to inflict harm by looking, especially envious looking. Indeed, the word *video* is derived from a Latin root that also gives the word *invidia*, meaning envy, or jealousy, and our word *invidious*. Some psychoanalysts see that envy as focused above all on food and eating, and on my desire to take the food from the mouth of my sibling – hence the association between looking and poison, in the tradition of the cockatrice, or basilisk, a mythical creature capable of killing both with its stupefying gaze and with its mephitic breath. Women, for so long the victims of avaricious looking, have also often been credited with a magical power to injure through the eye. Girolamo Fracastoro, in his treatise *On Sympathy and Antipathy* of 1546, declares that 'there exists in the nature of some persons a poison which is ejaculated through their eyes by evil spirits', a poison that is the more effective because of the heightened susceptibility of the eyes when the potential victim of fascination is being praised. To such a conception of the eye's powers and susceptibility belongs the extraordinary superstition, taken seriously by Aristotle, Saint Thomas Aquinas, and later commentators, that if a menstruating woman looks into a mirror, she will cause its surface to be coated with blood. The *Acts* of the Academy of Paris of 1753 record a version of this superstition, in solemnly affirming that an old woman who had approached a mirror and looked into it for some time had left upon it a film of filth, which, when gathered and investigated, proved to be poisonous. But it is not just ugliness that blocks looking. The beauty of women is often associated with veils, which both screen out and draw in the hungry eye. The relationship between the face of the female star on the cinema screen and the magical, glowing light of the screen itself was often emphasised by the use of soft focus, achieved by the veiling of the camera, or even the smearing of the lens with petroleum jelly. Beauty blears the eye; its blearing is its beauty. The cinema screen is both shiny, immaculate, untouchable, and sticky with our longings.

We fear, we men hitherto somewhat more than we women, that what we look at will gobble us up with the greed with which we ourselves want to eat it. We make it responsible for our hunger, suspecting it of wanting to poison us. The wicked queen in *Snow White* moves naturally from the operations of the mirror to those of the poisoned apple. After succumbing to her stepmother's powers, Snow White herself is turned back into a mirror, put on show in her glass coffin. Vision is always invidious, and, to the degree that it is hungry, also enveloping, and envenoming.

How do you forestall the powers of the evil eye, the powers of the fascinator, who can consume you with a look? Many mythologies and folk beliefs cohere around the idea that the only way to do this is to trap or deflect the gaze of the fascinator with an object called a *fascinum*, which would often be an obscene or ridiculous picturing of a phallus. The *fascinum* is a counter-charm to the fascinating powers of the eye, a way of screening-out looking. Perseus traps the poisonous, consuming look of the Medusa, the Gorgon who is both gorgeous and gorging, which would otherwise turn him to stone, in a mirror. He gives her back her own ugly, avaricious rage, or, rather, forces her into the image of the ugly, avaricious rage which is all he can make of her.

Ours has become a world of screens, a world that endlessly and on all sides calls out 'look here' to our overstuffed but still insatiable eyes. Screens are everywhere: on the street, in shop windows, at the desk, on the back of the airline seat, projected against the sides of buildings, winking at us from the mobile phone or the palmtop. The world of neutral surfaces, brick walls and the blank back sides of things is progressively being screened off, as the older meaning of the screen as something behind which something invisible may be going on is replaced by the newer conception of the screen as something on top of which things are being made available to sight.

Screens represent at once the jeopardy and the making safe of the eye. They are food for the eye's endless, unassuageable appetite, even as they are a place where the eye may come to rest. If our gaze can be fixed by a screen, then we might be protected from its own hunger, even as we consent to be consumed by it. Our restless lines of sight are endlessly interrupted, by images that offer themselves for ocular appropriation, calling us to let our look linger, and offering to allow the dangerous exercise of the eye unchecked. And yet such images also lure and solicit, like the amulets and emblems intended to gather up and turn aside the evil eye, and to that degree may seem to capture the gaze to which they appear merely to succumb, exercising their own form of fascination over us.

Screens are also increasingly credited with active powers, the powers to attract the look, to petrify us in the act of looking. Watching the screen in the cinema, one in a sense merely receives the visual impressions that have been deposited on the screen by the projector. It has not always been believed that the eye was passive in this way. The belief that looking involved the projection of streams or particles or effluvia from the eyes survived long into the early modern period in Europe. This is where our word *influenza* comes from: the victim of flu is under the influence, or the inflowing, of this malign force. However, the experience of the cinema screen also puts each viewer in the place of the projector, gathering back the fantasy that it *itself* projects outwards. The complication of who is doing the looking and from where is even greater in the case of the television screen. The fact that the projection occurs from behind the screen rather than in front of it, and therefore comes through the membrane of the glass rather than being reflected back from that surface to the eye of the spectator, makes things more complicated. Now the surface itself appears to be expressive, rather than merely receptive. While the cinema screen has an obverse (you can go behind the screen and see the images projected back to front from the other side), the TV screen and the VDU have no back. You can go into them, but can never get behind them. This complication of the hypothesis of the surface seems to encourage fantasies of the video screen not only as a kind of eye, but also as a kind of mouth, as in David Cronenberg's *Videodrome*, which dramatises fantasies of video screens that begin to bulge outwards to envelop the viewer.

The arrival of the screen into modern consciousness is perhaps marked by an essay by a psychoanalyst called Bertram Lewin in 1946. Lewin was struck by a patient who spoke of the experience of seeing her dream roll itself up like a window blind and roll away from her as she was trying to recall it for her analytic session. He came to the view that she was visualising the screen upon which dreams are 'projected', a screen that is usually as invisible as the cinema screen because of the engrossing nature of the dream-contents playing over its surface. Lewin postulated that this dream screen, which sometimes also becomes apparent in the blank screen of certain dreams without visual content but with a high erotic charge, derives from the primary experience of infant sleep. The screen represents the breast, which, as it approaches, loses its volume and visibility; the flatness of the screen represents both the undifferentiation of tactile contact with the skin, and the more specific experiences of the loss of ego boundaries in the oral satisfactions of feeding. In fact, the dream screen is the effect of a merging of identities centred specifically on the mouth, and on a substitution of orality for perspective, of eating for seeing. There is no terror of being eaten in this experience, since there is no other being to threaten the infant, who, in his condition of satiety, has 'eaten himself up, completely or partially ... and become divested of his body – which is then lost, merged in its identification with the vastly enlarged and flattened breast, the dream screen'. [3]

One may wonder whether this idea of the dream screen, if generalised, would tell us more about the dreamlike nature of the experience of the cinema, or about how dreaming might have started to have become a specifically cinematic experience. Perhaps it is not just that movies have learned how to work like dreams; perhaps it is also we who have learned to dream like the movies.

But there is another feature of Lewin's analysis that can highlight something about screens. Dreams testify to the release of crazily incoherent thoughts, images and feelings, which threaten all the time to wake us up. The screen, Lewin says, has the function of keeping us asleep by holding the dream together, like a skin. Or it is the image of the dream itself, in its own integrating function.

Screens are of course like mirrors, and mirrors are always dangerous moments of encounter between different worlds and states of mind. Mirrors can feed you back yourself, joyously entire, and shiny with youth. Surely it is for this reason that idealised forms of the human body, whether they be the beefcake or the glamourpuss, are nowadays always represented as shiny, as though some of the silvering or glister had rubbed off on their skins. And do we not speak of the silver screen?

But mirrors also testify to the possibility of the breaking off of this continuity. The Lady of Shallot sees her mirror 'crack'd from side to side'; Narcissus is finally engulfed in the mirror of his self-love, as he reaches forward to embrace his watery image. Narcissus falls into his dream, while the Lady of Shallot is forced into tragic wakefulness, but death results in both cases. Mirrors represent not just the suspension of the world in dream, but the threat of the dream's interruption. The wicked stepmother wants the mirror to tell her her truth, but it eventually tells her the intolerable truth of the beauty of another.

The shininess of screens and mirrors is a sign of their ambivalence; shine is a sign both of something organically moist and of something mineral or metallic. The lustre of the silver screen solicits touch, even in seeming to prohibit it, as something profane. The beauty and inviolability of our screens has something to do with the horror of touching an eye, or having your eye touched. This is surely the reason for the continuing popularity of the glossy finish of the photograph, perhaps the first portable screen. This sheen signifies the magical preciousness that we wish the photograph to retain, giving the eye notice that it is a tangible thing which looking is insufficient to encompass. The gloss of the photograph is an ideal, untouchable skin, though its untouchability also suggests its quality of tenderness, that word that signifies both the quality of something touched and the manner of our touching. This image has been touched and can touch us back. Perhaps it is for this reason that we feel called to handle photographs, both to caress their glossy surfaces and occasionally, in sadness or anger, to gash and efface them. The gloss of the photograph signifies it is more than human perfection, and therefore its vulnerability to the attentions of fingers, and the scratches, creases and corrupting smears of greasiness they can impart. This quality of the photograph is transmitted to the surfaces of other technological objects, such as the vinyl gramophone disc, tape (now boxed protectively in cassettes) and the CD, in the reverent kind of touch that it seems to teach us to use in handling it, a touch in which we keep the living, vulnerable surface of the object intact, instinctively preferring to hold it by its edges. When they first appeared, we were told that CDs were incorruptible; but nobody ever wanted to believe it, and we were glad when we discovered that, like living beings, they were indeed vulnerable to erosion and to the damage wrought by our tactile attentions. The practice of 'scratching', the manipulation in live performance of vinyl records, which grew up the club culture of the 1980s, at once rescued the possibility of damage in a world of incorruptible and immaterial data and preserved this ideal delicacy in our relationship to objects, drawing attention to the surface that would be as sensitive to our attentions as the skin of another person.

The projected images of cinema are shadowed by the techniques of reproduction and enlargement that made the living environments of the twentieth century a phantasmagoria of signifying surfaces. If anything and everything can become a screen, then everything has the capacity to bear faces and exposed bodies. The harsh banality of brick and metal, the sides of buildings, cars and buses, are capable of being made the vehicle for visible flesh. Anything can wear a face; anything can have, or become, a *front*. The new function of the material world, to be the support or carrier of images, means that the world literally makes eyes and makes faces at us.

It appears that as soon as you have screens, you must have skinflicks. The intense attentiveness that we are called upon to pay to images of naked human skin that fill our screens (why do we speak of screens being filled, unless in acknowledgement of the desire for engorgement?) passes across to actual skins, as people have started to make screens or visual display units of their own skins. The cult of tattooing, piercing, scarification and other kinds of skin-marking in the West has little enough to do with a desire to return to or rediscover the 'primitive', as is often claimed; rather, it is an embrace of the principle that anything and everything can become a screen. If a screen is an idealised form of the human skin, then it is perhaps only to be expected that human beings should come to make screens of their skins.

Films through the twentieth century sought to burst out of their flat, merely optical condition, to become palpable, to touch us, to move us, whether to shivers, screams or tears (literally, in the case of the famous Lumière brothers' sequence of a train arriving at a station, which is said to have caused the audience at a cinema in 1895 to flee in panic from the train, which appeared to be bursting through the screen). Contemporary films return obsessively to what might be thought of as this primal threat of cinema, that its contents will be so powerful and real that they will burst through the screen upon which they are displayed, and that the petrifying gaze of the Medusa may result in one being swallowed up in her mouth or decapitated wound. The woundings, flayings, lacerations and eruptions of bodies in contemporary film, whether in violent thrillers or in science fiction and 'body-horror' films, such as *Alien* and *The Fly*, expose the viewer to a kind of bodily disintegration that is both provoked and oddly assuaged by its very visibility. The desire to cut into the skin is evidenced not just in the display of lacerated bodily surfaces on our screens, but also in the ritualised piercing, cutting, scarring and branding among sadomasochists, modern primitives and other enthusiasts of what a grisly bureaucratic phrase calls 'body modification'. This apparent assault upon the surface is always in the end for the purposes of display and the leaving of visible marks; its larger purpose is not to display the mark, but to summon and make manifest the surface or screen upon which the mark may be made and retained. Such practices may evidence the depletion, and as a consequence the violently emphatic reassertion, of the function of the skin as a magical surface, whether screen or mirror, which serves, as does the *fascinum*, to capture and make safe the power of the oral eye.

But perhaps all this is just a prelude to something a little more disturbing. We have learned with the development of touch screens, and screens activated by eye movement (and soon, we hear, by internal willing or wishing alone), to make screens responsive to our touch, to make looking and wishing into a kind of touching. Perhaps this heralds a world in which we will be so thoroughly immersed that the screen will have no visible edges any more; or, to look at it the other way round, we will have moved into such intimate contact with our screens that we will have taken them into us, so that they lie sunk beneath our surface. If the world becomes indistinguishable from a screen, then the screen melts away, and we, like Alice, will melt through the mirror, as it melts through us. The screen, the function of which has for so long been to capture and keep safe the voracious eye, will have eaten us up.

Notes

1 This chapter is an expanded transcript of one of a series of four talks broadcast in the United Kingdom on BBC Radio 4 from 9 to 30 January 2000, offering 'philosophical adventures in the everyday'. The programmes were produced by Tim Dee.

2 For further reading in this area, see Augé (1995, 1998, 1999), Clucas (2000), Connor (1999, 2000), de Certeau (1984, 1997), Leiris (1938/1988), Lingis (1994) and Merleau-Ponty (1962).

3 This may help explain why the lowering of the lights in the cinema brings on such a storm of slurpings and crunchings. Jean Piaget records that when he asked a group of children where they thought dreams took place, one of them said that he dreamed in his mouth.

References

Augé, M. (1995) *Non-places: An Introduction to an Anthropology of Supermodernity*, trans. J. Howe, London: Verso.

Augé, M. (1998) *A Sense for the Other: The Timeliness and Relevance of Anthropology*, trans. A. Jacobs, Stanford, CA: Stanford University Press.

Augé, M. (1999) *The War of Dreams: Studies in Ethnofiction*, trans. Liz Heron, London: Pluto Press.

Clucas, S. (2000) 'Cultural phenomenology and the everyday', *Critical Quarterly* 42 (1): 8–34.

Connor, S. (1999) 'CP: or, a few don'ts by a cultural phenomenologist', *Parallax* 11: 17–31.

Connor, S. (2000) 'Making an issue of cultural phenomenology', *Critical Quarterly* 42 (1): 2–6.

de Certeau, M. (1984) *The Practice of Everyday Life*, trans. S. Rendall, Berkeley, CA: University of California Press.

de Certeau, M. (1997) *Culture in the Plural*, trans. Tom Conley, Minneapolis: University of Minnesota Press.

Deleuze, G. and Guattari, F. (1994) *What Is Philosophy?*, trans. H. Tomlinson and G. Burchill, London: Verso.

Leiris, M. (1938/1988) 'The sacred in everyday life', in D. Hollier (ed.) *The College of Sociology 1937–9*, trans. B. Wing, Minneapolis: University of Minnesota Press.

Lingis, A. (1994) 'The society of dismembered body parts', in C. V. Boundas and D. Olkowski (eds) *Gilles Deleuze and the Theatre of Philosophy*, London: Routledge.

Merleau-Ponty, M. (1962) *The Phenomenology of Perception*, trans. C. Smith, London: Routledge.

11 Suits you, sir

That obscure desire of objects

Robert Grafton Small

If shopping is the answer, what was the question?

(Jiricna 2003)

As they walk out, Hunter says to White Mike, 'I read somewhere that even if you're really broke, you'll survive, because there is so much food in New York just thrown away on the streets that it's nearly impossible to starve.'
  'You have to want to eat.'

(McDonell 2002: 12)

On Buchanan Street in Glasgow is a rather up-market store called Frasers. I get in there when the sales are on and I'm feeling full of myself. One lunchtime, alone – again, my dear – among the cut-price shirts, I hear a voice from across the display: 'What size are you?'

He's tall, broad and deep, a genuinely big man.

'Fourteen and a half.'

'That's not a collar – it's a watchstrap.'

Need I say he's no shop assistant? It matters, yes, but less than you might expect in a culture of style and confrontation, of being smart and feeling the smart. . . . Not of the gaze, however; we all have the right to look, to inspect, to invent the other (Derrida 1998: i, xxxvi). What does leave a – question – mark is the big man's expectation that I should somehow account for my side of our material interests. This mutual dependence upon the retailed and the retold – I'm telling you what I told him – is how we commonly make sense of the world, its messages and its margins (Douglas and Isherwood 1980: 72).

The exchange in Frasers was rule bound – he had to ask as I had to answer – and clearly a consumption of forms, a form of consumption, though we both bought nothing. Yet ours was hardly a free relationship (Douglas and Isherwood 1980: 58), without force; this taxonomy of a gender, dressing and addressing itself, showed me the symbolic assertiveness, the violence, implicit in punchlines. So I learned a small part of what it meant to be a grown-up there, a man maybe. Elsewhere and later, I'd realise the bloods, the studs, using public urinals, usually unbuckle themselves before undoing their flies, each leathery belt end the curve of an uncircumcised penis.

I too am the object here of a local agenda, addressing that obscure desire for community, its nature and composition. Through its structures and, above all, its discourse, this imposition of a particular social order denies or displaces every other, creating borders (Westwood 2003: 278), perimeters that must be policed to maintain dominance and contain threats. My accent says I'm an incomer – an 'outsider' is the end of a loaf, a crust – but I've a chance to speak for myself, within limits, to work a place where I might fit, a hole, or whole, just big enough for a citizen.

What's on offer, then, apart from shirts? An invitation: to a future that's already history, an object obscured by its own passing. The imperial system nowadays is a measure of age more than anything to those schooled and scaled in metric. I know I'm a thirty-seven neck yet I don't think of myself that way. Nor, for one, does Beckett (1991), who acts as his own translator, redressing an address to himself, so he can write to us more clearly. Is this creative reflexivity, a preferred self knowingly under erasure, or a refutation, an escape, from everyday existential doubt?

Fittingly, on the same frontier between French and English, one Gap has opened up another by labelling clothes my size in doubly unfamiliar terms, not Small, as I am used to, but XS/TP – Extra Small or Très Petit. With that happy coincidence of name and shape no longer secure, am I now some essence of myself or are mass-produced fashions leaving me behind, literally and metaphorically? Though a big man in these parts can lack bulk if he's got character, this is a matter for those who know him, and reputations curdle whether they're personal or Parmalat. In any representation of presence, our darker imaginings are unspoken perhaps, never absent (Falk 1994: 188).

These are also the semiotics of commerce (Eagleton 2000: 126), the ambiguities I've met spending time, and similar amounts, on clothes from Glasgow's charity shops rather than the chain-store sales. Many of the donated items, the offerings on offer are unsurprisingly, a little worn, faded physically and as symbols of belonging, yet passé? Only if they look new on you, which they won't, and at prices that make the most of a budget. There's an ethical element, too, in the recycling, especially of branded products, a – self-aware? – form of counter-consumerism that supports good causes, by shopping. The extreme version involves no money at all: simply try on something you like and walk out in it, your grubby cast-off still warm on the hanger and waiting to go back into stock.

Is this barter by the needy, organising their own relief, a forgotten form of shoplifting from a time before security tags, or greed and ruthless opportunism? Recast, these questions play a part in other theatres of exchange, other acts of desire. The scene is a howff in Motherwell, not a tavern in Eastcheap, one Sunday in August. Enter the prince of thieves, a career criminal with an offer:

'Fancy a pint, Rab?'

'Naw, ah've got tae get doon the road . . .'

'It's his fiftieth birthday.' Quickly, now . . .

'Aw, fuck – wait a minute.' The operator hits a button on his mobile. 'Right, you, get up the jeweller's and steal a watch. It's Rab Hood's fiftieth the day.'

I might have said Rab Sma', but reflexivity can be a little arch and, besides, wilful obscurity is not the object. You recognise the call for an alias. That phone was used openly and though the man was named, the howff wasn't, meaning where else would we be? The gesture itself was public like the bar and open-handed, too spontaneous, surely, to be showing off: look how I take care of my friends. Indeed. Both house and players found the whole performance unremarkable, despite the perverse echo of filching from Oxfam. How kind is making a present of what's unworn and wanted – and still hot? A Hood incriminated by hoods? Many Happy Returns . . .

This casual criminality is a cultural product, of lives made possible by organised illegality (Mars 1983: 28–33; Douglas 1996: 93–94). Yet even here, the gift economy has its hidden costs. Rab got his watch – he waited, he could hardly not – but the bracelet needs a link taken out, and he doesn't know which jeweller to avoid. The same quixotic morality is codified in the speed dialling that links the thief to his runner and the demands of a take-away society. Every day we want, and every day we choose, many of us to enrich our lives by blurring the boundaries between knocked off and knock-off, the real thing at an unreal price and the knowing fake, the sought-after copy.

A friend of mine, on holiday last winter in Cyprus, sent me a postcard which listed, along with the cheap brandy and breathtaking walks, her delight at a 'genuine ten-pound Rolex'. She's well aware of what she's doing: she's being ironic and buying a token of her actual as opposed to her symbolic poverty, a false signifier with true significance. All this is relative, though. Off-season trips still cost money, and mocking your own deceit with a mock-up (Eco 1986: 19) suggests the skills of a practised consumer. None more so than a Hilton heiress – in these enlightened times, the judgement of Paris ('Pendennis' 2004) takes a woman from the Apple:

> Who wants the new Louis Vuitton bag if there are tons of Canal Street fakes out there? We all want the brand new next-season exclusive Prada bag that's impossible to get. No one would want caviar if it was cheap. If I had tons of caviar all the time, I wouldn't want it.

Not the spectre of surplus value, the value of surplus: White Mike understands. Excess is the mark, the meaning, of common products, surplus a sign of desire – the unwanted thrown away (Winterson 1991: 3). Yet does meaning have an excess when I can pick up ordinary objects like a ballpoint pen with no maker's name, just BALLPOINT PEN in pale capitals on the see-through plastic? How transparent. An identity asserted – this is not a pipe – or denied, doubled into nothingness? A barb maybe, a poison-letter pen to anyone with a loose grasp of written English?

The rest of us are so at home these days with semiotic slippage, we'll eat out off it, lapping up layers of contradiction in the course – courses – of our daily lives. At Undershaw's, a highly successful and signally low-priced restaurant (Rayner 2004), one reason behind the cheapness of the meals lies beneath them on the plates: 'the logo of a dismal and now deceased American place called Babe Ruth's'. Struck out, bankrupt and broken, but usable where branded crockery can be gazed at and glazed over, where hunger is everything. When we're asked, though, what we want, here or anywhere else, our choice is curiously limited, by an ideology of industrialised consumption.

This oh-so-familiar order – Toyotas in Augsburg, burgers in Tokyo – is a product of products in order, as we become workplaces in and of ourselves for the making of meaning (Venturi 1996: 116–117). The goods we traffic in, like the languages we use, give shape to our everyday worlds, allowing each of us the means to an identity, some sense of belonging, extending us physically and symbolically. In these terms – cash or credit – shopping is never simply for necessities, an oxymoron in any culture, or a distraction, a pastime; it's a re-creation of our selves and our orthodoxies.

Those little pleasures we find in recognising the right thing, right now, and possessing it somehow, with money, a word or a glance, these are only insignificant until they're misjudged. Then we're embarrassed, by the shared incompetence, of course – you, I, did what? – and oddly anxious to make good (Goffman 1976: 206–207), each momentary lapse a reminder, of the abyss and our immanent being, the skill beneath the skin. There's also a refrain: 'You've conditioned me to need you because I've had it your way' (Mingus 1975: 216). The base line in every transaction – the bottom line, the suppressed reading – is the threat of imminent exclusion.

We've grown up in cultures of abandonment and decay, where consumers are consumed, each of us with a sense of being incomplete, emergent, an endless process of becoming (Jardine 1996: 436). Here, the urge to maintain ourselves with the range of our possessions is more a duty, a social obligation, than a formative desire (Douglas and Isherwood 1980: 104). Yet if like so many, you're market-forced – your job, your place in some old industrial hierarchy, has been traded for flexible hours and minimal pay – what then? Yours is not a rebel life of belonging on the margin, but one of marginal belonging, which is no life at all and barely an existence.

Shaped by desires that can't be met, this is the sinking world, of loan sharks and illegal moneylenders, and housing schemes where retail outlets mean mail-order catalogues and the iconography of forced choices: obscure brands or badly made, relentless easy terms. . . . There's a grim joke in one set of poor reproductions picked out by another – poverty in forms, deforms

(Smith 2004), and earthly delight: everything new a sign of old debts paid, to be shown off, shared, among your neighbours.

What matters, then, even here, is not simply the possession and decoding of things (Flusser 1999: 86); we're all more concerned with their public consumption, as forms of speech or spectacle – the speech of forms, their translation into non-things (ibid.: 87). This communal inventiveness is the lip gloss on our neophilia, and our own reinvention, yet any archaeology of the frivolous (Derrida 1987: 118–119) reveals a deeply layered social text, underpinned by some decidedly nineteenth-century anxieties (Eagleton 2000: 111).

Beneath the streets of Glasgow is an underground railway called colloquially the Clockwork Orange. It's a single line with parallel tracks laid in a circle and trains coloured – you know. I get down there when the weather's bad and I'm not up to walking. Or talking, though many do, whether they're with friends or just close to someone else. Newspapers, too, are common, and paperback riders, beetle-browed against the rocking of the rolling stock. The ads, unmissable above each window, are stared at rather than read, while shoegazers prefer the floor and headsets, the hissing of public angst.

iPod? I don't. My privacy is a bookish quiet, the silence inside my hooded Lacoste. Like the coming of metric, I'm living with a generation of technology that's living without me, that others cannot live without. House to Einstürzende Neubauten, they inhabit everyday worlds built around aesthetics and objects I recognise but do not own, desires that don't possess me. What else might be shaped along and beyond this line of readings? Perhaps the self as object – the desired end – and those objects – not just the shirts – desired in reaching that end, a dialectic of obscured identity.

If so, we're witness to another industrial revolution in which, paradoxically, the product is not an abstract idea repeated endlessly, a tape-loop train of thought (Pesce 2004: 45); it's 'a unique work that has been created in response to an individual's needs and preferences'. This way, we make ourselves to suit ourselves, and differ day by day, yet everything we are is rooted in tangles of goods and traded values, of ownership and understanding, a rhizomic rather than radical culture. As crime and punish meant Fedor before Foucault, my own notes from the Underground could track the originals more closely – a sickly man, retired – but I'd have to live with the comparisons. Erasure or cocksure? Censure. A gag diverts the threat – humour me.

Acknowledged or not, these recycled signs are scarcely readings. At some level, they depend, like any knowing play of surfaces, on shared depths and evocations easy as ABC: *When Smokey Sings* we hear Motown's back catalogue, with echoes of the Jackson Five, and Elvis in a gold suit. What goes unnoted is the implicit social arrangement; icons to unbranded goods, our every act of consumption is a commercial endorsement of one organisation or another, a shaping of structures that shape us. We're seduced by the prospect of premium products sold cheaply (Purvis 2004: 34), yet rarely ask how this might be possible and still profitable enough to support, say, Wal-Mart wall-to-wall.

In short, corporate sponsorship, of a perverse and cruel kind. Our mutual enrichment is underwritten by the distresses of globalisation (Klein 2001): workers who barely make a living, and competitors who can't, their economies distorted by trade deals and haulage where go means far from green. These elongated chains of distribution hold supply and demand apart, bringing us what we want – the world, and we want it now – dismissing what we don't. The same market forces have already shaped cities (Davis 1992: 227–228), turning physical into cultural distance, a structural and aesthetic suppression that puts ugliness elsewhere, with the other, beyond boundaries of decency and taste.

Our appetites also have limits, changing with our expertise as consumers. Even when we're not normally collectors (Venturi 1996: 120), 'objects fascinate us because they exhibit at once skill, pride and wit', like exhibitions that show familiar forms to a similar audience. Long before Damien Hirst repackaged pharmacy, Claes Oldenburg (1996: 44) pushed the Museum of Contemporary Art in Chicago with a close-up of green pills – his message in a bottle. Using the side of a nearby building, so it might be mistaken at first for an ad, he supplied three magazine clippings which were worked up one after another, over a period of years, into wall paintings, ending with the emerald tablets in 1972. Green means going . . .

My own maintenance dose is more modest, the steroids white, and pastel pink, the supplements – compound Jacques – an ill-suited oily yellow. I consume these products daily as I would any other, in displaying my fitness to belong. The alchemy of acceptance, though, is far harder to prescribe when we enjoy advertising, and promotion generally, for itself, not as a necessary part of possessing an object. Wrapped – rapt – in the discourse of commercial speech, what we desire may not be things at all but their meanings (Twitchell 1996: 10–12). Why else should we attach conversational, human, qualities like wit and character to goods with no innate significance, or value to the practically useless?

We've been doing this work for some while (McLuhan 1967), extending our public and private lives from their drugged extremes to the virtual intimacies of electronics, finding ourselves in dislocation. Wired in every sense, the world finally makes sense. Momentarily. These ordinary understandings are the result of an extraordinary traffic: industrial multiples on a domestic scale, designed to be identical yet never twice the same – differing in significance, not significantly different. The brands, the repeat purchases that hold us as consumers, are themselves products of dynamic instability, signs and objects we reuse to keep fresh.

It's inevitable, then, that Fukuyama moment should become history, undone by the enduring inequalities of market-based democracy. Fine art from proletarian lumps may suggest a precedent for the ten-pound Rolex but the generation gap makes Oldenburg's inversion another class of joke, displaying rather than dispensing cultural capital. Indeed, there's some social distance – place out of matter – implicit in every new possession that's dated by decay elsewhere; its traces and its owner's symbolic renewal begin in the tracks of cast-offs, caste marks of the bought and sold. We commonly trade across these margins in valuing each other's status – what size are you? – and moral standing: those cosmetics weren't tested on animals, were they?

A barefaced lie might not be enough, and a bare face would be going too far. Belonging is part of our make-up (Wolpert 2001: 56); we need to be known this way for our selves, and besides, desire is conditional, encultured in every consumer. Ask the parents who feed a 3-year-old chips for breakfast, or order their child a double egg and bacon cheeseburger, liquidised with gravy (Choudhari *et al.* 2004). When the industry catering to these people is more concerned by fat customers than fat profits, popular self-expression has clearly taken a powerful form, in the growing demand for bigger portions. What, though, can the bloated hunger for, if they are no longer outfaced by overeating in public, or bothered by obesity?

We're back with White Mike: they want to eat – they have to. Given the effort involved, and the investment, do they need to be seen gorging, their lives part performance art, a vernacular of felt fat now Beuys has made felt and fat aesthetically acceptable? Are we witnessing, instead, another style of conspicuous consumption, an excess of self to celebrate the self, hoggery after Hogarth maybe? Either way, these are visual tropes, memes of a market-based culture, embodying entrepreneurial expansiveness and the individual's right to choose. Shaped by a society we shape, we are modelled after our own desires, deep-fried Mars bars an' aw . . .

Modern life is rubbish, the blur of discarded signs and objects a record of our wants, as meaningful as everything we value – for the moment. Need alone is no longer enough to order this arbitrary commerce (Derrida 1987: 134–135); our ability, our urge, to acquire has become an end in itself, reducing goods to tokens, valued for their transience, their value transient. We understand them in similar terms, making sense to suit ourselves from the swirl of signifiers we inhabit yet never settle. Rab Hood's howff could be home to any of us with aspiration, or none.

I hope – to eat, usually, in a neighbourhood restaurant, and not too much else, or too much. I've been their customer so long and so often, conversation has almost disappeared, which I like. My order doesn't change either, which they like, as work disappears. This is commercial still: is it an exchange? One evening in particular, I'm at my favourite table when an undue wait for an overdue waiter prompts help being fetched from the bar. These things happen, and the staff are flexible enough to cope with little question:

'What chef is on tonight?'

'Jamie.'

'But who's doing the cooking?'

This is an exchange: is it commercial still? Backstage has been brought –

allowed – front of house (Goffman 1976: 115–116, 225), a compliment or carelessness?

My accent forgotten in my quiet, do I pass for a native here? More plausibly, the babel of incomers locally – students, say, and tourists – has talked us all into reworking our lives by living them, as members and makers of a mongrel culture, a transient society. Practically also, if I keep coming back, I must be happy enough with the service and aware, surely, of how it's provided. Perhaps. Perhaps, again – I don't know that Jamie can hear – the waiters are letting me listen while they dig up the chef. The joke, though, is freshly served, and piquant for a product of industrial catering.

Hardly everyone's taste – an unsavoury smack of resistance? – or the only translation, just my version of me now treating me then as a text, a place of work about a workplace. Similarly, any reader, any reading, finds a meaning to fit, reworking what I've done, and left undone. As I am, exposed by my dimly hoped-for obscurity. Yet objectively, if that's the desire, why write at all? Where's the need, the demand? In Beckett (1992: 37), echoing Beckett to become himself: 'Devised deviser devising it all for company.' Not organisation, you'll notice; those in company object to being organised, made an object by others. My – our – waiters aren't for Godot: they're playing themselves.

As their audience, their collective other, we're the eternal return that endorses their emerging identities (Derrida 1988: 84–85). Richard Klein's (1997: 33–34) is in endless returns to breakfast – an upstate diner, the warmth of the grill and the cook who slips him extra toast, thick with butter and significance – a symbol of solitude shared, spread – but a cold medium, or hot? We're in this too, immanent as the next, and equally guilty – community is a shared responsibility. Each of us adds to the spectacle of being by becoming, by representing ourselves again and again, Cindy Sherman, maybe, without the fetishes (Lowry 2000: 6), yet all the desires and the goods, the cargoes of cult objects.

Off Otago Lane in Glasgow is a rather downbeat bookshop called Voltaire and Rousseau. The stock's second-hand and the customers prefer not to talk; their appetites are private still, personal, though the books are hardly the objectionable kind. I get in there whenever I can. One time, remembering Kafka was anorexic (Rice 2004), an artificially little man – what size was he? – I came across a translation I had to buy: that's not *Amerika*, it's *The Man Who Disappeared* . . . (Kafka 1996).

References and further reading

A, Martin (forthcoming) *The misInformation*, London: Random Readings.

Beckett, S. (1991) *Mercier and Camier*, trans. S. Beckett, New York: Grove Press.

Beckett, S. (1992) *Nohow On*, London: Calder Publications.

Bourdieu, P. (1990) *In Other Words: Essays towards a Reflexive Sociology*, trans. M. Adamson, Cambridge: Polity Press.

Choudhari, H. (2004) 'Restaurant customers "getting greedier"', *Guardian*, 25 March, http://society.guardian.co.uk/publichealth/story/0,,1177609,00.html.

Davis, M. (1992) *City of Quartz*, London: Vintage.

Derrida, J. (1987) *The Archeology of the Frivolous*, trans. J. P. Leavey, Jr, London: Bison Books; Lincoln: University of Nebraska Press.

Derrida, J. (1988) *The Ear of the Other*, trans. P. Kamuf, London: Bison Books; Lincoln: University of Nebraska Press.

Derrida, J. (1998) *Right of Inspection*, trans. D. Wills, New York: Monacelli Press.

Dostoevsky, F. (1992) *Notes from the Underground and The Gambler*, trans. J. Kentish, Oxford: Oxford University Press.

Douglas, M. (1996) *Thought Styles: Critical Essays on Good Taste*, London: Sage.

Douglas, M. and Isherwood, B. (1980) *The World of Goods: Towards an Anthropology of Consumption*, Harmondsworth, UK: Penguin.

Eagleton, T. (2000) *The Idea of Culture*, Oxford: Blackwell.

Eco, U. (1986) *Faith in Fakes: Essays*, trans. W. Weaver, London: Secker & Warburg.

Falk, P. (1994) *The Consuming Body*, London: Sage.

Flusser, V. (1999) *The Shape of Things: A Philosophy of Design*, trans. A. Mathews, London: Reaktion Books.

Fukuyama, F. (1992) *The End of History and the Last Man*, New York: The Free Press/Macmillan.

Goffman, E. (1976) *The Presentation of Self in Everyday Life*, Harmondsworth, UK: Penguin.

Jardine, L. (1996) *Worldly Goods*, London: Macmillan.

Jiricna, E. (2003) Royal Academy of Arts, London, 1 December.

Kafka, F. (1996) *The Man Who Disappeared (Amerika)*, trans. M. Hofmann, London: Penguin Books.

Klein, N. (2001) *No Logo*, London: Flamingo/HarperCollins.

Klein, R. (1997) *Eat Fat*, London: Picador.

Koolhaas, R. *et al.* (eds) (2001) *Harvard Design School Guide to Shopping*, New York: Taschen.

Lowry, J. (2000) 'From the site of desire to the scene of destruction: photography and the work of Cindy Sherman', in G. Knape (ed.) *Cindy Sherman: The Hasselblad Award 1999*, Göteborg: Hasselblad Center.

McDonell, N. (2002) *Twelve*, London: Atlantic Books.

McLuhan, M. (1967) *Understanding Media: The Extensions of Man*, London: Sphere Books.

Mars, G. (1983) *Cheats at Work: An Anthropology of Workplace Crime*, London: Unwin Paperbacks.

Marx, K. and Engels, F. (1998) *The Communist Manifesto*, trans. S. Moore, London: Verso.

Mingus, C. (1975) *Beneath the Underdog*, Harmondsworth, UK: Penguin.

Oldenburg, C. (1996) *The Multiples Store*, London: The South Bank Centre.

'Pendennis' (2004) 'Tax on both your houses', *Observer*, 29 February, p. 31.

Pesce, G. (2004) 'Modern man', *Blueprint*, no. 216, February: 44–46.

Purvis, A. (2004) 'Loaded! Why supermarkets are getting richer and richer', *Observer Food Monthly*, no. 34, January: 32–38.

Rayner, J. (2004) 'Gothic splendour', *Observer Magazine*, 25 January, p. 67.

Rice, M. (2004) 'Still at war with our bodies', *Observer Review*, 1 February, p. 4.

Smith. D. (2004) 'You'll be lucky to live to 60 here', *Observer*, 14 March, p. 14.

Twitchell, J. B. (1996) *Adcult USA: The Triumph of Advertising in American Culture*, New York: Columbia University Press.

Venturi, R. (1996) *Iconography and Electronics upon a Generic Architecture*, Cambridge, MA: MIT Press.

Westwood, R. I. (2003) 'Economies of violence: an autobiographical account', *Culture and Organization* 9 (4) (December): 275–293.

Winterson, J. (1991) *The Passion*, London: Bloomsbury Publishing.

Wolpert, J. (2001) *Malignant Sadness: The Anatomy of Depression*, London: Faber & Faber.

12 Refocusing

A Bergsonian approach to organization

Stephen Linstead

Henri Bergson has been for many years relegated to a footnote in most philosophical texts, especially those in the North Atlantic analytical tradition, his work having been widely critiqued by Russell (1914) and others and subsequently dismissed decades ago, with the exception of treatments such as those by Carr (1919), Alexander (1957), Pilkington (1976), Kolakowski (1985) and Lacey (1989). Until recently, he fared only marginally better in the Continental tradition, but in the first two or three decades of the twentieth century he was perhaps the world's best-known philosopher, with the public presence and celebrity these days afforded to actors and musicians. Nevertheless, it may seem unusual to turn to the work of a philosopher who has been neglected for over sixty years to illuminate contemporary organization theory, however creative he may have been. In a world that is characterized by constant change; where chaos theory seeks to explain conditions of complexity, instability and emergence; where the habitual nature of problem solving (paradigms, culture) produces false or factitious problems (puzzles) for us to "solve"; where creativity and perpetual learning are prerequisites for organizational competitiveness; where novelty is prized; where environmentalism is forcing us to rethink the nature of the relation of organisms, communities and organizations to their environment and to each other; where knowledge, capturing the implicit and preserving organizational memory are key concerns; where time and space are being collapsed into virtuality; where the body is reasserting itself as a social and psychological phenomenon in new and different ways through cyborgs and prostheses; where a new spirituality and concern with ethics are emerging in both the natural and the organizational sciences; where the image has become the dominant metaphor in postmodern social organization; where difference and multiplicity are key problems in understanding identities; where new evolutionary theory is now emerging in psychology and organization studies; where language is seen as unreliable in the process of representation; where critical realism struggles to offer a viable alternative to positivist empiricism and postmodern textuality, genealogy and deconstruction; and where action and experience are seen by many as the foundations of social networks, it seems hard to imagine that a philosopher whose reputation was at its peak during the Great War could have anything relevant to say. Yet, however remarkably, Henri Bergson did address these matters in a way that remains vital and accessible, and indeed speaks directly to many of our contemporary concerns in organization studies.

Bergson's influence was wide, and often unacknowledged by those who appropriated him. Indeed, it was perhaps so wide that it was dissipated across too many areas for its distinct force to be clearly discerned, and never comprised a unified programme. Often identified with vitalism, for example, Bergson was never a vitalist as such, and critiqued vitalism's simplistic tendencies (Burwick and Douglass 1992); similarly identified as a Heraclitan process philosopher, he explicitly held back from identification with full process metaphysics. Gilles Deleuze (1988) coined the term "Bergsonism" in his eponymous essay with deliberate irony, for Bergson wrote each of his works without regard to his previous ones, with no sense of progression or teleology, and often changed, contradicted or shifted his views. Indeed, just as his view of life was of constant change, his view of philosophy embodied in his practice was of a discipline that must itself be constantly changing. Bergson could be said to have initiated a cult of change, but one without a programme (Carr 1919). Consequently, his work was taken up by thinkers in various other disciplines, in particular phenomenology (notably through Alfred Schütz, Maurice Merleau-Ponty and Emmanuel Lévinas, impacting on social constructionism and ethics); existentialism (through Martin Heidegger and Jean-Paul Sartre); process philosophy (notably Alfred North Whitehead – see Rescher 1996) and more recently post-structuralism (notably Michel Foucault, Jacques Derrida and Gilles Deleuze). His dialogues with the American pragmatists John Dewey and William James have also had influence that has re-emerged in the postmodern pragmatism of Richard Rorty (see Bergson 1999; Griffin *et al.* 1993). In the realm of literature, his concept of time influenced Paul Valery and John Dos Passos, but had most impact on Marcel Proust, to whom Bergson was related by marriage, in *The Remembrance of Things Past*. Even a work that Bergson considered to be minor, *Laughter*, was regarded by Arthur Koestler as being a major influence on his book *The Act of Creation*. It is through these interpreters, all picking up the aspects of his work that most interested them and creating their own versions of it, that we have come to know Bergson. Yet this is exactly what his own philosophy predicted in arguing that the process of perception is not the replication of its object, but an act of *replying to it*, in that representation as a translation of stimulating sense data always entails interest, selection and creation.[1] This chapter can therefore be considered as a *reply* to Bergson, one that seeks to work with his ideas on contemporary organizational problems.

Bergsonian thinking: revenge as organizing through focus

The noble Brutus
Hath told you Caesar was ambitious.
If it were so, it was a grievous fault,
And grievously hath Caesar answered it.
Here, under leave of Brutus and the rest –
For Brutus is an honourable man;
So are they all, all honourable men –
Come I to speak in Caesar's funeral.
He was my friend, faithful and just to me.
But Brutus says he was ambitious,
And Brutus is an honourable man.
He hath brought many captives home to Rome,
Whose ransoms did the general coffers fill.
Did this in Caesar seem ambitious?
When that the poor have cried, Caesar hath wept.
Ambition should be made of sterner stuff.
Yet Brutus says he was ambitious, and Brutus is an honourable man.
You all did see that on the Lupercal
I thrice presented him with a kingly crown,
Which he did thrice refuse. Was this ambition?
Yet Brutus says he was ambitious,
And sure he is an honourable man.
I speak not to disprove what Brutus spoke,
But I am here to speak what I do know. . . .
. . . O masters, if I were disposed to stir
Your hearts and minds to mutiny and rage,
I should do Brutus wrong, and Cassius wrong,
Who, you all know, are honourable men.
I will not do them wrong. I rather choose
To wrong the dead, to wrong myself and you,
Than I will wrong such honourable men.
    (Mark Antony, speaking in William Shakespeare's *The Tragedy of*
Julius Caesar, Act 3, Scene 2 (Wells and Taylor 1987: 1107–1108)

As I have mentioned that this chapter could be considered a reply, it seems instructive to turn to one of the most famous replies in all literature. Mark Antony, in delivering his reply to Brutus's public justification of the murder of Caesar, is forced, because he is constrained in being allowed to speak only if he does not condemn the conspirators, to work through irony, layering irony upon irony as the sense of indignation of the people, who were previously enthusiastic in their support of Brutus, mounts – towards eventual mutiny. Mark Antony repeatedly returns to the phrase "honourable man" (or men), and each time it recurs with greater irony. Irony could be said to increase because at each stage of the speech a "deeper and more shocking contrast" is made between what an honourable man should have done and what Brutus actually did and its consequences, or Mark Antony's account of them (Moore 1996: 46; Sperber and Wilson 1981: 295–318).

But is it accurate to say that *irony* increases? If so, does the sense of indignation in Mark Antony's stage audience increase similarly? For Bergson (1889/1910), the answer would be no, at least in so far as an increase in irony or indignation is not a quantitative increase comparable to an increase in temperature. Human mental states are not the same as physical states of matter, and change qualitatively. What occurs is that a focal thought (in this case the honourableness of Brutus) is brought into relation with a growing constellation of acts, consequences, recollections, connections and loyalties, and as this context amasses, and the dissonance between this context and the focal thought is emphasized repeatedly, the focal thought becomes tenable in fewer and fewer aspects, and the irony more comprehensively depicted and hence more striking.

As Moore (1996: 46–47) draws out from his discussion of Sperber and Wilson's (1981) comments, this Bergsonian view has profound implications for cognitive science and social psychology, and, I am suggesting, for organization theory. Our attempts to measure social and psychological phenomena from personality factors to motivation to organizational culture are potentially thrown into confusion if we accept that extroversion, for example, is not stronger or weaker in a personality, but a quality of a shifting relationship embedded among other shifting relationships, affected by them, and whose quality shifts with its relevance and pervasiveness as a focal thought. Indeed, in considering motivation as an example, Bergson would question the idea that motivation consists of the satisfaction of needs or desires that become stronger or weaker in intensity the closer they come to being satisfied. He consistently argued against the identification of separate mental states such as jealousy, enthusiasm, desire (or indeed motivation) which were said to vary in intensity, being stronger or weaker and which led to attempts to measure changes in their quantity. This is another example, for Bergson, of the spatializing tendency in human thought, which separates moments, lays them out as if upon a table and by such separation institutes immobility and stasis as the natural state of things, rather than mutability.

Bergson's (1889/1910) view is that we make the error of assuming that once we have identified *a* desire we can determine its strength by a method such as introspection or behaviour analysis (Moore 1996: 47). The differences between merely fancying something, wanting something enough to make plans to get it and being so overcome with passion for something that it becomes an obsession are recognized by Bergson, but he would deny that they were differences in the *intensity* of desire. As Moore puts it, such intensity consists in:

The role of desire, or the extent in which it is embedded in us, the extent to which it systematically colours our mental states.... The intensity of a desire resides in the extent to which it is a *focal* desire, rather than in any quantitative measure analogous to a measure of force in mechanics.

(1996: 47; emphasis added)

We could illustrate this by taking Moore's example of a desire for revenge, but exploring it in an organizational context, where it appears to be common enough everywhere except the academic literature. Let us suppose that Judith has prepared a recommendation for the adoption of experiential learning incorporating outdoor activities into the programmes of her business school. She is enthusiastic and eloquent in her advocacy of the development, and has done her homework on the benefits and drawbacks. But when she presents the proposal in a departmental meeting, Martin, her boss, scathingly and sarcastically rejects – indeed, ridicules – it, insisting that the programme take on more "hard" subjects. The rejection is personal, and Judith feels humiliated and patronized. There are several ways in which this situation might develop. The sting of the insult might be one that is easily returned, if the culture allows it; such adversarial battles may be an everyday occurrence and Judith may know she will not have long to wait before she is able to get one over on Martin. She may therefore be little affected by the incident, and it will not colour her other perceptions of Martin, her ideas about him, her other work plans or personal projects in or outside work. On the other hand, power and gender imbalances may mean that realistically she will never be able to directly turn the tables, and so the sting may be submerged and unreturned for some time, perhaps never, or perhaps diverted onto another object. Judith may sit back patiently and wait for her moment, or she may just shrug it off. Again, it will not affect much else in her life. *However*, she may also experience the incident much more sharply – every time she hears Martin's voice it may recall to her his patronizing snub; every time she hears him laugh at a joke in the school bar it may remind her of the occasion when she was the butt of his caustic humour; even a smile may bring back echoes of his smug and self-satisfied grin. She may begin to detach herself from people who appear to be close to Martin lest they are "in on the joke" against her. She may distance herself from things that remind her of the outdoor aspects of the training she had advocated because they recall her discomfort; she may even come to reject her original position herself as a means of self-protection. She may begin to mistrust her own fresh enthusiasms, not just in work settings, but in reading a new novel or watching a new television programme, and be wary of sharing them with others lest they become the focus of a similar mocking rebuttal. Here her wish to redress the intolerable aspects of Martin's insult by an adequate form of retaliation has become the focus of many of her other thoughts and possible actions. The difference between the two cases, which we might commonly describe as a difference in the *strength* of Judith's desire for revenge, in fact, as Moore (1996: 48; emphasis added) would argue, "actually consists in the extent to which that desire *acts as a focus for other thoughts and tendencies*, and colours them".

This everyday example – which reconstructs the problem of motivation as importantly relational and cultural rather than purely individual and psychological – gives us an idea, I think, of the potential power of the thought of Henri Bergson, which questions the appropriateness of the mechanistic thinking that often works behind the scenes of our most common assumptions, and indeed reverses the direction in which we commonly think – "thinking backwards", as Moore terms it, using the intellect against itself to reveal the power of what Bergson calls intuition, the body and the emotions offering a more genuine insight into the nature of reality than the symbolic representations through which the intellect works.

Almost without exception, the various accounts of motivation deployed in management literature, education and practice, whether "content", "process" or "expectancy" theories (see Laurie and Cherry 2001 for a summary of the approach), construct motivation as a commodity produced by some form of mental and emotional interest-based calculus. Maslow, for example, even in attempting to move beyond assumptions of economic man, merely incorporates social and spiritual dimensions into an expanded version of mechanistic economic thinking, reproducing bourgeois social values as essentialized determinants of action. In the "motivating machine" of expectancy theory, the result of the interaction of valency and expectancy is *force*. If selves were billiard balls, such mechanistic motivation theory might be appropriate, but selves are much more complex than this – for a start, they are fluid and emergent, multiplex, formed and re-formed in contexts, and self-reflexive. In other words, they can often decide whether to be motivated or not, and they can frequently choose what motivates them, regardless of whether circumstances are favourable or unfavourable. Of course, they are equally capable of being driven, unconsciously or consciously but without apparent option, by things that motivation theory would not recognize as motivators (as with our concept of revenge) and of being moved to be creative or inventive for no instrumental reason at all, other than the sheer joy of what Bergson calls creative involution. For Bergson, the different levels between the physical and the metaphysical are constantly crossed in both directions, rather than the lower levels setting the conditions of operation of the higher levels of the system or the higher levels controlling the lower levels, and it is the occasions of such interpenetrative crossings, which refocus and thus reorganize the hierarchy, that ought to be of interest (for a related discussion on physicality, causality and free will, see Searle 2001).

Of course, if selves are not fixed in the way that motivation theory assumes, these fluid selves are not particularly amenable to the sort of personality theory that lends itself to testing and scoring either. Anyone who completes such tests over a period knows that they become more difficult to answer the more reflexive and self-questioning we become and the more self-knowledge we acquire, and more than one answer would become equally credible over time. People experienced in using or responding to these tests can reproduce different profiles at will, and yet claim that they are not being entirely dishonest. Models of personality that feature the "big five" characteristics, sixteen personality factors, four dimensions in combination or similar lose the dynamic and multiplex quality of human identity which realizes itself in interaction with a changing world, and others in it, as a changing part of that changing world, acting on and in that changing world as a subject whose sovereignty and identity are always becoming, never fixed, as is the meaning and significance of the world itself. Mood or intuition may be more useful concepts than interest, or even emotion in the way it is often constructed in psychology; fluid desire more useful than motivation; organization or organizing focus than structure; (hermeneutic) invention than caused or learned responses in considering the patterns, choices, reproductions and eccentricities that constitute the phenomena that we label personality. Indeed, much of what we may discover through personality testing is about the discourse of the subject in modernity as reflected through particular technologies of the self rather than anything we might consider independently as constitutive of the "person" and of which human behaviour is merely symptomatic.

One problem of Western thought has been its inability to separate space and time; it is immensely difficult to talk about the one except to some degree in terms of the other. For Derrida, of course, this is a product of the sequencing and spatializing practices of writing, where the spatialization of inscription attempts to create a difference that could be rendered translatable across time. It could be argued that Zeno's paradoxes are only paradoxes because of the metaphorical shift implied in them; they are spatial paradoxes expressed in terms of time, and thus a product of the visual, frontally oriented thinking that has dominated Western thought. Bergson attempts to break the frame in several ways, especially through his interest in surprise and phenomena that cross levels of awareness. Another dimension of organizational life that has particularly suffered from spatialization and frontal thinking is that of culture. Culture is grounded in practice, and therefore always has to have a dynamic and creative aspect. Its distinctiveness arises from the ways in which the tensions between rules to govern and occasion action and spontaneous and often transgressive actions that occur in the world give rise both to varieties of the production of meaning and to new forms of social practice. Culture, approached from a Bergsonian rather than a functionalist point of view, would be about process, but *process-in-tension*. Like personality, it would not be seen as fixed, but with characteristics of fluidity and multiplicity as well as of order and stability. Culture, like desire, could then be seen as an outcome of collective processes of *social focal organization*, in which what is commonly regarded and measured instrumentally as the strength of culture, values and beliefs would be considered to be a result of continual refocusing of attention, rather than revalorization of cultural elements, within a meaningful yet ambiguous complex of the practical, social, symbolic, intellectual, intuitive and the embodied.

Following this line of Bergson's thought and enacting his method of thinking in an unaccustomed direction therefore has considerable implications for understanding organizational processes, including organization development and change, knowledge creation and diffusion, and innovative product development (Calori 2002; O'Shea 2002; Wood 2002). In what follows, I will sketch out some of the major themes in Bergson's thought before returning to consider how his treatment of change – a dominant and almost defining theme across his work – might be usefully incorporated into our thinking on organizational change.

Becoming Bergson: a historical stroll through Bergson's work

Henri Bergson was born in Paris in 1859. His musician father was a Polish Jew, and his Catholic Irish/English mother came from Doncaster in the north of England. Bergson travelled considerably from an early age, and spent time in Switzerland, France and England, where his mother lived until her death at the age of ninety-eight. Something of a youthful prodigy, educated at the Lycée Condorcet, when only seventeen he won an open competition for an original solution to a mathematical problem, and later in the same year he solved a further perplexing problem (which Pascal claimed to have solved but had left unpublished). Bergson went on to study at the École Normale Supérieure and the University of Paris from 1877 to 1881, subsequently working as a philosophy teacher in a succession of *lycées*. Some later commentators have considered his school course books to be important in the understanding of his overall philosophy (Hude 1989–1990; see Moore 1996 for a critique). In 1898, he became a professor at the École Normale Supérieure until he was appointed to the chair of philosophy at the Collège de France in 1900. He resigned in 1921 in order to dedicate himself to his writing on morality and religion and to his work in international relations and politics on behalf of the League of Nations. He was awarded the Nobel Prize for Literature in 1927. During this latter period, although he wrote only one book, *The Two Sources of Morality and Religion* (1932/1977), Bergson was something of a cult figure, and his charismatic and brilliantly delivered public lectures often attracted large crowds. Despite having become more attracted by his mother's Catholicism than by his Jewish heritage, and being offered the opportunity to be excused registration, Bergson identified himself as a Jew under the Vichy government in 1940 as a sign of solidarity with those being persecuted. In his will, he states, "I would have become a [Catholic] convert, had I not seen in preparation for years the formidable wave of anti-Semitism which is to break upon the world. I wanted to remain among those who tomorrow will be persecuted" (1937, quoted in Burwick and Douglass 1992: 6). So he did. Bergson died in 1941 at the age of 81, having stood for hours in a queue of Parisian Jews registering with the Nazi government and contracted bronchial pneumonia.

In his first major work, *Time and Free Will* (1889/1910), based on his doctoral thesis, Bergson argued that false problems about the will and its freedom have arisen from a false phenomenology of mental states that have been conceived in spatial terms. Bergson argued that human experience of real life is not as a succession of clearly demarcated conscious states, progressing along some imaginary line (from sorrow to happiness, for example), but rather a continuous flow in which these states interpenetrate and are often unclear, being capable of sustaining multiple perspectives. Bergson made the distinction between the analytical concept and the personal experience of time. While the physicist observes objects and events in succession, as time ticking away on the dial of a clock, which can be marked and measured accordingly, we are conscious of and experience time as *duration* – a constant flowing process, with no end points and beginnings, where sometimes those (usually pleasurable) hours seem to fly by as seconds and at others (think of that "Monday morning feeling") hang so heavily as to make a day seem as burdensome as a week. This inner experience is qualitative, heterogeneous, dynamic, unpredictable and non-linear – indeed, it *invents* time, as every moment brings with it something radically new (Mullarkey 1999a: 9). Bergson argued, against the mechanistic science and psychology which were dominant at the time, that "real time" is experienced as duration and apprehended by *intuition*, not through separate operations of instinct and the intellect, thus prioritizing intuition (but not completely rejecting intellect). While critics of his work suggest that Bergson did not satisfactorily show that intuition could work apart from intellect, this is not such a damaging critique, as Bergson's ontology is not one of either/or, and his dualisms are not exclusive; it is more important that the intellect could not work without intuition.

In *Matter and Memory* (1896/1991), perhaps his most dense and difficult work, Bergson argued that philosophical (and other) method needs to be developed according to the nature of its subject matter. What is good for philosophy may not be good for mathematics, for example, but this can be driven down to more local and empirical levels as method emerges from the grounding of intuition in experience. He develops the concept of the *image*, which, in contrast to the traditional distinction between objects and representations, can exist without being perceived. The body then becomes the centre of "virtual actions" that require pure perception – that is, we know they are there – but recognition (that is, giving them significance and meaning) requires memory. Habit-memory is the body repeating familiar action, but pure recollection is non-active, though it may occasion action. Memory produces different layers of states of consciousness, grounded in the image called the "body", which moves through planes of consciousness and self-consciousness between body and spirit, a "reaching up and down" (Moore 1996: 5). These ideas of the body as image and the transitions between planes of awareness emerge as the basis of some of Deleuze and Guattari's (1983, 1987) thought, including the *body-without-organs* and planes of intensity. In a series of short studies, Bergson explored examples of phenomena that involve crossing of the levels. *Laughter* (1900/1999) considers the breaking through of the mechanical into the social; 'The dream' (1901/1985) considers the working of the intellect, in divining clues, when dislocated from the purposes of reality construction; and 'Intellectual effort' (1902/1985) considers how memory and intellect work to produce the effort required to cross between one scale of consciousness to another – to instantiate images from ideas, or to generate intellectual schemes from images.

In *Introduction to Metaphysics* (1903/1998), Bergson moves on to explore whether there is a possibility of formulating a general position emerging from these more focused studies. He argued that it is intuition that offers direct access to the "real world" and therefore discovers truth rather than the analytical operations of the intellect, which too often get entangled in the factitious – the artificial world of false problems rather than the apprehension of pure process. Bergson at times in his work suggests that intuition is an aleatory phenomenon, related to moments of insight; at others, it is presented as the true method of philosophy, as "first philosophy" in contrast to intellect as the appropriate method of mathematics (Mullarkey 1999b). But here Bergson argues that intuition represents absolute knowledge, and distinguishes it from analysis, which offers relative knowledge. Bergson dismisses "dog-leg" approaches which are characteristic of analysis, which depends on taking a point of view outside either the object or our own inner experience, knowing the object only through ways of representing it which spatialize; the representation is always decentred relative to either the object or our experience of it, outside of either, and hence something is lost in the process. Analysis seeks to recapture this lost element by creating more points of view, relativizing representation, yet cannot escape the trap created by the process of detachment, the irony of disengagement from the object which it seeks to possess more fully. The sidestepping of the object by this analytical dog-leg consists of a systematic and reductionist simplification of the object's qualities in order to make them more manipulable in terms of already known categories – a movement of the object into a different space, which for Bergson is *translation*. Intuition, on the other hand, pursues not what can be made to seem familiar within the object, but that which is unique to it, and consequently may be inexpressible or unrepresentable. It is "knowable" only by the intuitive process of "intellectual sympathy", placing oneself within the object – or, as Deleuze might put it, *becoming-object* – in order to know it without expression, translation or representation. For Bergson, this is the truth of the object, accessed by a truer empiricism than the abstracted empiricism that is the obsession of representational analytical strategies. As Chia (1996: 209–211) points out, the influence of Bergson on deconstruction can be seen in the deconstructive commitment to destabilize representation, to open up symbolic closings, to release the play of the system in the interests of human emancipation – that is, emancipation from tyrannies of representation. But it would be inaccurate to say that Bergson sets his metaphysics directly against representation, and particularly metaphor, *per se*: while he calls for us to "dispense with symbols" (Bergson 1938/1992: 162, 230, 241; Mullarkey 1999b: 152), he also exhorts us to "use metaphors seriously" (Bergson 1972: 980). Metaphor is not some kind of peephole on reality, but should itself be fluid, embodying the processes of that reality. It is the use of symbol and metaphor in ways that arrest this fluidity to which Bergson objects – in a way that has resonances with Kristeva's distinction between the symbolic and the semiotic.

Bergson's next major work is perhaps his best known, as his shift toward metaphysics enabled him to consider directly the "big issues" of the day – evolution and relativity – on their own terms. The concept of *élan vital*, "vital/creative impulse" or "living energy", was developed in *Creative Evolution* (1907/1998). Bergson argued against both mechanist and finalist theories of evolution, the former breaking down the process into its parts, but being unable to account for the process itself which animates them – that is, the pro-creative force of life. Finalism works back from the present evolutionary state as the end point, but as a result cannot account for future development, just as it cannot adequately explain why this end point should be most appropriate over all other possible end points. As the human intellect has developed in the course of evolution as an instrument of survival, it comes to think, mimetically and inevitably, in geometrical or "spatializing" terms that are inadequate to grasp the ultimate living process. It is the creative urge, for Bergson, not the Darwinian concept of natural selection, nor the Lamarckian one of incremental progression, that is at the heart of evolution. As we have seen Bergson argue, intuition goes to the heart of "reality", and enables us to find living philosophical truth, beyond philosophical problems and paradoxes that are bound up with language and forms of representation. *Élan vital* is not to be thought of as a organismic or personal property, but as immaterial force, whose existence cannot be scientifically verified but is nevertheless implied by all scientific endeavour, and provides the imperative that continuously shapes all life. It is an intransitive urge towards "the constant elaboration of novel forms without end" (Ansell Pearson 1999: 157), a creative *in*volution as well as an evolution, in which evolution is inventive and has duration; it is a lived, continuing experience rather than a series of discrete events, enmeshed in transverse rather than simply linear relations. This concept here has much in common with Deleuze's understanding of fluid desire, and provides the basis of a non-Hegelian approach to desire (Brewis and Linstead 2000).

In *Duration and Simultaneity* (1921/1999), Bergson addresses Einstein's theory of relativity, from which he had distanced himself in 1911. Bergson had earlier argued that Einstein, in establishing relativity by identifying the difference between the observer's experience of phenomena, including time itself, according to different observations from different perspectives, was reproducing the carving up of flow into moments in a way that was foreign to that experience. In *Duration and Simultaneity*, Bergson argues that Einstein's theory is important in establishing relativity in order to break down the false absolutes of Newtonian science, but further that Einstein's shifting perspective actually implies the existence of pure motion, the inescapable flow of being in time. Einstein rejected Bergson's views, and Bergson was at the time widely regarded as having lost his public debate with Einstein, who felt there were serious flaws with Bergson's mathematics (Bergson himself became dissatisfied with this and felt he could not prove his theory mathematically, and declined to revise the volume further in the 1930s). Nevertheless, natural scientists have become increasingly drawn to Bergson in recent years as his ideas are close to those of the "new science" (Gunter 1969; Čapek 1971; Papanicolaou and Gunter 1987) and resonate with the insights of complexity theory, both of which have received almost faddish attention in the strategy and change management literature (Axelrod and Cohen 2001; Olson *et al.* 2001; Sanders 1998; Stacey 2001; Stacey *et al.* 2001).

After his debate with Einstein, Bergson's work received increasingly less attention. His last major work, *The Two Sources of Morality and Religion* (1932/1977), emphasizes how morality and religion arise from the social nature of humanity, and contains a remarkable last chapter foreseeing a world in the shadow of nuclear weapons which seems even more relevant and poignant in the wake of the attacks on the World Trade Center and the Pentagon. These essentially closed systems arise, paradoxically, out of an operation of the intellect in self-interest – ultimately the pursuit of *self*-interest returns us to the necessity of morality, while the intellectual pursuit of knowledge through science returns us to religion, a point that more recently natural scientists such as Paul Davies have made. They are thus not oppositional to intelligence, but, as Moore (1996: 130) notes, its antinomies, being a product of social intelligence rather than organismic instinct. In this work, Bergson argues that intuitive, mystical access to the divine or the sacred is what renders essentially static systems of religion and morality dynamic, making explicit the connection between empiricism and ethics running through his whole work, which Mullarkey (1999b: 3) argues is "an ethics of alterity fleshed out in empirical concerns".

In a late collection of his essays, including both early and later work, Bergson made some more sceptical remarks about the scope of metaphysics and the concerns of philosophy as being too "big" and on too grand and abstract a scale, and – not untypically – appears to distance himself from aspects of this middle-phase work, perhaps moving to a position that is closer to the one he held before *Introduction to Metaphysics* (Bergson 1938/1992: 1, cited in Moore 1996: xvii; Bergson 1938/1992: 135–136, cited in Moore 1996: 10). But of course, for Bergson such a position could never have been final, just a product of one of many Bergsons attempting to actualize a virtual Bergson, still becoming.

Bergson, change and organization

If he had turned his attention to it, how would Bergson, the philosopher of change, have seen organization? Almost certainly he would have seen it as a process, part of a system of apprehension of its object which changed the nature of the object and was therefore part of it. It could be thought of as a non-discursive conversation with the object which changes the participants. Here attempts to organize in terms of stopping the flow of process are deathly; they kill off that which is vital and urgent in process in order to stabilize it temporally and create, as a false problem, a situation where movement has to be reinscribed or reinserted into the system. But the simple opposition of a metaphysics of substance/presence to a metaphysics of change/process that sees organization as the antithesis of process is inadequate, as Chia notes, for "change implicates its other. That other is *organization*" (1999: 224). Chia argues that organization is not a fixed entity, with established patterns, but a "repetitive activity of ordering and patterning itself" which, we should add, is itself changed by the activity of its repetitive engagement with reality in flux. Organization, we could say, is at best a *tendency* and never a *state*. But if change implicates its other, then change must also be implicated *by* its other. Change must always to some degree be organized to be thinkable. We could not meaningfully preserve a concept of change without a differentiated concept of non-change or stability. Indeed, at an abstract level, the use of a term such as change is itself an attempt to stabilize change as a concept, as if change and non-change are differentiated as states, then the differentiation of objects associated with these states under different values of t is implied. In reality, of course, our *experience* tells us that things do not stay the same, and it is practically important and necessary for us to have some account of how things have changed or are changing in order to continue to recreate our social world. But the language that we use is even more problematic than Chia implies and may have the opposite effects to those intended. As Mullarkey (1999b) argues, if change is the fundamental quality that underpins human life, then philosophy itself cannot be exempt from this and must itself change. Accordingly, the concepts of philosophy, including metaphysics and including change itself, must change, and perhaps radically. From such a meta-perspective, it could be argued that not only do we not have adequate language *of* change (Chia 1999; Chia and King 2001) or *for* change (Ford and Ford 1994, 1995), but a better reflection of experience would be a language with no term for change at all, but which constantly reflected change as a condition in its other terms. As Bergson was aware, "language, as the instrument of the intellect, is a great deceiver" (Moore 1996: 141), as it alienates us from our own intuitive knowledge of our experience. Indeed, if change is a focal concern of all our activities and experience, naming it might have a decentring effect by setting bounds to it and creating areas of specialization and concentration: change management, change process consultancy, post-change impact assessments and readiness for change diagnoses, determining and forecasting rates of change. The problem here is exactly that which Bergson embodied in his work, as we have noted: the challenge not of thinking forwards from the concept (such as change) into experience, but of thinking backwards from experience and using the intellect against itself in the interests of intuition. Whereas Chia rightly notes that simply relaxing the controlling approaches to change in organizations that are currently dominant would produce change, and allow creative novelty to emerge, we need to bear in mind that organizations as social constructions still need some *organizing* if we are to sustain our social world in a recognizable form. The process, then, to borrow another of Bergson's concepts, might be seen as one of shifting tensions and relaxations, expansions and contractions, with organizing not as the opposite pole of the dualism to change, as its absolute other, but as a shifting qualitative relation between order and change which might at different times display more patterning than others, more evidence of environmental intervention than others, more creation and surprise than others.

Henri Bergson's invitation – RSVP

The difficulty of summarizing Bergson's complex and nuanced thought seems emphatic when we consider how we might *reply* to his work – to think (backwards) with Bergson, to think on from him, to combine his work with that of others, and to apply it to areas Bergson did not consider.

There are many possible Bergsons; indeed, he would expect new ones to arise constantly, and no one overarching system to contain them. He is accordingly often seen as the enemy of reason, and Berlin condemned him as advocating "the abandonment of rigorous critical standards and the substitution in their place of *casual emotional responses*" (Berlin 1935 cited in Mullarkey 1999a: 5, also p. 14n13; emphasis added). Yet despite the recognition in Bergson of the full importance of the non-formal and informal, simplification is not friendly to the quality of Bergson's ideas; precision and clarity, and indeed his insight, are as much in the style of his writing and the way in which he uses metaphor than in any content of the ideas which can be extracted and properly translated in précis as his writing embodies the flow of which he speaks, and translation can only attempt to fix this flow, however temporarily. One can only hope to respond and remain in motion. I hope, however, that this introduction gives sufficient indication of the power and continuing potential of Bergson's ideas to be reactualized, even a century after many of them were first instantiated, speaking to us with a voice still fresh and vibrant. My comments should be viewed as illustrations of how Bergson can be used in organization and management theory, taking their place among others already attempted, but also as an invitation to explore much further (Boje 2000; Calori 2002; Letiche 2000; O'Shea 2002; Wood 2002). Indeed, Bergson's work, consistent with his philosophy of change and motion, which did not fear self-contradiction, could itself be seen as a standing invitation to engage with and creatively evolve with it as we organize the actualization of the virtualities of our own accounts. As Bergson (1932/1977: 296) argued, "action on the move creates its own route, creates to a very great extent the conditions under which it is to be fulfilled, and thus baffles all calculation". In theory and in practice, we can have a hand in making our own luck, to create *casual organization theory* not as a programme, but as a quality of a field in motion. It is an invitation that continues to merit reply.

Note

1 Deleuze goes a step further in seeing his treatment of Bergson (and others) as an act of copulation, or "buggery" as he puts it, producing a monstrous progeny.

References

Note: References to Bergson give the date of the original French publication of the work, rather than the earliest translation, followed by the date of the English edition used.

Alexander, Ian W. (1957) *Bergson: Philosopher of Reflection*, London: Bowes & Bowes.
Ansell Pearson, Keith (1999) "Bergson and creative evolution/involution: exposing the transcendental illusion of organismic life", in John Mullarkey (ed.) *The New Bergson*, Manchester: Manchester University Press.
Axelrod, Robert and Cohen, Michael D. (2001) *Harnessing Complexity: Organizational Implications of a Scientific Frontier*, New York: Basic Books.
Bergson, Henri (1889/1910) *Time and Free Will: An Essay on the Immediate Data of Consciousness*, London: George Allen & Unwin.
Bergson, Henri (1896/1991) *Matter and Memory*, New York: Zone Books.
Bergson, Henri (1900/1999) *Laughter*, Los Angeles: Green Integer.
Bergson, Henri (1901/1985) "The dream" (Le Rêve), in *L'Energie spirituelle*, Paris: Presses Universitaires de France.
Bergson, Henri (1902/1985) "Intellectual effort" (L'Effort intellectuel), in *L'Energie spirituelle*, Paris: Presses Universitaires de France.
Bergson, Henri (1903/1998) *Introduction to Metaphysics*, Kila, MT: R. A. Kessinger Publishing.
Bergson, Henri (1907/1998) *Creative Evolution*, Mineola, NY: Dover.
Bergson, Henri (1921/1999) *Duration and Simultaneity, with Reference to Einstein's Theory*, Manchester: Clinamen Press.
Bergson, Henri (1932/1977) *The Two Sources of Morality and Religion*, Notre Dame, IN: University of Notre Dame Press.
Bergson, Henri (1938/1992) *The Creative Mind* (original French title *La Pensée et le mouvant: essais et conférences*), New York: Citadel Press.
Bergson, Henri (1972) *Mélanges*, ed. A. Robinet, Paris: Presses Universitaires de France.

216   Stephen Linstead

Bergson, Henri (1999) "A letter from Bergson to John Dewey", introduction by Ryu Jiseok, trans. John Mullarkey in John Mullarkey (ed.) *The New Bergson*, Manchester: Manchester University Press.

Berlin, Isaiah (1935) "Impressionist philosophy", *London Mercury* 32 (191): 489–490.

Boje, David M. (2000) "Phenomenal complexity theory and change at Disney: response to Letiche", *Journal of Organizational Change Management* 13 (6): 558–566.

Brewis, Joanna and Linstead, Stephen (2000) *Sex, Work and Sex Work*, London: Routledge.

Burwick, Frederick and Douglass, Paul (eds) (1992) *The Crisis in Modernism: Bergson and the Vitalist Controversy*, Cambridge: Cambridge University Press.

Calori, Roland (2002) "Organizational development and the ontology of creative dialectical evolution", *Organization* 9 (1): 126–151.

Čapek, Milič (1971) *Bergson and Modern Physics: A Re-interpretation and Re-evaluation*, Dordrecht: D. Reidel.

Carr, H. W. (1919) *Henri Bergson: The Philosophy of Change*, London and Edinburgh: T. C. and E. C. Jack.

Chia, Robert (1996) *Organizational Analysis as Deconstructive Practice*, Berlin: De Gruyter.

Chia, Robert (1999) "A 'rhizomic' model of organizational change and transformation: perspective from a metaphysics of change", *British Journal of Management* 10: 209–227.

Chia, Robert and King, Ian (2001) "The language of organization theory", in Robert Westwood and Stephen Linstead (eds) *The Language of Organization*, London: Sage.

Deleuze, Gilles (1988) *Bergsonism*, trans. Hugh Tomlinson and Barbara Habberjam, New York: Zone Books.

Deleuze, Gilles and Guattari, Félix (1983) *Anti-Oedipus: Capitalism and Schizophrenia*, London: Athlone.

Deleuze, Gilles and Guattari, Félix (1987) *A Thousand Plateaus: Capitalism and Schizophrenia 2*, London: Athlone.

Ford, Jeffrey D. and Ford, Laurie W. (1994) "Logics of identity, contradiction and attraction in change", *Academy of Management Review* 19 (4): 756–785.

Ford, Jeffrey D. and Ford, Laurie W. (1995) "The roles of conversations in producing intentional change", *Academy of Management Review* 20 (3): 541–570.

Griffin, David Ray, Cobb, John B. Jr, Ford, Marcus P. and Gunter, Peter A. Y. (1993) *Founders of Constructive Postmodern Philosophy: Pierce, James, Bergson, Whitehead and Hartshorne*, Albany, NY: SUNY Press.

Gunter, Peter A. Y. (1969) *Bergson and the Evolution of Physics*, Knoxville: University of Tennessee Press.

Hude, Henri (1989–1990) *Bergson I and II*, Paris: Éditions Universitaires.

Kolakowski, Leszek (1985) *Bergson*, Oxford: Oxford University Press.

Lacey, A. R. (1989) *Bergson*, London: Routledge.

Laurie, N. and Cherry, C. (2001) "Wanted: philosophy of management", *Reason in Practice* (now *Philosophy of Management*) 1 (1): 3–12.

Letiche, Hugo (2000) "Phenomenal complexity theory as informed by Bergson", *Journal of Organizational Change Management* 13 (6): 545–557.

Moore, F. C. T. (1996) *Bergson: Thinking Backwards*, Cambridge: Cambridge University Press.

Mullarkey, John (ed.) (1999a) *The New Bergson*, Manchester: Manchester University Press.

Mullarkey, John (1999b) *Bergson and Philosophy*, Edinburgh: Edinburgh University Press.

Olson, Edwin E., Eoyang, Glenda H., Beckhard, Richard and Vaill, Peter B. (2001) *Facilitating Organization Change: Lessons from Complexity Science*, New York: John Wiley.

O'Shea, Anthony (2002) "The (r)evolution of new product innovation", *Organization* 9 (1): 113–125.

Papanicolaou, A. C. and Gunter, P. A. Y. (eds) (1987) *Bergson and Modern Thought: Towards a Unified Science*, Chur, Switzerland: Harwood Academic Press.

Pilkington, A. E. (1976) *Bergson and His Influence: A Reassessment*, Cambridge: Cambridge University Press.

Rescher, Nicholas (1996) *Process Metaphysics: An Introduction to Process Philosophy*, Albany, NY: SUNY Press.

Russell, Bertrand (1914) *The Philosophy of Bergson*, London: Macmillan.

Sanders, T. Irene (1998) *Strategic Thinking and the New Science: Planning in the Midst of Chaos, Complexity, and Change*, New York: Simon & Schuster.

Searle, John (2001) "Free will as a problem in neurobiology", *Philosophy* 76 (298) (October): 491–514.

Sperber, Dan and Wilson, Deirdre (1981) "Irony and the use–mention distinction", in Peter Cole (ed.) *Radical Pragmatics*, New York: Academic Press.

Stacey, Ralph D. (2001) *Complex Responsive Processes in Organizations: Learning and Knowledge Creation*, London: Routledge.

Stacey, Ralph D., Griffin, Douglas and Shaw, Patricia (2001) *Complexity and Management: Fad or Radical Challenge?*, London: Routledge.

Wells, Stanley and Taylor, Gary (1987) *The Complete Oxford Shakespeare*, vol. 3, *Tragedies*, Oxford: Oxford University Press.

Wood, Martin (2002) "Mind the gap? A processual reconsideration of organizational knowledge", *Organization* 9 (1): 151–171.

13 The becoming of organization and the organization of becoming

Martin Brigham

Introduction

It is said that 'philosophy is the logic of multiplicities'.[1] It is the memory of this future that is examined in this chapter, with the intention not of being able to say a simple 'yes' or 'no' to multiplicity, but of being able to work through and beyond its limits. Multiplicity goes by many names, including becoming and difference, and is deployed as a philosophical concept and a basis for social and political contestation. This chapter is concerned with a philosophy and politics of becoming, multiplicity and difference set out in the works of Nietzsche and Bergson, and Deleuze's writings on Nietzsche and Bergson. In examining their approaches to the 'being of becoming', or what can be termed 'becoming human' and 'becoming organization', this chapter suggests that there are both resonances and common targets of criticism in these philosophers' projects. In order to grasp the kind of philosophical and political contribution Nietzsche, Bergson and Deleuze are concerned with, it is critical to understand that their abiding motivation is to disinter concepts of becoming, multiplicity and difference:[2] Nietzsche depicts active and reactive forces, Bergson sets out qualitative and quantitative differences, and Deleuze refigures Nietzsche and Bergson into virtual and actual multiplicities.[3] It is this privileging of becoming as active force, qualitative difference and virtual multiplicity in conjunction with an alleged dismissive opposition to socio-cultural phenomena as expressions of negativity and delimitation that constitutes the basis for the denigration of these philosophers' ideas.

It is helpful to orientate Nietzsche, Bergson and Deleuze within recent social science theorizing. Nietzsche has been a critical influence on postmodern thought in the study of organizations (Cooper and Burrell 1988) and in the problematization of long-held principles of moral and political philosophy (Ansell Pearson 1991, 1997a; May 1999; Patton 1993). Similarly, Bergson is currently deployed as an alternative approach to organizational change (Chia 1998, 1999, 2003), to reconfiguring the ontological status of organizations (Letiche 2000; Linstead 2002) and the human condition (Ansell Pearson 2002; Mullarkey 1999a, b; Watson 1998). Deleuze is now an influential philosopher (Ansell Pearson 1997a, b, 1999; Deleuze 1988; Grosz 1999; Patton 1996, 2000), cited across studies of science and technology (Law 2002; Latour 1999) and organization theory (Burrell and Dale 2002; Cooper 1998; Jackson and Carter 2000).

It is also useful to situate being and becoming as invoking political and cultural debates that conjoin and intersect with philosophical concerns. 'Becoming human' or 'becoming organization' is not only a philosophical question, as 'becoming' is currently deployed into management thinking and policy initiatives that signal a shift from Fordism to the 'new times' of the knowledge economy (see, for example, Giddens 2001). Harvey (1989) describes Fordism as a political and economic management strategy that comprised standardized manufacturing and mass consumption and gained increased momentum in the reconstruction of Western economies after the Second World War (see also Lee 2001: 7–20). In achieving mass production, Tayloristic principles enabled organizations to achieve significant economies of scale, but in order to connect political and economic policy to 'being' and 'becoming', Fordism must be understood as much more than an approach to economic and manufacturing management. It is rather, as Harvey (1989: 135) remarks, 'a total way of life', in which the 'image of standard adulthood was supported by specific patterns in the organization of people's working lives and in the organization of their intimate relationships' (Lee 2001: 10). It is in this sense that aligning the political and economic management of a national economy and individuals' public and private aspirations can be understood as constructing Fordist stability as 'being'. This 'way of life' comprised large and stable organizations providing long-term employment, 'jobs for life', internal career progression and relatively well-delineated career paths. It is constitutively supported by intimate relationships characterized by lifelong marriages, strict divisions between men as the principal bread-winners and domestic labour done by women, and between adults and children. The adult is the 'human being', who should be 'stable, complete, self-possessed and self-controlling', and in the child 'human becoming' in contrast is 'changeable and incomplete and lacks the self-possession and self-control' (ibid.: 5).

Harvey (1989) sets out how Fordism's advantages of stability were problematized in the early 1970s with the over-supply of goods contributing to recessionary tendencies, competition from low-cost manufacturing economies in South-East Asia and an incremental approach to investment and innovation associated with creating institutional rigidities. In Harvey's terms, the shift from Fordism as 'human being' to post-Fordism as 'human becoming' comprises a turn to 'the idea that business has to become more knowledgeable in a turbulent and constantly fluctuating world' (Thrift 1997: 30) and to a generalized indeterminacy in analysing cultural phenomena. But similarly, this is more than a business strategy for competitive advantage. It marks out another way of life, with, for example, equivalences between 'human becoming' and lifelong learning, 'boundaryless' careers with atypical employment patterns (see Heelas 1996), 'workplace becoming' as continual innovation that 'reinvents the corporation' (Brown 1991), and 'organizational becoming' as the unravelling of classical forms of organizational structure into 'virtual organizations' that consolidate organizational and individual flexibility and short-term management strategies (see Ackroyd 2002). For these new times of restructuring capitalism, management and ownership of creativity and innovation, and the dissolution of existing organizational boundaries *qua* becoming, are the new knowledge economy asset. As a 'way of life', human becoming similarly supports adulthood around particular notions of flexibility in which, for instance, intimate relationships are continuous for as long as both partners consider this appropriate, and relationships are subject to ongoing renegotiation (see Lee 2001). Despite the liberatory rhetoric of the individual or organization freed from social and historical legacies, there are distinctly 'hard edges' to such open-ended conceptions of the human subject and organization. Thrift (1997) suggests that not only are existing capacities and protections challenged, but conceptions and comportments of becoming are narrowly framed, and associated with only certain activities. Such one-dimensional conceptions can be partly explained by the under-theorized connections between politics and philosophical concepts of becoming, and partly occur because even 'notions of radical indeterminacy can be turned to all manner of ends, not all of which are pure or pleasant' (ibid.: 51). How then to account for 'becoming' as the stuff of life, so to speak, when its meaning is converted into a strategy of competitive advantage in the knowledge economy?

In order to respecify philosophical and political thinking in relation to the human subject and organization, this chapter is organized into five sections. The next section sets out being and becoming within philosophical debates and delineates the relations between being and becoming into a typology of nihilism. The argument that is introduced is that the condition for re-evaluating socio-historical assumptions of human subjects, organizations and cultural phenomena generally involves not so much a critical working against some*thing* as a genealogical articulation that is *through and beyond* relational effects. The second and third sections introduce Nietzsche and Bergson respectively, elaborating how each constructs becoming, difference and multiplicity as the 'ground' of the human condition. This provides the basis for the fourth section, which examines in more detail how Nietzsche, Bergson and Deleuze cannot be reduced to being against pre-existing notions of the human subject or enduring forms of organization as such, but rather are much more nuanced in approach. It is rather the limits and consequences of particular forms of multiplicity and the associated implications for evaluation that are the crucial issue for Nietzsche, Bergson and Deleuze. It is contended that 'becoming human' and 'becoming organization' are not reducible to social or historical legacies, although such becomings are constitutively implicated in re-evaluations of the cultural, technical, natural, psychological and historical. The conclusion takes up the implications of the impossibility of a simple choice between humans as possessive or relational selves (see Lee and Brown 2002) and approaches to organization as distal or proximal (see Cooper and Law 1995) by proposing the concept of assemblage and technico-affective relationality as both critical and creative for thinking organization, philosophically and politically.

Being and becoming and a typology of nihilism

Philosophers of becoming, multiplicity and difference are interested in problematizing the metaphysical tradition that runs through Western philosophical thinking. This treats being and identity as primary, and becoming and difference as derivative or secondary. It constitutes, Patton (2000) suggests, a moral vision of the world that privileges stability, organization and hierarchical relations.[4] Beardsworth (2001) sets out how this dominant metaphysical tradition involves splitting the world into 'two worlds, two instances, two principles'. For Beardsworth, the proposition of two worlds is a life-denying 'metaphysical nihilism' that is premised upon a divide between the transcendental–disembodied–abstracted and the empirical–embodied–lived. Such schemas and evaluations are nihilistic from the first instance, says Beardsworth, because they are concerned with getting away from our 'mean little world' (see also Nietzsche 1968) of becoming human. Attempting to challenge this must mean attempting to unravel the historical hierarchy between being and becoming, and articulating a philosophy of becoming, but it also means not lapsing into a second form of nihilism. This second type of nihilism is associated with the first in the sense that it is bound up with the realization that the metaphysical categories important to the history of Western thinking (unchanging being, discrete causalities, etc.) are no longer so convincing. This is, then, the 'all too human' shock that metaphysical categories do not articulate the world or have formal objective status. Beardsworth (2001) terms this 'passive nihilism' as a sense of an exhausted world with no meaning and a human spirit that motivates questions phrased as 'so what!' or 'what for?'. It is, in other words, a nihilism that accompanies the disorientation and distress felt by the loss of a simplified metaphysical world of being and unity.

For Nietzsche, Bergson, Deleuze and others, these life-denying forms of nihilism invoke the moment of philosophy's stillness and the simultaneous clarion call to work through and beyond these nihilisms in order to reclaim the future for humankind as a becoming human. Beardsworth's (2001: 38) typology, which draws on Nietzsche for inspiration, terms this 'active nihilism'. This is a search for an alternative to metaphysical beliefs through the re-evaluation of metaphysical schemas, which are nihilistic from the beginning, *and* the banalities of passive nihilism, which is a response to the loss of these metaphysical certainties. Beardsworth (2001: 40) suggests that active nihilism marks out a way of thinking of the 'complexity of the "now" ... as an immanent relation between "genealogy", "energetics" and "ethics"'. It denotes the task of philosophy and politics in general and the human subject in particular of becoming more than it is *through and beyond* present categories of thought and their simple repudiation. It is, specifically, an approach to the genealogical character of the present set in motion by assemblages of, for instance, economic-administrative rationality, techno-scientific practice that attempts to overcome tendencies towards metaphysical and passive nihilism.

The connection between philosophical and political activity becomes clearer with this typology because what is at stake is an examination of the constitution and justification of the state of contemporary thought in relation to the human subject, organization and cultural forms which are 'matters that concern the community as a whole' (Ansell Pearson 1991: xii). It is, then, to the conditions and characteristics of these challenges, their implications and responses that this chapter is concerned. It is also concerned with the inadequacies of invoking an inversion of the hierarchy between being and becoming on the basis that inversion does not alter the relation between elements nor changes the nature of those elements. 'You do not do it with a sledgehammer, you use a very fine file', Deleuze and Guattari (1988: 160–161) caution; 'we are in a social formation; first see how it is stratified for us and in us and at the place where we are'. The intention here is not, then, so much to straightforwardly discard or topple pre-existing cultural identities, the human subject or the status of organization, but to evaluate each of them in a particular way by examining how they are constituted and what forms they take (see Patton 2000: 29).

Deleuze and Guattari (1988, 1994) provide a way into thinking about becoming human and becoming organization as through and beyond some kind of search for original being or identity. Their philosophical task is to cease treating becoming or multiplicity 'as a numerical fragment of a lost Unity or Totality or as the organic element of a Unity or Totality yet to come, and instead distinguish between different types of multiplicity' and to work through the ontological, political and ethical implications of this by distinguishing 'between different types of multiplicity' (Deleuze and Guattari 1988: 32). This means that the task of philosophy and politics is the construction of 'a non-contradictory, non-dialectical consideration of difference, which would not envisage it as the simple contrary to identity, nor be obliged to see itself as "dialectically" identical with identity' (Descombes 1980: 136 quoted in Patton 2000: 31). Deleuze and Guattari's lifelong concern was, in other words, to think of becoming, multiplicity and difference in ways that do not refer back to an a priori identity or the fantasy of a future unified identity. In order to articulate a conceptual framework of becoming, they draw upon inspiration from Nietzsche and Bergson, and it is to these philosophers that the following two sections are concerned.

Active and reactive forces and the will to power

Nietzsche (1968, 1994) sets out the cultural battle between different modes of evaluation in a post-theological age in terms of active and reactive forces or noble and slave moralities. In order to theorize what he considers the necessity of a new myth that can form the basis of a new politics, morality and ethics for the human condition (see Safranski 2002), Nietzsche (1994: 21–27) discerns forces as either 'active' or 'reactive'. The difference between active and reactive forces is that

> In order to come about, slave morality [reactive force] first has to have an opposing, external world, it needs, physiologically speaking, external stimuli in order to act at all, – its action is fundamentally reaction. The opposite is the case with the noble method of evaluation: this [active force] acts and grows spontaneously.
>
> (ibid.: 21–22)

Beardsworth (2001: 45) writes that, for Nietzsche, 'what is good is originally what is noble, that is, what discharges spontaneously, what is oriented towards the outside. The bad [that is, the reactive] in this schema constitutes that which blocks the path of this original affirmation'. In Deleuze's (1983) reformulation of Nietzsche, forces come in many forms: social, psychical, moral, biological, political, to name a few. These forces are relational in that they denote the potential for affecting others and being affected,[5] and here the concept of force is close to 'power' as a 'capacity' to do or be certain things, and denotes an important aspect of force as power as nothing inherently objectionable.[6] Deleuze (1983) thus delineates Nietzsche's active forces as affirming and producing differences and, in distinction, reactive forces as negating and denying difference. It is the active that is the nature of things and that confronts the human subject as becoming rather than the force of the reactive conceived as identity. Reactive forces are, then, expressions of forces of 'adaptation, regulation and conservation', whereas active forces comprise the power of transformation and the ability to 'impose forms onto the world' (see Patton 2000: 60). In Nietzsche's terms, reactive forces occur when an *effect* of a force is understood as a *cause*.

The transformation of capacities through active forces is described by Deleuze and Guattari (1988) in terms of becoming and is illustrated by the mutual transformation afforded by the well-known example of the wasp and the orchid. This 'double capture' of forces of one assemblage by another illustrates how capacities undergo transformation through a relation that does not, according to Patton (2000: 54), occur through dialectical change, as change does not necessarily take place by weakening another. Deleuze and Parnet (1987: 2) write:

> The orchid seems to form a wasp-image, but in fact there is a wasp-becoming of the orchid, an orchid becoming of the wasp, a double

capture since 'what' each becomes changes no less than 'that which' becomes. The wasp becomes part of the orchid's reproductive apparatus at the same time as the orchid becomes the sexual organ of the wasp.

It is because of the becoming-wasp-of-the-orchid that active forces are associated with another key Nietzschean concept: that is, the 'will to power'. For Nietzsche, the will to power, which is internally divided between active and reactive forces, gives priority to the expansive character of active force because this is *the* immanent principle through which the human condition is to be conceived, rather than one power among others. Yet contrary to much traditional political thought (e.g. Hobbes' *Leviathan*), which equates power with domination, Nietzsche's will to power as a form of power 'refuses any perspective according to which the fundamental drive is to preserve or to increase the power of the body concerned' (Patton 2000: 50). The will to power is, then, not about discharging energy in order to reach some kind of teleological end point or aimed at acquiring power to dominate others, but rather the discharging of energy itself.[7] 'Force here assumes a very broad sense which has no necessary connection to violence', although in particular contexts there will be an uneven distribution of capacities, so that, for instance, 'the law may prevail over racially discriminatory public opinion; in another, public opinion may force politicians to override the rule of law. In this sense, a certain stable or precarious but always reversible balance of forces will be established' (Patton 2000: 52).[8]

It is Nietzsche's exposition of active and reactive forces that Cooper and Burrell (1988) suggest is so instructive for rethinking organization analysis.[9] Cooper and Burrell (ibid.: 92–93) trace the historical displacement of the 'object of organizational analysis' from 'a process in the continuing mastery of the social and physical environment' to 'organization as a quasi-stable collection of things or properties'. This distinction between active forces as superior, a 'kind of prime energizer' from which the human emerges and acts, is counterposed to the inferior or reactive force that is representation and 'talking about' or representing some*thing*. It is these reactive forces that constitute a search for pure and ideal forms that pre-date the everyday world. Cooper and Burrell (ibid.: 101) continue, 'what we find at the so-called origin of things is not a reassuring state of perfection, now lost but still reclaimable; instead there is disparity, difference and indeterminacy'. The claim of perfect origins is replaced with a 'search for instabilities' that is a process of 'differential contestation'.

Deleuze (1983) argues that Nietzsche's philosophical project is marked out by a re-evaluation of the values of cultural phenomena and that it is the 'qualitative dimension of the will to power' as the expression of active forces that constitutes the potential for a genealogical re-evaluation of the present. Put simply, difference, as active force, is the 'ground of being' of becoming, and this posits an ethical position and normative stance. It is in this critical and creative sense, then, that normative values can be articulated against the particular quality of the will to power deployed, as either active or reactive, in a particular context (Patton 2000: 60). Here Nietzsche, who is often regarded as the seer of postmodernism and equated with the contention that all perspectives are somehow equivalent, rejects out of hand the claim that all truth claims are subjective to the extent that it is the quality and mixture of forces that is taken as the basis for evaluation. The surrogate for truth and hope articulated by Nietzsche, in contrast to liberal versions of post-modernism and conventions of critical thinking, resides not, then, in the human subject or the organization as such, but in the approach to them and the implications that are then drawn:

> [T]his is not the moral form of critique which judges against what should be, rather it is a genealogical critique which judges what is by determining the quality of the forces present and their affinity with one or other character of the will to power. The result is a complex and nuanced system of judgement.
>
> (Patton 2000: 62–63)

This confrontation with becoming as active force denotes an engagement with a particular relation and quality that Nietzsche wishes to privilege 'so that it can say "yes" to itself even more thankfully and exultantly' (1994: 22). Nietzsche describes this selective concept of being as becoming as the 'eternal return' of the different. In Deleuze's (1983: 48) terms, this means that it is returning itself 'that constitutes being in so far as it is affirmed of becoming . . . identity in the eternal return does not describe the nature of that which returns, but, on the contrary, the fact of returning for that which differs'. In this sense, evaluations reflect the quality of forces, either active or reactive, and can be judged normatively through the quality of forces deployed.[10] This does not mean, however, that reactive forces do not return, but

> rather their returning involves a becoming-active. . . . The eternal return of reactive forces involves a contradiction; reactive forces cannot return, where returning names the being of becoming, simply because they have not begun to leave themselves, they want to remain what they are.
>
> (Ansell Pearson 2000: 201)

This privileging of the quality of active force is, then, premised on a partisan concept of being as a becoming human and, as Patton (2000: 65) observes, is no less moral in its consequences than the dominant traditions of Western philosophy that privilege being as unchanging identity.

Quantitative and qualitative multiplicities and *durée*

Bergson (1983, 1991, 2000) is similarly interested in re-evaluating the philosophy and politics of being and becoming through multiplicity and

difference (see also Ansell Pearson and Mullarkey 2002).[11] Bergson's philosophy is premised on the proposition that the life-world cannot be characterized as Cartesian, but rather is characterized by the inseparability of the
mind, body and world (see, for example, Bergson 1991). This forms the
basis of his connectionist proposition of the absolute continuity or immanence, which Deleuze and Guattari (1994) term 'the plane of immanence',
between the human subject and matter. There are, for Bergson, only differences in degree between human perception and the heterogeneity of
matter.[12]

Bergson (1991: 9–10) suggests that philosophy often gets into difficulties
because of concepts associated with matter. The reduction of matter to perception is a mistake, as is the idea that matter can produce perceptions. For
Bergson, matter is described as

> an aggregate of 'images'. And by 'image' we mean a certain existence
> which is more than that which the idealist calls a representation, but
> less than that which the realist calls a thing – an existence placed
> halfway between the 'thing' and the 'representation'.... It would
> greatly astonish a man unaware of the speculations of philosophy if we
> told him that the object before him, which he sees and touches, exists
> only in his mind and for his mind or even, more generally, exists only
> for mind ... on the other hand, we should astonish him quite as much
> by telling him that the object is entirely different from that which is
> perceived in it, that it has neither the colour ascribed to it by the eye
> nor the resistance found in it by hand.

These classical antinomies relating to representations and matter are problematic for Bergson as they are either 'now idealistic' or 'now realistic'. They
are 'badly analysed composites', in Deleuze's (1988: 28) terms, to which the
appropriate response is not an attempt to resolve the problematic they set
up, but to do something different with its mutual disappointments.[13] From
the assumptions of monism and immanence, Bergson argues that human
consciousness is not representational. Rather, the 'qualities of the world that
we experience are not the qualities of miniature representations inside our
heads ... they are qualities of the world itself' (Watson 1998: 6), and thus
perception puts the human subject into matter not external to it (see
Deleuze 1988: 25). The interpenetrating relation of perception and matter is
central to Bergson's philosophical approach because it is the selection of
'matter forces' appropriate to the requirement for practical action that constitutes a 'cerebral volume' or 'zone of indeterminism'. It is this 'zone of
indeterminism' for Bergson that denotes the potential of ethical evaluation
and becoming human, although this indeterminacy cannot be conceived
outside of what he terms *durée*, which is a relation of matter and a memory
in which memory cannot be reduced to psychological recollection.

Bergson's difficult concept of *durée* is his response to the dissatisfactions of idealism and realism. *Durée* is articulated through the distinction between temporality as *temps*, which is time understood in spatial terms – that is to say, time as chronological, abstract and concerned with quantity and size.[14] Time as *temps* is a pragmatic resource in Bergson's terms where what is perceived is what is necessary for calculative action and from which embodied experience is missing. Time as *durée*, in contrast, is qualitative and embodied, and thus does not comprise the putting together of discrete units of time. Bergson (1991) argues that time as *temps* is incapable of grasping the real facts of time and that it is in fact more a manner of speaking than the reality of temporal experience. Time as *durée* is an indivisible limit between past, present and future that is made up of sensual and embodied experience from which time as a series of quantitative moments is plucked (see Chia 1999: 216).[15] *Durée* is an ever-changing process of differences in kind without beginning and end from which the heterogeneity that is the ground of becoming human is actualized in perception. It invokes, then, a permeating flow of activity that is 'above the turn' of the human condition's tendency to utilitarian thought and action. It is in this sense that Bergson's *durée* as multiplicity echoes Nietzsche's eternal return as the being of becoming.

Bergson's elaboration of quantitative and qualitative difference provides another way of approaching time as spatial extension (i.e. discrete past, present and future) and time as *durée*. Spatialized temporality is equated with quantitative differences or differences in degree between perception and matter, and time as *durée* with qualitative differences or differences in kind between matter and memory.[16] In positing differences in degree as relations of matter and perception and differences in kind as relations of matter and memory, Bergson and Deleuze have a very particular concept of memory, which is memory as *durée* or, put another way, as a virtual multiplicity that is a heterogeneity that has its own particular ontological status.[17] The critical and creative concern here is to reformulate the contemporary understanding of time so that becoming human is *of* time rather than *in* time, a concern similarly articulated by Nietzsche's eternal return of difference. In this important sense, Grosz, writing about Nietzsche, Bergson and Deleuze, says that each 'conceptualises time as becoming, as an opening up which is at the same time a form of bifurcation or divergence. Each conceives of *time* as *difference*' (Grosz 1999: 3–4).

Perception or consciousness occurs for Bergson when particular aspects of the world are selected or 'actualized' that are relevant to the human condition.[18] Deleuze (1988: 25) writes that from this 'cerebral interval, in effect, a being can retain from the material object and the actions issuing from it those elements that interest him . . . [but] it is not an object plus something, but the object minus something, minus everything that does not interest us'. This 'minus everything' is the virtual multiplicity that nevertheless remains real as the 'totality of impressions, impulses, sensations, possible actions and utterances . . . [in fact] our body is awash with forces that never quite make it to consciousness' but nonetheless affect our behaviour in concrete ways as the 'virtual field of energy traversing and binding the connectivity of the social . . . that is immanent to this non-human fabric of the "virtual"' (Watson 1998: 7–8). Bergson's target here is to problematize a psychological conception of memory which Ansell Pearson (2002: 167–205) elaborates as an attempt to think memory as an ontology of difference. This entails an enlargement of perception in order to make visible 'forces that are ordinarily imperceptible. Although invisible forces – molecular affections and perceptions – are not time they are intertwined with its passages, intervals, echoes, and tunnels' (Deleuze 1998: 72 quoted in Ansell Pearson 2002: 171). For Bergson, reducing the past to psychological recollection corrupts 'the past' because it renders an ontology of the past as a virtual multiplicity inoperative.[19]

Developing an ontology of the virtual that overcomes the problems Bergson associates with psychological recollection therefore requires the dispelling of a number of illusions, a crucial 'one being that memory only comes into being once an actual perception has taken place' (Ansell Pearson 2002: 174). In other words, the illusion is that the past only comes into being once it has been retrospectively constituted in the present. Memory conceived as differences in degree is here a diminished conception of memory that cannot go beyond psychological recollection, because 'the difference between perception and memory is simply one of intensity or degree, in which the remembrance of a perception is held to be nothing other than the same perception in a weakened state' (ibid.: 175). Perception requires the 'powers afforded by memory', which means granting an ontology to memory – that is to say, its own particular being, which comprises differences in kind that mark out becoming human. For Nietzsche, the identity of what returns eternally is not prescribed in advance because it is the returning of time, not something in time – that is to say, the time of virtual multiplicity that returns.

Ansell Pearson (2002: 179) continues that Bergson gives the being of the past 'an extra-psychological range', and that 'which is not actually lived and no longer active may cease to belong to consciousness without thereby ceasing to exist' (for example, an object that does not cease to exist just because perception of it ceases). This means that the human condition is one through which we do not simply live the past again through better or worse recollections (with, say, more comprehensive archives); that is, 'it is not a question of rendering actual what is simply virtual and making the two identical', because 'being is always of the order of difference' and memory is a virtual multiplicity that is 'a movement of differences and time' which by its nature denotes the impossibility of equivalence between the virtual and the actual (ibid.: 176).[20] It is with this conceptual move to problematize memory as psychological recollection that Bergson and Deleuze invoke memory as the ontological ground of difference and change as the movement of differences in kind that do not refer back to a priori identities. The implication of this is that if the virtual, as an immanent ontological totality of the past, is not a former present, then this begets a future that is not simply a future of the present: to think in terms of the ontology of the virtual is constitutive of Bergson's motivation to construct an approach that works beyond what he considers the pragmatic and utilitarian tendencies of the human condition.[21] In other words, with memory conceived as an ontology of difference rather than a psychological recollection, the critical and creative task that sustains Bergson, but also Nietzsche and Deleuze, is made clear: to salvage the human condition from determinism and redeem contingency for the future through the heterogeneity of the virtual.

It is becoming, divergence or 'difference differing' that is the key to understanding how and why Deleuze takes up and extends Bergson's ideas and how this conjoins with his concern with Nietzsche's notion of active and reactive forces. Deleuze (1994: 40–41) writes that the condition of a virtual ontology can 'be satisfied only at the price of a more general categorical reversal according to which being is said of becoming, identity of that which is different'. Instead of the dominant Western philosophical tradition of being first and becoming second, being is associated with a second principle that revolves around difference differing. For Deleuze, this amounts to nothing less than the fourth blow to the human subject after the Copernican, Darwinian and Freudian revolutions. Difference now has its own ontological status from which being is constituted of becoming: multiplicity is no longer conceived as an adjective.

Purifications, mediations and transformations

Nietzsche, Bergson and Deleuze share, I have suggested, a concern with a philosophy and politics of becoming, multiplicity and difference. Given this, it is not surprising to find that they have been subject to similar criticism: Nietzsche for reducing the human condition to the discharging of biological or individual 'instinctual' forces (see Lash 1990), Bergson for positing a subjective or religious-cum-mystical notion of *durée* (see Game 1997) and Deleuze for deploying becoming as 'pure' difference (see Badiou 2000). The general critique of their concepts is that a dichotomy is posited between force, memory or difference as a priori and social, political and historical formations as epiphenomenal; that is to say, they reverse the dominant tradition of being and becoming but leave its general hierarchy intact. Engaging with these critical comments means setting out how the relationship between active and reactive forces, memory and perception, and virtual and actual is more nuanced and complex than is often portrayed, and it also means 'overcoming lazy and self-satisfied appraisals' of concepts which 'guarantee only sad encounters are produced' (Ansell Pearson 2002: 8).

Nietzsche has been associated with attempting to construct a human subject that expresses active forces in an unabashed fashion above 'man and mountains'. Beardsworth is similarly concerned with the potential re-enactment of a dichotomy between active and reactive forces, with active forces becoming a new orthodoxy of forces outside cultural and historical differentiations. For Beardsworth (2001: 47), the focus on active force means risking 'a move back to the "original" valuation, the original noble valuation. At such moments the active destruction of metaphysics ("active nihilism") becomes a pure regression to the fiction of spontaneous discharge'. In response to such claims, Ansell Pearson (1991: 120) argues that, for Nietzsche, the categories that produce the human subject, cultural forms, and so on come out of an ordering that does not precede the world in a straightforward sense and cannot be demarcated into an a priori distinction of nature and culture.

Contra critical theorists such as Habermas, who claims that Nietzsche posits a primary and ahistorical nature, it is the eighteenth-century French Enlightenment thinker Rousseau rather than Nietzsche who betrays a desire that 'represents a search for origins which will validate the "original" in history as being more authentic because it is, in some fundamental sense, more "natural"' (Ansell Pearson 1991: 120). It is, he continues, Rousseau who endows human subjects with a natural and individualistic goodness in which the ambition of society can only be realized by the free choice of individuals who decide to join society and submit to its rules and regulations. Despite 'man's natural goodness', then, the lack of a higher moral society requires careful cultivation in order to be brought into existence. For Lee (2001), who examines being and becoming in terms of the politics of childhood, the dichotomy between natural goodness and potential higher morality in civil society is the Enlightenment expression of the gift of free will to humankind from god. Here human becoming occurs between the good but incomplete nature and the education of the human into a moral being. In this sense, 'Rousseau's mythic "nature" does its work before the work of culture, cultivation and education, and abandons the scene before socialization begins. If culture is the supplement to nature, then culture and nature would seem to work at different times' (Lee 2001: 112). For Rousseau, human becoming, and thus the possibility for good and bad free will, is delimited to the space and time between nature and culture rather than out of the mediations between nature and culture.

Yet as Ansell Pearson (1991) remarks, Rousseau's solution to the problem that all societies face – that is, determining what is natural and cultural and where human becoming takes place – remains more ambiguous than it might seem at first glance because Rousseau writes that a state of nature 'no longer exists, perhaps never did exist, and probably never will exist' (quoted in Ansell Pearson 1991: 55). Rather, Rousseau's state of nature, Ansell Pearson continues, is conceived in philosophical terms as a 'legal fiction' *and* as an actual historical condition that precedes civil society. By contrast, Nietzsche's genealogical approach, as a history of the present, comprises no such ambiguity, as 'only that which has no history can be defined' (ibid.: 56). Here the human condition cannot be rendered into an a priori division between the incompleteness of nature and the completing role of culture.

Rather, the particularity of the human subject is constituted by incorporations and interdependencies that construct the potential to act and be acted upon through assemblages that extend, supplement and delimit the human subject's capacities to discharge, defer and transform effects (see Nietzsche 1994: 38–40).

Bergson has similarly been charged with reducing the human condition to lived experience and psychological subjectivism, particularly with an alleged 'mysterious' notion of *durée* (Game 1997). Although the contention of psychologism is more warranted in earlier writing, says Deleuze (1989: 82–83; emphasis added),

> increasingly, he came to say something quite different: the only subjectivity is *time*, non-chronological time, grasped in its foundation, and it is we who are internal to this time, not the other way round. . . . Time is not interior to us, but just the opposite, the interiority in which we are, in which we move, live, and change.
>
> (quoted by Ansell Pearson 2002: 184)

Put another way, the human subject cannot be assumed to be a priori given or 'ready to hand' even to itself; rather, there is a temporality of becoming human or becoming organization that is an immanent virtual multiplicity. For Bergson in particular, I have suggested that this virtual multiplicity means going beyond the inadequacies of perception and recollection. But, importantly, this 'enlargement of reality' is not transcendent to the human, but rather an opening up to the immanence or continuity of becoming human with virtual multiplicity.

Bergson and Deleuze articulate this immanence through the pairings of 'virtual and actual' and 'possible and real', with the distinction between virtual and actual understood as *durée* and *temps* respectively, and the virtual and actual made distinct, in turn, from the possible and the real. The virtual and actual means, most simply, contesting the proposition that for something to be real it must be made up of a preceding possibility. In place of this, says Ansell Pearson (2000), constructing the 'radically new' necessitates the recognition that even possibility is constructed. This is why for Deleuze (1994) there is such a grave danger in confusing the virtual and the possible. The realization of the possible comprises resemblance (i.e. a good or bad copy) and limitation (i.e. the narrowing of possibilities), and this makes the relation of the possible and the real one of conceptual equivalence (see Deleuze 1994). Here the possible is 'both more and less than the real. It is more, insofar as the real selects from a number of pre-existing possibilities. . . . But it is also less, insofar as the possible is the real minus existence' (Grosz 1999: 26). Deleuze (1988: 98) suggests that the 'sleight of hand' at work here is that 'the real was expected to come about by its own means', and this means that 'it was possible at any time before it happened'. This is, for Deleuze, a 'projection backwards' or 'mirage effect' of the possible pre-existing the real but in fact being constituted after the real. The philosophical and political implications of overturning the notion of possible and real cannot be overestimated for Deleuze, because 'the possible' delimits the future by effacing its retroactive constitution as possibility and thus relegates the creative potentiality of the human to a secondary role. In Nietzsche's terminology this is to make the serious error of conceiving of something as a discrete cause that is in fact a relational effect.

The virtual is, I have suggested, immanent to the actual and induces actualization, and as such the virtual 'possesses a full reality by itself. The process it undergoes is that of actualisation' (Deleuze 1994: 211). Actualization is produced as an effect rather than restricted or contained within a subset of causal possibilities. Because the virtual, as an ontological multiplicity, is immanent but does not resemble the actual, which diverges from the virtual, actualization is understood as constituting genuine newness. The movement between the virtual and the actual, then, 'requires a certain leap of innovation or creativity, the surprise that the virtual leaves within the actual. . . . The movement of actualisation is the opening up of the virtual to what befalls it' (Grosz 1999: 27). Here, realizing the possible is an acontextual approach as possible realities are already given, and actualization, in contrast, is situated within particular temporal and spatial assemblages in which the virtual simultaneously exists and takes the actual away from itself.[22] Actualizing the virtual

> is to create divergent lines which correspond to – without resembling – a virtual multiplicity. The virtual possesses the reality of a task to be performed or a problem to be solved: it is the problem which orientates, conditions and engenders solutions, but these do not resemble the conditions of the problem.
>
> (Deleuze and Guattari 1994: 212)

It is, then, this immanent but irreducible connection and movement between virtual and actual that means that contexts, boundaries and identities are 'up for grabs'.[23]

Bergson and Deleuze are concerned with providing the actual with more 'life' than is visible in the actual (Ansell Pearson 2000). This comprises the movements and intersections in both directions between virtual and actual multiplicities, and this means 'threading' cultural phenomena towards the virtual (see Deleuze and Guattari 1994: 122). Ansell Pearson (2000) argues that those who are critical of the concepts of active forces, *durée* or virtual multiplicities usually neglect this immanent relation between virtual and actual. Instead, there is a desire to know whether forces, differences, multiplicities are either 'of this world' or 'from outside of it' in order to make the accusation that becoming is a mysterious and transcendent phenomenon. This is an illusion, Ansell Pearson (ibid.) continues, that requires continual exposing, because active forces, *durée* and virtual multiplicities are not transcendent to the human condition and must be understood as 'neither inside nor outside the world'. Rather, forces, multiplicity and difference become *with* the world, and as such the world exists as a becoming human or 'becoming world'.[24]

Beardsworth (1996, 1998, 2001) makes a similar argument about becoming in terms of the mediated organization of forces. For Beardsworth, active and reactive forces come out of a mediated history from which distinctions between the social, the organizational, the physiological, the psychological and, in particular, the technical emerge in the first place. In this important sense, then, forces are posited as immediately beyond a priori 'instinctual forces', conceived as ahistorical. The human condition, according to Beardsworth, is constituted by the right to make promises, to defer action in time and space, and the ability to transform the future through a genealogy of the present. Nietzsche (1994: 39) writes that in order to be able to discern the future,

> man must first have learned to distinguish between what happens by accident and what by design, to think causally, to view the future as the present and anticipate it, to grasp with certainty what is end and what is means, in all, to be able to calculate, compute – and before he can do this, man himself will really have to become *reliable, regular and automatic* ... so that he, as someone making a promise is, is answerable for his own future!

Here Nietzsche describes the process of becoming human as occurring through and beyond calculability, repeatability and organization. For Beardsworth (2001: 48–56) this 'humanization' comes out of the *non-human* transformations invoked by technics (from *techne*, defined as both the arts of mind and practices). The will to power, then, denotes not the arbitrary discharging of the will outside of the cultural, historical or technical, but expressive action that is conditional on, and emerges out of, willing the necessity of the human condition as non-human from the first instance. On this point, Colebrook (1999: 121) adds that articulating the denial of the will to power through a genealogy of the effacement of effects invokes active forces and returns a cause to a relational effect. Nietzsche is, then, not simply against notions of human identity, organization or calculation as such, but against a particular approach to cultural phenomena understood in terms of the reformulation into active forces that constitutes identities, formations and activities and that is imperative for critical and creative responses. This is not, then, so much an overcoming of the human or the death of the subject as a becoming human that is effaced by causes conceived as foundations. Here the human subject is in fact the precondition for becoming human in so far as it is evaluated as an effect that thus invokes the will to power.

May (1999: 15–17) also problematizes the association of active force with thought beyond the human and suggests that what is required is a more nuanced form of judgement that does not simply pit active and reactive forces against one another, but examines their reciprocity yet irreducibility to each other. Here, positing reactive forces as 'illusory' or 'false' and active forces as 'primary' is sustainable only to the extent that these are illusions or falsifications because they are approached through a reactive form of judgement that delineates relational effects into foundational causes. Put simply, the illusion is not that the human subject or cultural forms really exist or not, but rather the illusion is that particular effects are ahistorical and conceived as a priori causes. For May (1999: 37), this means that evaluations cannot occur in the abstract and that, for instance, pity

> is bad when, *inter alia*, it has the 'insane' aims of abolishing suffering – insane because suffering is inseparable from living, because suffering is in large part, both cause and effect of our growth in power and creativity and 'sovereignty'.... By contrast, pity is good when it has the '*converse*' object: namely, those who resist suffering, those who cannot bear to be (or to witness others being) 'broken, forged, torn, burnt, made incandescent, and purified'. Something is fully a value only if it is specified in terms of the functions (and the motives they express) in the life of a particular type of individual.

This motivation towards evaluating pity, which is applicable to cultural forms generally, is also Bergson's notion of intuition as an 'enlarged reality' (see Mullarkey 1999a). For Bergson, 'intuition' is not a spontaneous or subjectively embodied experience, but a 'supra-intellectual' competency that comes out of the effort and attention directed towards 'the detail of the real'.[25] It is in attending to the processes that constitute, for example, dichotomies that invokes intuition in the intellect, the virtual that unravels the actual or differences in kind immanent to differences in degree (ibid.: 159–160). This is, similarly, why Nietzsche (1974: 85) remarks that 'the growth of consciousness may be danger' to 'instincts', but to the extent that senses show becoming, they do not lie. Instincts are understood here not as a priori, psychological or ahistorical forces, but as Bergson's intuition that comes out of a practice that approaches the condition of the human, of organization, and so on, through a genealogy of the present: it is in this sense, through and beyond the present, not against it, that Nietzsche writes of 'incorporating knowledge and making it instinctive'. Reactive forces, time as *temps*, actual multiplicities are the 'scars of the past', but 'even here, and especially here, the reconstitution and working-through of the past calls upon an art of existing ... in which these scars bear their own fruit' (Ansell Pearson 2002: 195).

The proposition that reactive forces are necessary 'illusions' or 'falsifications' is further complicated because although becoming human or becoming organization is an expression of active force, reactive forces provide something to 'become otherwise' and engender the expression of active forces. This is another way of expressing the mediated history of becoming in which 'pure' active forces, if such unmediated forces were possible, would be an expression of power that would remain crude and unreflective:

> Nietzsche interestingly suggests that slavish traits [that is, reactive forces] are crucial to motivating it [that is, active forces, becoming]. . . . For the slave's feeling of vulnerability, the gnawing question mark he (in contrast to the master) places over his identity and power, and his restless dissatisfaction with his lot, can all provide decisive impetus to the highest realms of thought and art and self-mastery. . . . He, unlike the master [that is, active forces], is a painful problem to himself; and in his search for relief from the pain and for a solution to the problem he is driven to feats of thought, imagination, self-discipline, and artistry for which the self-assured master simply lacks comparable motivation.
>
> (May 1999: 46–47)

The human subject, organization and cultural forms generally are posited as always a composite of reactive and active forces such that neither can be equated with becoming alone: active forces or virtual multiplicities cannot be understood as only coerced into reactive forces or actual multiplicities, because they are constituted through a mediated history. Similarly, Beardsworth (2001: 50) argues that forces are not simply active or reactive, because forces are radically unstable and mutually defining, and as such, 'the categories against which Nietzsche sets much of his thinking – causality, finality, purpose, the subjectivity of the will – are the result of a long process that designates the human as such and therefore designates them *as also* active' through a becoming human that is a constitutive technics (see also Brigham 2001).

Mullarkey (1999a) similarly elaborates the importance of mediations, purifications and transformations with regard to Bergson's later writing and terms this the 'circle of quality and quantity'. Bergson changes his emphasis over time, Mullarkey (ibid.: 143) argues, from actual multiplicities revealing virtual multiplicities to a relation in which 'quantity seems to subtend quality' and that 'sometimes a difference in degree can be so immense that it creates a difference in nature'. Here relations of virtual and actual or quality and quantity are, despite irreducibility to one another, mutually reciprocal. Bergson's immanent and irreducible 'internal division' of quality and quantity is also Patton's (2000) description of the 'internal complexity' in Nietzsche's concept of active and reactive forces. For Patton (ibid.: 63),

> active forces may become reactive, and acquire an affinity with the reactive rather than the affirmative quality of the will to power, or the possibility that reactive forces may become active and acquire an affinity with the affirmative dimension of the will to power.

The implication of this is that the particular meaning and evaluation of a given phenomenon requires the 'patient and meticulous practice of genealogy' to produce a 'becoming otherwise'.

Conclusions: philosophy, politics and assemblages

The relationship between being and becoming has been fundamental to philosophical and political thinking in the Western imagination. The previous section sets out how it makes little sense to talk of being and becoming outside of constitutive purifications, mediations and transformations, and how the oppositions and reversals between being and becoming must be returned to their particular history in order to be thought anew. In relation to this, these concluding remarks are concerned to make three points: first, the importance of evaluating phenomena in a particular way; second, the implications of such an approach for what phenomena are worth attention; and third, how the relationship between the philosophy and politics of being and becoming can be understood.

This chapter has argued that for a philosophy and politics of becoming to be meaningful, it must comprise more than a simplistic reversal of the relative priority of being and becoming and the association of becoming with change in contemporary capitalism. Chia (1999: 211), for example, quotes Kanter's use of process theorists to bolster the observation that economic circumstances are continually uncertain as evidence of the conflation of becoming with the legitimacy of re-engineering organizations' structures and practices.[26] This chapter has argued that in contrast to these reductionist associations and their critiques, what is in fact critical and creative is the way in which evaluation of becoming takes place rather than becoming *per se*. Put another way, instead of situating analysis as either for or against being or becoming, a genealogical approach has been set out orientated towards an evaluation that is *through and beyond* the dichotomy of being and becoming.

The contemporary emphasis on becoming in social and organization theory and associations with new forms of individualism and virtual organizations requires problematizing because it is bound up with two Procrustean tendencies. First, novel philosophical concepts relating to the relationship between forces, differences and multiplicities are rendered subtly complicit with the restructuring of capitalism around a knowledge economy and a narrowing of what is conceived of as becoming human and becoming organization. Second, emphasis on becoming as the basis of contemporary experience is discerned as meaning being against historical legacies and outmoded forms of sociality. Contra these one-dimensional depictions, this chapter has argued that Nietzsche, Bergson and Deleuze are not in any sense straightforwardly against human subjectivity, organizational forms or cultural phenomena as either good or bad, or proactive or defeatist. Neither are they interested in invoking multiplicity or difference as some kind of unfettered ode to spontaneity.

I have argued that the task of philosophy for Nietzsche, Bergson and Deleuze is to think beyond the human condition. Their approach is not, however, concerned with providing a critical analysis based upon dismissing or rejecting the uses and abuses of the philosophical concept of becoming as evidence that the term is empty and not worth analytical attention. In this sense, critical approaches are characterized by contesting becoming and examining whether it can be empirically accounted for and how far it is representative of the alleged emergence of a knowledge economy. Although critical approaches are valuable in Nietzsche, Bergson and Deleuze's terms, such approaches bring about an intensification of the contested 'problem of becoming' rather than 'problematizing becoming'. In their terms, this is restrictive because of the dependence on a form of critique that simultaneously and paradoxically sustains 'becoming' as an object of analysis. The way in which phenomena are evaluated is not, then, to use Deleuze and Guattari's broad cultural metaphors, reducible to a straightforward choice between the arborescent tree as being, or liberatory rhizome as becoming, as there are knots of arborescence in rhizomes and rhizomatic stems in roots. The task at hand is, instead, to put thinking on its way with an approach that overcomes the choice between being and becoming through a form of analysis that articulates the way in which relations are continually in construction, being extended or are collapsing, or composed of offshoots that are falling apart or starting again. This is not a new or different dualism, say Deleuze and Guattari (1988: 20); rather, it is a

> problem of writing: in order to designate something exactly, inexact expressions are utterly unavoidable. . . . We invoke one dualism in order to challenge another. We invoke a dualism of models only in order to arrive at a process that challenges all models.

Deleuze and Guattari (1988) propose the concept of assemblages as instructive for conceiving what phenomena are worth attending to in order to work through and beyond dichotomies (see also Cooper 1998). 'Assemblage' is from the French *agencement* and can also be translated as 'organization' or 'arrangement'. For Deleuze and Guattari, assemblages are comprised of technico-affective relations that are constitutive extensions, supplements and mediations. The analytical focus on assemblages denotes the contention that the human subject or the status of organization cannot be located and exclusively depicted within the realm of the human subject or organization as such. This means that being or becoming is also problematic and presages an analysis that articulates the relational constitution of effects through assemblages that simultaneously constitute capacities to act and be acted upon.

The focus on assemblages denotes the interdependencies and irreducibility of discursive and non-discursive relations. This is also expressed in terms of 'forms of content', which are also termed 'machinic assemblages' and comprise interactions, corporeal bodies and practices and 'forms of expression', which are termed 'assemblages of enunciation' and comprise utterances, speech acts and statements (see Patton 2000: 44).[27] The human subject is the 'borrowings', distributions and displacements of these machinic and enunciative assemblages, and it is these constitutive mediations and extensions that provide the basis for a critical and creative analysis of becoming human and becoming organization. Beardsworth (2001) is similarly concerned with becoming human and becoming organization as constituted by an originary rather than epiphenomenal technics and symmetrically eschews the contention that technics has been added to the nature or culture. Neither humans nor technics can be considered as a priori independent or autonomous, although capacities, or the deficiency of them, can be mutually incorporated, exchanged and transformed. Becoming human and becoming organization also come out of movements of territorialization and deterritorialization. For Deleuze and Guattari, 'deterritorialization' is another way of expressing Nietzsche's active forces, Bergson's qualitative multiplicity and Deleuze's virtual multiplicities. There are, then, different 'lines' or 'processes' that make up assemblages. Subjects and organizations

> are composed of different kinds of 'lines': molar lines that correspond to forms of rigid segmentation ... molecular lines that correspond to the fluid and overlapping division ... and finally, lines of flight that are paths along which things change or become transformed into something else.
>
> (Patton 2000: 86)

Deleuze and Guattari (1988: 394–415) illustrate technico-affective becoming human through the transformation constituted by assemblages of human–horse–plough (see also Lee 2001: 113–117). The human–horse–plough assemblage can be understood by the symmetrical analysis of non-discursive and discursive relations that are the limit and support one another, and it is in the relations of human–horse–plough that becoming human is defined (see also Latour 1999; Law 2002). For horses to become mounts, they had to be captured and trained to respond to commands so that humans could borrow their legs and lungs and move faster and over greater distance. But the human subject changed no less than the horse, because the capacity of knowing about horses' strengths, fears and how to stay mounted while on the move did not pre-date humans' capacities as 'riders'. The provisional human–horse assemblage, as an actual and virtual multiplicity, is also always subject to movement when it comes up against other assemblages. In their example the assemblage of agriculture diversified the human–horse assemblage because it 'made it possible to use heavier ploughs than before, to dig deeper furrows than could be dug using oxen' (Lee 2001: 114). Yet symmetrically, the horse–plough assemblage is not a simple cause of sedentary forms of agriculture, as this would presuppose a technological rationalism; rather, it is constitutive of the problematic of becoming human:

> the heavy plough exists as a specific tool only in a constellation where 'long open' fields predominate . . . where the land begins to undergo tri-ennial rotation, and where the economy becomes communal. Before-hand, the heavy plough may well have existed, but on the margins of other assemblages that did not bring out its specificity.
>
> (Deleuze and Guattari 1988: 399)[28]

Here, although horses are not a priori mounts, humans have not always been riders or farmers of long open fields and iron has not always been used for producing ploughs. Each of these is brought into being through an ontolog-ical labour of non-discursive and discursive relations that is the movement between actual and virtual multiplicities, reactive and active forces, quanti-tative and qualitative differences.

The turn to a relational ontology, now established within the social sci-ences, marks out the constitutive role of the distribution of technics, prac-tices and discourses in becoming human and becoming organization, but there remains a question of how to account for the experience or persistence of affects when the human subject and organization are understood as rela-tional. This chapter has argued that becoming human and becoming organi-zation cannot be understood outside of a technico-affective history of translations, purifications and mediations, and that these relational affects are set in motion by, for instance, techno-scientific, economic-administrative and political economy assemblages and that these assemblages are deployed and possess human subjects and organizations in different ways in different places and times. This necessitates an approach that analyses the minutiae of how affects constitutively construct human becoming or becoming organi-zation, but also how circulating affects come out of relationality and become capacities or incapacities that belong to the particular subjects or organi-zations. Lee and Brown (2002: 277) illustrate this with the example of a small child traumatized by fear during a 'scary' theatre performance. The young boy becomes capable of a possessing 'persistent memory of fear by virtue of his peculiarity as a child'. Here there is a sense of a possessive human condition in which the task of responding to, discharging or dispos-ing of affects falls upon a particular subject alone, but, more generally, incorporating and responding to affects is 'a job for which we may all, at times, be singularly ill equipped'.[29] It is, then, the incorporations, deferrals and dispersions of technico-affective assemblages that mark out the human condition as irreducibly becoming *and* being, relational *and* possessive, and organizations as proximal *and* distal.

In concluding, I want to suggest that the connections and complicities between philosophical concepts and contemporary politics in relation to being and becoming remain under-theorized in social and organization theory: multiplicity, becoming, difference each require ongoing ontological, political and ethical determination and specification. This chapter has argued that the relationship between the philosophical and the political should be characterized as an open-ended, temporary and ongoing resolution between concepts, discourses and practices, and that it is this relation that constitutes the potential for complicity and indeterminacy. In terms of specifying the relationship between being and becoming, it means that once this connection is made between politics and philosophy, it becomes incumbent to articulate thinking and acting through a genealogy of present dichotomies. This genealogical approach, an evaluation 'from within', necessitates the detailed examination of how disjunctions and connections between being and becoming are constructed and consolidated as a condition for their re-evaluation. In constructing a way through and beyond current antinomies, thinking the philosophical and the political means invoking the contemporary expressions of being and becoming in order to turn assumptions and effects back on themselves as a means to different ends.

Acknowledgements

An initial version of this chapter was presented at Sub-theme 32: 'Odysseys of organizing: philosophy in search of the other', EGOS 17th Colloquium, Lyon, France, 5–7 July 2001. Thanks to the stream organizers and participants for helpful questions and comments.

Notes

1 See Deleuze (1995: 147). 'Difference must be shown differing' (Deleuze 1994: 56).
2 Others concerned with multiplicity include Derrida, Foucault, Irigaray and Lyotard.
3 This does not mean that these philosophers can be reduced to one another, however, or that it is adequate, for instance, to 'describe Deleuze as a Bergsonian, not simply because of the many sources he draws on, but rather because of the highly innovative character of his Bergsonism' (Ansell Pearson 2002: 3). Nietzsche, Bergson and Deleuze are often considered enigmatic, frustrating and difficult to approach, partly because for each there were changes in emphasis in their writing over time. More importantly, Nietzsche, Bergson and Deleuze do not fit into a conventional approach that breaks down ideas into discrete segments, and each had a lifelong commitment to articulating a philosophy of multiplicity that required the continual invention of unfamiliar ways of thinking and sensing.
4 Plato and Hegel are often associated with philosophies that presuppose the primacy of identity and the subordination of difference. For more detail, see Patton (2000: 29–32).
5 Affect is 'the passage from one experiential state of the body to another and implying an augmentation or diminution in that body's capacity to act' (Deleuze and Guattari 1988: xvi).

6 Offering advice or support to a friend is to act upon the actions of another, for instance, but this is not in itself necessarily against the interests of the person over whom it is exercised. Rather, 'in some respects, the exercise of power is what shapes and determines those "interests"' (Patton 2000: 59).

7 'It follows that Nietzsche's understanding of power must be distinguished from the homeostatic principle which underpins the Darwinian conception of nature' (Patton 2000: 50). 'English Darwinism', which is a reactive formulation of life, is premised on differences of degree, rather than differences in kind: active forces as differences in kind emphasize 'the priority of "form shaping forces" that give new directions and interpretations. . . . "Adaptation" is a secondary effect which takes place only after formative powers have exerted their influence' (Ansell-Pearson 1997a: 92). See also Beardsworth (1996).

8 'The will to power is essentially creative and giving: it does not aspire, it does not seek, it does not desire, above all it does not desire power. It gives' (Deleuze 1983: 85).

9 Despite the widespread usage of their aphorism 'the production of organization', the Nietzschean character of their approach has passed without much scholarly analysis. The first move towards this Nietzschean-inspired organizational analysis is the recognition that organized activity is reactive and defensive and that active force is superior. This entails a 'genealogy of system and organization [that] begins with the recognition that representations and structures derive from a more fundamental process of materiality and energy' (Cooper and Burrell 1988: 105).

10 Deleuze and Guattari's (1988) approach to evaluation is similarly partisan and gives priority to what they variously term 'lines of flight', 'deterritorialisation' and 'becoming-minor' through processes described as 'rhizomatic', 'the body without organs', and 'the plane of consistency'. See Cooper and Burrell (1988: 104–105) for a discussion of the active forces and organizational analysis, and Patton (2000: 65–67) for an examination of the benefits and dangers of different forms of evaluation.

11 Bergson shares Nietzsche's concern with becoming, although there is little evidence that Bergson was familiar with his writing (Ansell Pearson 2002).

12 Even the term 'perception' is problematic, as 'the classical language of perception is misleading in that it implies a world outside, a mind inside, and a series of intermediate channels through which information is passed' (Watson 1998: 6).

13 As Latour (1999: 24) writes, 'you cannot do to ideas what auto manufacturers do with badly conceived cars; you cannot recall them . . . retrofitting them with improved engines or parts, and sending them all back again, all for free. . . . The only solution is to do what Victor Frankenstein did *not* do, that is, not to abandon the creature to its fate but continue all the way developing its strange potential'.

14 Time as *temps* is a misunderstanding of time, says Ansell Pearson (2002: 178): '1) that the past can be reconstituted simply with the present; 2) that we pass gradually from one to the other in terms of discrete steps; 3) that the passing of time takes place in terms of a chronological "before" and "after"; 4) that the activity of the mind takes place in terms of mere additions of elements, as opposed to changes in level, leaps and the reworking of closed and open systems'.

15 For Bergson, *durée* is understood as a qualitative multiplicity, which is 'an internal multiplicity of succession, of fusion, of organization, of heterogeneity, of qualitative discrimination, or of difference in kind; it is a virtual and continuous multiplicity' (Deleuze 1988: 38).

16 Quantitative and qualitative differences, which are also termed discontinuous and continuous multiplicities by Bergson, are renamed actual and virtual multiplicities by Deleuze (1988).

17 Bergson's and Deleuze's assumption of monism should not be conflated with the idea that it is one thing in the conventional philosophical sense. Rather, 'the renewed thinking of the One Deleuze undertakes constitutes an intrinsic part of his overriding commitment to pluralism' (Ansell Pearson 2002: 3). Deleuze proposes that the 'universe of memory is a pluralistic one' where 'monism = pluralism' (see Ansell Pearson 2002: 179).

18 The distinction here is between memory in the virtual and perception in the actual (see Ansell Pearson 2002: 177).

19 It is important to acknowledge, says Ansell Pearson (2002: 196), that the contemporary human subject remains focused on practical action based on a psychological present, and, as such, inhabiting 'the virtual plane of existence' happens only now and again and in particular and rare contexts. This 'virtual plane' is another way of expressing what Nietzsche proposes as the new ideal for the human condition: *Übermensch*, translated as 'overman'.

20 Ansell Pearson (2002: 201) connects Nietzsche's active and reactive forces to Bergson's memory in the sense of recollection as 'only investing traces' to memory as virtual 'that no longer rests on traces'.

21 The emphasis Ansell Pearson (2002: 190–197) places on an ontology of memory is contrasted with the account given by Mullarkey (1999a: 51–57), another commentator on Bergson, who privileges perception discerning perception as a multiplicity of presents. For Ansell Pearson (2002: 197), this form of actual multiplicity deprives the virtual of its ontological reality and 'has the effect of situating the self purely on the level of psychology'.

22 The notion of situated action goes some way towards virtual multiplicities, although the virtual means more than experienced judgement in relation to a particular contexts (see Flyvbjerg 2001). Ciborra (1999) describes how objects, people and boundaries get 'lifted out' of routine activities and reordered by 'improvization'; that is to say, plans and procedures become 'up for grabs'. For Ciborra, improvization marks out something fundamental to existence. He notes (ibid.: 86–91) that improvization is more than decision making with judgement or calling on the resources of previous experiences as 'vast regions of the past are enacted at that very moment'. Ciborra draws on Heidegger's notion of *Augenblick* to denote a 'moment of vision, that is a movement in which our Being is conscious of itself and its possibilities vis-à-vis the world, rather than being dispersed in the ordinary chores and interests of everyday life'. Bergson develops a non-phenomenological approach, which Ciborra makes reference to, but does not elaborate on. For more on a temporal approach to studying organizations, see, for example, Gherardi and Strati (1988) and Kavanagh and Araujo (1995).

23 In order to make the virtual and the actual distinct from the possible and the real, Deleuze (1994: 209–211) sets out the determination of the virtual content of a multiplicity as differen*t*iation and the divergence of actualization as differen*c*iation. This means, in other words, a particular understanding of different/ciation where differen*t*iation means making something *determinate* and differen*c*iation means producing something *different* in a particular context (see also Patton 2000: 38).

24 Ansell Pearson suggests that it is those who accuse Bergson and Deleuze of positing a transcendental realm (e.g. Badiou 2000 and Game 1997) who are in fact responsible for positing a transcendent realm. Game (1997: 117–124) argues that discontinuities come out of embodied ruptures to chronological

time. This is, for Deleuze, much more unfathomable and mysterious than the concepts of *durée* or virtual multiplicity, as it is becoming that is somehow outside of the actual.

25 This is what Deleuze (1994) describes as a 'superior empiricism'. See also Ansell Pearson (2002: 12–13, 170–174) and Mullarkey (1999a: 158, 179–180).

26 The conclusion that Chia (1999) reaches contrast to the approach developed in this chapter. Chia (1999: 225) concludes that 'merely relaxing the deeply entrenched organizational and institutional habits, which keep "organizations" together and which enable them to be thought of as "thing-like", is itself sufficient to allow change to occur of its own volition. It is this "hands-off" attitude towards organizational change which is the implicit advocacy of this process metaphysical mindset'. This conclusion reveals a desire to separate phenomenal experience to 'let it be' from social, political and historical forces. Chia (2003: 111) similarly remarks, 'social reality is always already an abstraction from the brute reality of our pure empirical experience . . . what remains absolute is the immediacy of our unthought lived experience'.

27 The relational character of assemblages is further delineated into assemblages of 'content' and 'expression' as non-discursive and discursive relations, and 'territorialization and deterritorialization' as the movements and transformations of assemblages that are reactive and active forces, quantitative and qualitative differences, and actual and virtual multiplicities. Transformations are not reducible to changes in the content of non-discursive activities, but are simultaneously bound up with discursive expressions. The example that Deleuze and Guattari (1988: 66–67) provide is of an individual pronounced guilty by a judge who then becomes a 'criminal'. Here technologies act as expressions of a particular discursive content of 'guilty'. Judging an individual as 'criminal' has effects on this subject's movement which cannot be understood outside a particular set of non-discursive practices (e.g. imprisonment or tagging). Here the assemblage of enunciation that expresses 'guilty' only has effects through time and space to the extent that it is interwoven with non-discursive relations such as prison cells or electronic tags. The 'criminal' undergoes an incorporeal transformation in the sense that the individual is put into very different sets of non-discursive relations without a direct material transformation of the individual as such (see also Wise 1997: 63–64).

28 Assemblages are mixtures of forms of content and forms of expression, and both can be discursive and non-discursive. On this, Deleuze and Parnet (1987: 70–71) argue that the invention of a tool is never sufficient for its adoption and that 'a tool remains marginal, or little used, until there exists a social machine or collective assemblage'.

29 Patton also makes the connection between a particular affective history and a form of evaluation that works towards overcoming by invoking active forces. Patton (2000: 63) writes, 'take the example of illness or injury which separates the healthy individual from his or her powers and limits possibilities for action. While it is clearly a reactive force, its value depends on the nature of the subject and how it responds to the illness which act upon it. The same physiological state may weaken some powers but also open up new possibilities of feeling or being about new capacities for acting and being acted upon. . . . Depending on how the illness is lived, we must ask whether it is the same condition or the same illness in each case.' See also Deleuze (1983: 67).

References

Ackroyd, S. (2002) *The Organization of Business*, Oxford: Oxford University Press.

Ansell Pearson, K. (1991) *Nietzsche contra Rousseau*, Cambridge: Cambridge University Press.

Ansell Pearson, K. (1997a) *Viroid Life*, London: Routledge.

Ansell Pearson, K. (1997b) (ed.) *Deleuze and Philosophy*, London: Routledge.

Ansell Pearson, K. (1999) *Germinal Life*, London: Routledge.

Ansell Pearson, K. (2000) 'Pure reserve: Deleuze, philosophy and immanence', in M. Bryden (ed.) *Deleuze and Religion*, London: Routledge.

Ansell Pearson, K. (2002) *Virtual Life*, London: Routledge.

Ansell Pearson, K. and Mullarkey, J. (2002) *Henri Bergson*, London: Continuum.

Badiou, A. (2000) *Deleuze: The Clamor of Being*, trans. L. Burchill, Minneapolis: University of Minnesota Press.

Beardsworth, R. (1996) 'Nietzsche, Freud and the complexity of the human: towards a philosophy of failed digestion', *Tekhnema* 3: 113–141.

Beardsworth, R. (1998) 'Thinking technicity', *Cultural Values* 2 (1): 70–87.

Beardsworth, R. (2001) 'Nietzsche, nihilism and spirit', in K. Ansell Pearson and D. Morgan (eds) *Nihilism Now!*, Basingstoke, UK: Palgrave.

Bergson, H. (1983) *Creative Evolution*, trans. A. Mitchell, Lanham, MD: University Press of America.

Bergson, H. (1991) *Matter and Memory*, trans. N. M. Paul and W. S. Palmer, New York: Zone Books.

Bergson, H. (2000) *Duration and Simultaneity*, trans. L. Jacobson and M. Lewis, Manchester: Clinamen Press.

Brigham, M. (2001) 'Life enhancement now, now, now', *Ephemera* 1 (4): 374–394.

Brown, J. S. (1991) 'Research that reinvents the corporation', *Harvard Business Review*, January–February: 102–111.

Burrell, G. and Dale, K. (2002) 'Utopiary: utopias, gardens and organization', in M. Parker (ed.) *Utopia and Organization*, Oxford: Blackwell.

Chia, R. (1998) 'From complexity science to complex thinking: organization as simple location', *Organization* 5 (3): 341–370.

Chia, R. (1999) 'A "rhizomatic" model of organizational change and transformation: perspectives from a metaphysics of change', *British Journal of Management* 10: 209–227.

Chia, R. (2003) 'Ontology: organization as "world making"', in R. Westwood and S. Clegg (eds) *Debating Organization*, Oxford: Blackwell.

Ciborra, C. (1999) 'Notes on improvisation and time in organizations', *Accounting, Management and Information Technologies* 9: 77–94.

Colebrook, C. (1999) 'A grammar of becoming: strategy, subjectivism, and style', in E. Grosz (ed.) *Becomings*, Ithaca, NY: Cornell University Press.

Cooper, R. (1998) 'Assemblage notes', in R. C. H. Chia (ed.) *Organized Worlds*, London: Routledge.

Cooper, R. and Burrell, G. (1988) 'Modernism, postmodernism and organizational analysis: an introduction', *Organization Studies* 9 (1): 91–112.

Cooper, R. and Law, J. (1995) 'Organization: distal and proximal views', *Research in the Sociology of Organizations* 13: 237–274.

Deleuze, G. (1983) *Nietzsche and Philosophy*, trans. H. Tomlinson, London: Athlone Press.

Deleuze, G. (1988) *Bergsonism*, trans. H. Tomlinson and B. Habberjam, New York: Zone Books.

Deleuze, G. (1989) *Cinema 2*, trans. H. Tomlinson and R. Galeta, London: Athlone Press.

Deleuze, G. (1994) *Difference and Repetition*, trans. P. Patton, London: Athlone Press.

Deleuze, G. (1995) *Negotiations 1972–1990*, trans. M. Joughin, New York: Columbia University Press.

Deleuze, G. (1998) 'Boulez, Proust and time: "occupying without counting"', *Angelaki* 3 (2): 69–74.

Deleuze, G. and Guattari, F. (1988) *A Thousand Plateaus*, trans. B. Massumi, London: Athlone Press.

Deleuze, G. and Guattari, F. (1994) *What Is Philosophy?*, trans. H. Tomlinson, London: Verso.

Deleuze, G. and Parnet, C. (1987) *Dialogues*, trans. H. Tomlinson and B. Habberjam, London: Athlone Press.

Descombes, V. (1980) *Modern French Philosophy*, trans. L. Scott-Fox and J. M. Harding, Cambridge: Cambridge University Press.

Flyvbjerg, B. (2001) *Making Social Science Matter*, trans. S. Sampson, Cambridge: Cambridge University Press.

Game, A. (1997) 'Time unhinged', *Time and Society*, 6 (2/3): 115–129.

Gherardi, S. and Strati, A. (1988) 'The temporal dimension in organizational studies', *Organization Studies* 9 (2): 149–164.

Giddens, A. (2001) *The Global Third Way Debate*, Oxford: Polity Press.

Grosz, E. (ed.) (1999) *Becomings*, Ithaca, NY: Cornell University Press.

Harvey, D. (1989) *The Condition of Postmodernity*, Oxford: Basil Blackwell.

Heelas, P. (1996) *The New Age Movement*, Oxford: Blackwell.

Jackson, N. and Carter, P. (2000) *Rethinking Organizational Behaviour*, London: Prentice Hall.

Kavanagh, D. and Araujo, L. (1995) 'Chronigami: folding and unfolding time', *Accounting, Management and Information Technologies* 5 (2): 103–121.

Lash, S. (1990) *A Sociology of Postmodernism*, London: Routledge.

Latour, B. (1999) 'On recalling ANT', in J. Law and J. Hassard (eds) *Actor Network Theory and After*, Oxford: Blackwell.

Law, J. (2002) *Aircraft Stories*, Durham, NC: Duke University Press.

Lee, N. (2001) *Childhood and Society*, Buckingham, UK: Open University Press.

Lee, N. and Brown, S. (2002) 'The disposal of fear: childhood, trauma, and complexity', in J. Law and A. Mol (eds) *Complexities*, Durham, NC: Duke University Press.

Letiche, H. (2000) 'Phenomenal complexity theory as informed by Bergson', *Journal of Organizational Change Management* 13 (6): 545–557.

Linstead, S. (2002) 'Organization as reply: Henri Bergson and casual organization theory', *Organization* 9 (1): 95–111.

May, S. (1999) *Nietzsche's Ethics and His War on Morality*, Oxford: Oxford University Press.

Mullarkey, J. (1999a) *Bergson and Philosophy*, Edinburgh: Edinburgh University Press.

Mullarkey, J. (ed.) (1999b) *The New Bergson*, Manchester: Manchester University Press.

Nietzsche, F. (1968) *The Will to Power*, trans. W. Kaufmann and R. J. Hollingdale, New York: Vintage.

Nietzsche, F. (1974) *The Gay Science*, trans. W. Kaufmann, New York: Vintage.

Nietzsche, F. (1994) *On the Genealogy of Morals*, trans. C. Diethe, Cambridge: Cambridge University Press.

Patton, P. (1993) *Nietzsche, Feminism and Political Theory*, London: Routledge.

Patton, P. (ed.) (1996) *Deleuze*, Oxford: Blackwell.

Patton, P. (2000) *Deleuze and the Political*, London: Routledge.

Safranski, R. (2002) *Nietzsche*, London: Granta.

Thrift, N. (1997) 'The rise of soft capitalism', *Cultural Values* 1 (1): 29–57.

Watson, S. (1998) 'The new Bergsonism: discipline, subjectivity and freedom', *Radical Philosophy* 92: 6–16.

Wise, J. M. (1997) *Exploring Technology and Social Space*, London: Sage.

Conclusion

Thinking on . . . the need for philosophy of management and organization

Stephen Linstead and Alison Linstead

In their call for philosophy of management in 2001, Laurie and Cherry identified six areas to be included in its scope:

1 presuppositions of management theory and practice;
2 concepts at the core of management;
3 representations of management and the managerial myths informing management theory;
4 management methodologies;
5 the relevance and applicability of philosophical techniques and skills;
6 the application of philosophical disciplines to issues facing managers.

Their general argument is that philosophy must be simultaneously analytic, prepared to more accurately describe and theorize its phenomena and how they relate and interact, and prepared to prescribe, to engage with practice and help to improve it – while resisting the temptation to be immediately practically helpful. This latter temptation is of course easily resisted in some areas of organization studies, where the opposite is often the case, and the way in which theory has distanced itself from its practical implications is often the target of criticism. Nevertheless, in this book we have tried to embrace an approach to philosophy in which the practical implications of the explorations we have undertaken, whether for practice or for further research, have been borne firmly in mind. Furthermore, we think that Laurie and Cherry's six core areas offer some potential for organization studies, with some modification.

First, we need to remember that organiz*ation* and organiz*ations* are not the same thing, and that organization as a process extends beyond either formal or informal organization across, as we read Bergson, life itself. Understanding organization, properly constituted, is an ontological as well as a practical issue; while most work done is likely to be in relation to or within organizations, organization is not the sole province of those who organize or are organized. Management we see as related to organization, and indeed we think that philosophy of organization should also be closely connected to philosophy of management, but management is the province of the managers and the managed in a way that is different from our understanding of organization.

Accordingly, the first of the core issues needs to be rephrased as *presuppositions of the theory and practice of organizing.* In this sense, Kakkuri-Knuuttila and Vaara readdress one of the core assumptions of organization science, that of causality, not to defend such an approach against its critics, but to review both the criticisms and the approach and to suggest new ways forward. In a different vein but at the same level, both Connor and Grafton Small challenge the assumptions made in organization theory about the qualities of the modern mind and the way sense is made in response to organized phenomena, with reference to image and commodification. The cultural phenomenology of organization emerges as an important new arena of investigation.

The second issue, recast as *concepts at the core of organization and management,* is addressed by Heracleous and Fellenz in terms of how such concepts change and mutate as they are transferred into organization studies from other disciplines, and they suggest how 'better' and 'worse' conceptual borrowings might be evaluated. Taking quite a different approach, Letiche and Maier interrogate the ideas of play and gaming through the concept of *glissement,* with reference to the film *The Matrix.* In so doing, they address the question of how to be inside or outside the game, and its consequences, and effectively introduce a concept from another domain to organization studies.

The third issue is *representations of organization and the myths informing theory,* and here Munro's title sets out the agenda perfectly. Although in some other chapters there are elements of this issue, Munro's focus is absolutely direct.

The next issue we would call *organization and management studies methodologies,* and here Kavanagh, Kuhling and Keohane analyse processes of rationality in operation, again through the means of media science fiction, but raise important issues about the relation of rationality to otherness and collectivity.

In considering *the relevance and applicability of philosophical techniques and skills,* we can turn to the software development of Wallemacq and Jacques, who combine the development of new representations of language and meaning in information technology with a careful underpinning derived from philosophical analysis. McKinley also applies meticulous analysis to examine concrete and social processes through which the field of study is itself constructed.

Regarding *the application of philosophical disciplines to issues facing organization theory and practice,* we have the contribution of Schipper, who looks at the dominant managerial issue of the day, knowledge management, from the perspective of a philosopher of knowledge, particularly with regard to the question of the question. His conclusions suggest that knowledge management may be asking the wrong questions to get the answers it needs. Linstead and Brigham respectively take the work of Bergson, combined with Nietzsche and Deleuze, again to suggest challenging new directions for organization theory as a *practice* that is both being and becoming, moving beyond current antinomies through refocusing and genealogy.

Selves, others, language, representation, myth, motivation, feeling, political praxis, collectivity, cause and effect, convergence and coherence, science, bricolage, objects and subjects, play, ethics – a small sample of what the contributors to this volume have touched upon and what remains to be done. The matters that are of interest to philosophy are not just of interest to philosophy, but have moral and practical and political import as well. Two examples will suffice. Laurie and Cherry (2001: 11) offer a lengthy quotation from a best-selling core organizational behaviour text on the subject of motivation and the motivational calculus. Thinking as analytical philosophers, they demonstrate that the ontological assumptions behind this approach produce instinct as unconscious calculus, claim an epistemological value for it and ontologize this into an account of how people behave. They claim that if such approaches are going to affect the ways in which managers make decisions about the motivations of their employees and, consequently, how they manage them, then this demands a philosophical investigation. It is hardly likely, though, that however seductive their apparent rationalities, such approaches based on false ontology could achieve optimal real-world outcomes. Similar examples could be found throughout organization studies, especially where probabilistic statistics are used to determine truth and validity at a methodological level, effectively displacing serious consideration of epistemological, ontological or metaphysical issues.

A second example can be found in the different Continental philosophical tradition. The recent work of Jacques Derrida has drawn increasingly on his readings of the work of Emmanuel Lévinas (Critchley 1999; Derrida 2000, 2001; Lévinas 1999). Lévinas argues that the self is not known through other simply by the process of recognition and reflection, as Hegel or Kojève would have it. For Lévinas, the encounter with the other imposes a responsibility on self which is in fact prior to self – to the extent that self is created as a response to the other. Derrida looks closely at the moment of the encounter and argues that in this moment the question of hostility/hospitality is raised; we do not know what to do or how to go on with regard to the other, and this is an ethical decision. For Derrida, ethics, then, is located not in the certainty of applying known principles to a situation, or in being true to the self, but in the dynamic *ethical moment* of doubt, uncertainty and responsibility, the response to the other which also *creates self*. The criticisms levelled at postmodern thought which allege that it can have no ethics because it refuses the ontological foundations on which ethics must be grounded are thus shown to have missed the point: it is not possible to *be* ethical, as ethics is achieved only through its dynamic becoming. The sorts of approaches drawn from moral philosophy, whether deontological or otherwise, that currently dominate business ethics render it static and distal, rather than dynamic and deeply interpersonal. In Derrida's terms, 'ethical philosophy', which assumes that 'men' of good conscience simply desire to know what it is proper to do in accord with reason, simply *avoids* its responsibility for the other, may develop quite elaborate rationalizations to do so, and indeed is capable of using reasoned ethical principles to behave in a way that is quite unethical.

Philosophy is capable of making huge differences once unexamined lives become reflexively available for interrogation. As we have seen from the chapters in this book, there is much to be gained from developing philosophy of organization and management; as our discussion of its possible focuses has illustrated, it has potential that is both broad and deep. As our two brief examples have shown, there is much to be done, and regardless of the philosophical tradition within which that is done, much current thinking can be turned on its head. We hope that this book has contributed to furthering the beginnings of philosophy that views organization as a legitimate and fruitful field, and an organization studies that takes philosophy not just seriously, but to heart.

References

Critchley, S. (1999) *Ethics – Politics – Subjectivity: Derrida, Lévinas and Contemporary French Thought*, London: Verso.

Derrida, J. (2000) *Of Hospitality*, Stanford, CA: Stanford University Press.

Derrida, J. (2001) *On Cosmopolitanism and Forgiveness*, London: Routledge.

Laurie, N. and Cherry, C. (2001) 'Wanted: philosophy of management', *Reason in Practice* (now *Philosophy of Management*) 1 (1): 3–12.

Lévinas, E. (1999) *Otherwise than Being or Beyond Essence*, Pittsburgh: Duquesne University Press.

Author index

Subject index